THE PEOPLE'S WAR

MEGAN BECK

Edited by Rachel Garber
Cover design by Romona Bovin
Formatted by Nola Li Barr

ISBN 978-0-578-90885-4 (E-Book)
ISBN 978-1-956-95203-2 (Paperback)

PROLOGUE

A STORY ON THE BEGINNING

In late December of 2019, life was chaotic, already in full swing. The holidays were over, New Year's Day was fast approaching, and resolutions were being made. The beginning of the year was the end of a decade, a time for a new way of life. Some looked forward to a rebirth of the Fitzgerald flapper era, others were ready for a different phase of life—having children, getting a dog, graduating college, electing a new president, or turning the big 4-0. It was, like every year, a time for change. But the world, as we knew it then, was not watching, and did not foresee what was actually waiting behind the curtain of this new decade. What no one saw coming was what felt like a cataclysmic-sized shift in the Earth's rotation. It began in a part of the world few Americans ever paid much attention to, a place where over eleven million people were living under oppression and a tyrannical dictatorship.[1] This is where a new virus was about to wrap the world's population around its finger and not let go. We do not know where the specific origins of this novel virus came from; the actual origins may never be known. By all accounts, the spread began on December 31, 2019 in Wuhan, China.

It began at Huanan Seafood Wholesale Market.[2]

In mid-December of that year, a man named Lan was working in one of the thousand Huanan seafood stalls in Wuhan when he began to experience symptoms that forced him to stay home. After losing three kilograms of weight in just a few days, he was eventually brought to a hospital specializing in infectious diseases. The date was December 19, 2019. It would be more than ten days before the name Corona began to crop up. During the interim, Lan was able to recover from the disease but not before learning that nearly all of Wuhan had been shut down during this time, including the crowded seafood market where he made the little money he could. And he was only the first of many.

A month later, a woman named Coco Han described having a cough that she could not shake. By now, word of the virus in China was growing rampant, but little was known about it. She and her mother fled to the hospital only to be greeted by frightened, panicked people from all over Wuhan who thought they might have this new virus. The doctors who examined Coco were not able to confirm her diagnosis at the time, as they were not authorized to do so. Being undiagnosed was very common with the early patients in Wuhan. Three days later, on January 23rd, the entire city was placed under lockdown. By February 19th, fatalities had hit over 2,000.[3] The name for this tragic time, and the extensive measures Wuhan and other cities in China took to stop it, became known as the "people's war."

And it was a war, a war for the soul of a city that did not know how connected it was until many of those inside its walls began to perish. But soon this war would wage across oceans, throughout other major cities, and infect millions of people worldwide. In less than a month, this novel virus known as COVID-19 shut down states, locked up innocent people in their homes and killed loved ones.

For me, it begins and ends with a birthday party.

---

1. Haley Ott, "China to test entire population of Wuhan for COVID-19 as virus reemerges," CBS News, August 3, 2021, https://www.cbsnews.-com/news/china-wuhan-covid-test-entire-population/ (accessed October 26, 2021).
2. Lily Kuo, "The weeks that changed the world: Inside Wuhan when a pandemic was born," The Irish Times, April 11, 2020. https://www.irish-times.com/news/world/asia-pacific/the-weeks-that-changed-the-world-inside-wuhan-when-a-pandemic-was-born-1.4226167 (accessed April 29, 2020).
3. Ben Westcott, Adam Renton, Jack Guy and Ivana Kottasová, "Global death toll from coronavirus exceeds 2,100," CNN, February 19, 2020, https://www.cnn.com/asia/live-news/coronavirus-outbreak-02-19-20-intl-hnk/index.html (accessed February 21, 2020).

1

IMPROV

In March of 2020, the word of the virus had begun to spread as quickly as the disease itself. At the time, my life was in full swing. We were right in the middle of the busiest season at the real estate office I own; my husband, Michael, and I were in the throes of raising four kids; and I still had my brother, Nick's, birthday party to plan and attend. So when the word came down from D.C. that the United States might enter a lockdown, it was not that I did not believe it, I just did not have time to even consider it. Lockdown? But what about all the things I have to do this week? We can't lockdown a country, I have a business to run and kids to feed. Little did I know just how different my life at that time was going to be very soon.

Thursday, March 12, 2020, the President of the United States announced an unprecedented (at the time) suspension of travel from Europe. That day I was also told I would become a teacher to my four daughters, ages nine, seven, five, and two. My kid's school announced that schooling would happen from home indefinitely. To top the day off, the stock market crashed. The following day, Friday, March 13, 2020, the President declared a national emergency concerning the coronavirus disease pandemic. This happened to fall on the day of my brother Nick's big surprise party that I had put a lot of effort into planning, and during the planning, it had been feeling a little extra special because it just so happened to be occurring on his actual fortieth birthday. Suddenly, the superstition of bad luck for Friday the 13th felt like it was coming true on an exponential level. I gathered all of our employees together and told them that come Monday we would begin working from home.

"This does not mean you are out of jobs or that business is slowing down," I told everyone, although that's exactly what I was told would happen. My business mentors weathered this particular storm by informing me and other mentees that we very likely would have to lay people off and that the housing market would start to dry up. It would be months before any of us realized how opposite that would end up being for the residential real estate market (which I will explain later on). For now, I knew I had to hold my head up high, smile, and reassure everyone, even myself, that this would be over quickly and nothing was wrong. As I spoke these words, the birthday theme rang in my ears and celebration plans flew through my brain like a film reel.

By around noon that day, all the news outlets were reporting the same story of the National Emergency nonstop. To see the media and everyone else saying the words out loud made me worried for my family and team at work. Then panic hit me like a bucket of water; what about the party? I had been planning this party for weeks. I couldn't let it get ruined. I called the improv theatre where we planned to have the party, and we spent a while going back and forth, debating about whether it was safe to still have the party. They didn't know what we should do, and I didn't know what we should do. Finally, after some time, we all agreed to go ahead and continue with the original plan.

That night my family and friends met at the Whole World Improv Theatre Co. in downtown Atlanta. The night was a blast, but there was a drip of fear that trickled like raindrops throughout the night. We did our best to celebrate Nick's fortieth birthday, but we all knew something was going on. We all knew if nothing else, that our grocery stores were empty and toilet paper had become the hottest commodity. It was a fairly small gathering, with a few of my brother's close friends, some of our cousins and aunts and uncles, and my sister, and we had the theatre all to ourselves, but none of us were wearing masks. At the time, there were very few reported cases in Atlanta and only one death in Cobb County, where I lived. We simply did not know how serious this was. At this point, we didn't even know *what* this was. It was unprecedented in our lifetimes to have the world shut down. Our fears were compounded by the virus being intangible to our community at the time, and yet it was clearly circling on us.

We ended the night with cheers to "many more," and then made our way back home. As I left the theatre, I knew I would not have traded the night for anything, and I was glad it came together. When I woke up the next day I was flooded with emails, texts, and voicemails all concerning the virus from friends, family, employees, and upcoming guests planning to stay at our Airbnbs. In this moment, we all knew that this was not going away. Life was changing trajectory, and this was just the beginning phase of what would become significantly different and very quickly.

As the morning turned into the afternoon, I rapidly began to feel how people were reacting and how drastically daily life was changing, for everyone. The reservations for the six Airbnbs we lease were starting to dry up right in the middle of the busiest season. In just one day, all of our current reservations were canceled, and all of the reservations we had on the books for the next few weeks as well. In that one day, the Saturday after the national emergency declaration, we lost $40,000 due to cancellations. And that was only the beginning.

I was at home with my four kids but I felt lost. I felt as if my world was falling out from under me. I needed a way out, an escape. And I knew that my kids did too. Come Monday, they would begin schooling from home, and now I would be stuck at home as well. We are a very active family. Our kids are in sports, musicals, and after-school clubs. If we find ourselves with a free weekend, it is certainly not spent at home. We love to explore the world and travel often when we aren't tied up with school and extracurricular activities. So, with four relatively young children suddenly at home, and without the possibility of getting out of the house other than to go for a walk outside, I was searching for some other type of escape. Then I had a fun idea. We would relocate where home is. Thanks to all the sudden cancellations, we had several vacation homes to choose from. I decided on Sandy Feet Retreat, one of the homes we own with our vacation rental business in Florida. I quickly told the kids to pack because the next day we were headed to the coast.

From Georgia to Florida, I was filled with fear. I jumped back and forth between worrying for the sake of the people on our planet, to going over projections for my company, to entertaining my four kids on a long car ride. They were understandably confused, but as all mother's know, that is when you can't let them see *your* fear. I had to stay strong for them and for myself. Luckily my Aunt Judi had decided to join us on this journey and was there the whole way; she was a godsend. All the kids love her, and so do I. We rocked out to music, we laughed, we played road games with license plates on the backs of cars along the highway, and we did our best to stay positive. Most of the kids didn't know what was going on. And how could they? I barely had a clue yet. I gripped the steering wheel with both hands, aware of how itchy my fingers were to tap through the news and emails and figure out what was happening.

As we neared Sandy Feet Retreat, a troubling sight crossed my windshield: it was a large billboard with a birthday cake in the center, brightly lit with lots of candles. I remembered the birthday party from two nights ago. And then I remembered something else: my birthday was only three days away. In seventy-two hours I would turn thirty-five. That's when my worst fear and most rational thought occurred to me all at once: will life ever be the same again?

It was past midnight. I was sleepless and exhausted all at once. We had been at the house in Florida for one day. My youngest, Maddie, couldn't sleep. An open box of Cheeze-Its sat on the coffee table. Bernie Sanders and Joe Biden were debating for the Democratic seat for the United States presidential election. It was early in the primaries and I wish I could have been more invested. But somehow this debate seemed less important. I wanted to change the channel, find out what was going on with this new virus. But I was scared. I held Maddie tight and watched the two candidates battle it out for the Democratic seat in the nomination for President. I wondered what the world would look like the next day, or the next day, or next year. I could only hope that whatever would happen, that the little girl in my arms and my other daughters sleeping upstairs would remain healthy and safe. I prayed as a mother that I could keep them that way. I kissed Maddie on the top of her head once more as another question was thrown at the candidates. Life, I thought, is scary and hard and stressful. That night was truly a time where I didn't know what would happen next. But as I watched Maddie start to close her sleepy eyes, I knew one certain thing about life. It is truly precious.

Later that same morning, after getting just a wink of shut-eye, I left the four sleeping kids with Judi and raced to the nearest grocery store. It was a madhouse with dozens of people shoving carts around and grabbing everything off the shelves. Luckily, I was able to grab many important necessities, as well as some fun treats for the kids. However, when I finally made it through the checkout line, I went to grab my wallet and felt my heart sink. I had left my wallet at the house. I cursed under my breath, and with the little patience left in me, pleaded with the store clerk behind the register to hold my cart until I returned. He graciously agreed, and I sped back to the house.

The entire drive back and forth, I kept wondering what I would be doing right now if everything was normal. One day my kids were in school and I was running my own business in Atlanta. Now, here I am participating in what felt like a relay race between a beach house and a packed grocery store in Florida. I couldn't help but imagine what the cartoon version of myself would look like right about now in one of those funny papers. I laughed the thought off as I parked, got back in the long line, and paid for my groceries. I got back to the house with the food and supplies and took a deep breath. Whatever the mad house was at the grocery store, at least I was not in charge there. I knew that as soon as I walked through the door of this new terrain, all four kids would be looking in my direction. I said a quick prayer, grabbed the groceries, and walked inside.

The next few hours were a blur as I tried my best to get all four kids to work on their first day of virtual school. I divided up spaces in the house for all the kids to have their own room to work quietly. Aunt Judi helped a ton and made sure the groceries were unpacked while I wrestled with the kids about what classes needed to be done and which pages to turn to in their workbooks. When I finally had a moment to check my phone, I saw that I had over 1,600 emails from work. I couldn't bear to look at them. It felt, in real time, like all hell might be breaking loose. But of course my immediate concern was answering the incessant question, "Mommy, what's four times five?"

The next day, despite being St. Patrick's Day, did not begin very lucky. Early that morning, Aunt Judi took our dog for a walk on the beach. In all the excitement, my dog jumped up on Judi, causing her to fall hard on the tough sand. She was left with a badly sprained hip. Soon the paramedics arrived and rushed her to the E.R. for X-rays. I only had enough time to recover from that when my sister, Stefanie, showed up with her three kids. She helped me tidy up Sandy Feet Retreat and pack my car back up. All together we headed to another vacation rental home we owned called Bayshore. In line with its name, it sits on the bay and had a pool and hot tub, which we hoped would keep the kids entertained. We also have a boat that was docked there. Little did we know that soon we would be banned from even going out on our boat. I often feel at peace staying at Bayshore but not this visit.

I only had seconds to enjoy the scenery before having to rush to pick up Judi from the hospital, drop her off at Bayshore, and find a walker. And when I say find a walker, I mean hunt one down as if it were the Holy Grail. Turns out, they were harder to find than one might think. I drove all over town to several recommended places and did not find a single one. Finally, we came across some luck. In desperation, I contacted the only person I knew that lives in the area, the cleaning lady for my vacation homes. Amazingly, she had an old walker that her dad had used, and she was able to lend it to me for Judi. By that time, I was exhausted, and that's when Michael showed up.

Michael had been in Atlanta covering our business from the home front while I juggled the kids and their school. We were happy to see each other and decided to really let our hair down that night. It was St. Patrick's Day and Michael, myself, and the kids all dressed up in green galore, with shamrock shirts and party hats to boot. We partied Irish style until bedtime. Then, after the kids were down, Michael prepared the traditional birthday breakfast cake that we do in our family. This one was for me, and I couldn't wait to eat it. I went to bed that night thinking of all that had happened in just a short amount of time. And I had a thought: If my life is so hectic in the middle of all of this, I wondered what other people around the world were going through alongside me.

The next morning, March 18th, was my thirty-fifth birthday. It had been five days since I told my team to work from home and three days since I had left Atlanta. And yet, so much had already happened. But for some reason, I could not get a random idea that I had out of my head. As we sat down to enjoy a delicious birthday breakfast cake, I began to form a plan. It made me laugh that in spite of all this, no matter how tired I was and how much I had to do, I wanted to do something else. That is who I am: if a million things aren't happening at once, I'll add one more thing in the mix. God only knows why. But this new plan was something small, a sort of curiosity that had begun to itch inside me, pushing me to seek out what others were going through.

You see, the world was changing fast around me from my

little corner of the world. I could see the early stages of how hard this pandemic was affecting so many people around me. Then later, I saw many changes over the course of a year. People lost loved ones and could not physically attend their funerals due to restrictions; people were stuck with kids they could not teach and bills they could not pay. Whole countries were shut down from planes coming in or going out. In the United States, people began moving all over the country like an irritated ant hill. Businesses were shut down "temporarily" and never opened back up again. One of my dear friends had to say her final goodbye to her grandmother through a closed window before she passed away because of a new thing called "social distancing" . . . later on in the pandemic we switched to calling this "physical distancing" due to the ability of humans to morph our definition of how to socialize into doing it from a distance. A family friend from Germany lost his father during quarantine and was then isolated even more in a local hospital, first with his wife as she gave birth to their son, and then by himself, away from his wife as she recovered and quarantined alone for a week. Nothing was as it had been before. Life had not been altered so fundamentally since the days of The Great Depression and World War II.

This was the year that I was most affected economically, socially, emotionally, and spiritually. And at this time, in March, I was not yet aware of the trials and tribulations of the rest of the world. I did not know that this would become a catastrophe for some, a heartbreak for one, a love story for another, and an earth-shattering revolution for everyone else. No matter where you were, who you were, or what you believed, COVID-19 in the year 2020 affected us as a human race so drastically, that most believed nothing would ever be the same again. All I knew was that this virus was everywhere, spread throughout the world. It was not a government conspiracy or some sort of scare tactic. It was not something to be taken lightly. It was a real pandemic with case numbers doubling every four days (until the world locked down) and the global death rate increasing daily.[1] It was, in a word, scary.

But hidden inside one of the biggest pandemics in our lifetime, I was able to talk with and seek out something else that arose from the wake of this. I found a droplet of hope, of love, of optimism, and of faith inside different people from all over the world. This was certainly a war. But unlike The Great Depression or World War II, this was a war for people by people. In the throes of a changing landscape, one wrought with fear and death, job loss and money loss, depression and anxiety, some were able to find hope through all of this. I did not know just how much hope could be stored away inside a single person until they are put to the ultimate test. But in these pages you will see the hope that rang out from the hearts and minds of people that might be just like yourself. Believe me, I saw it too.

The first true sign of hope comes from a young man from Venezuela.

Alessandro Cavedoni:
A Story on Perseverance

From the time he was a little boy, growing up in Venezuela, Alessandro loved music. It was his solace in a country that he could not escape, yet a place he knew he was not long for. He did not know when, or where, but he knew he and his family would move up in the world. Music helped him see those visions. Alessandro was and still is a gifted, dedicated violinist. He learned how to play at a very young age and continued to get better as he grew up. His sister, Camila, was equally as talented with an instrument. But the world they played the music in was not as peaceful as the music they played. The Cavedoni parents, Doris and Roberth, were politicians for thirteen years. They fought hard to see both Hugo Chavez's and Nicolás Maduro's fall from power. But their efforts, the same ones the children took on in their teen years, were met with danger and threats of death. The ultimate danger came when Alessandro himself gave up his gift of music and finally used his voice instead.

Alessandro and Camila often played their music at large rallies attended by the whole family in Venezuela. It was here where his parents would march and make grand speeches against the tyranny brought by men like Chavez and Maduro. Once, at a very large rally, Alessandro stood up as a young teenager and spoke to the crowd of thousands for approximately five minutes. He even quoted Simon Bolivar, former liberator of Venezuela, with the words, "When tyranny is the law, rebellion is a right."[2] This speech, in all of its courageous glory, tipped the scales for the enemy and brought danger to the Cavedoni's doorstep. Soon after the speech was made, a group of extremists from Maduro's side threatened to kill the kids by chopping them up into pieces, placing the pieces into bags, and sending the bags to their family.

Alessandro's mother knew this was real. She had her own brush with death years before in an attack on her life from people very similar to those now threatening her children. Despite the children's growing passion, she urged the family to flee Venezuela. So, after sixteen years of bravely fighting against the system that ruled their beloved country, the Cavedoni family fled their home. It would take a lot of work and luck to get a better home in a safer place. They could die on the way out of Venezuela, they could die on the way to the border, or even at the border. But they had to take the risk. And they did. On May

24, 2019, they left the dangerous country they called home and set out in search of American soil.

The family traveled to the Mexican-American border, where they were able to find a migrant's shelter. Countless families arrive and try to get in but are denied due to space and the system being overwhelmed. The shelters provide a free and safe place to stay while working through the asylum process to enter the United States. Alessandro's family was lucky to find a place for themselves, as men, women, and children were forced to sleep outside the shelters. Some get swindled by men offering help that only turns out to be a con. They are called "Coyotes," and they are very dangerous. Some families at the border are threatened, and even a few can be kidnapped or even killed by these men. Alessandro reflected on his journey in his journal that he later shared:

"It was not an easy trip for me and my family. In fact, it was tortuous. The Chavista Regime had made it difficult for Venezuelans to leave the country. The Venezuelan immigration has been considered the largest immigration in a decade (with more than four million immigrants in different countries, often compared to the Syrian Immigration). The Regime has increased the cost of passports (one passport could easily cost $2000), it has shut down borders, etc. Thankfully, my family and I had gotten our passports before the prices went up. Still, since we were being politically persecuted, we feared that if we got to an airport, the authorities would not let us travel (as they do with many other people). The best way to escape Venezuela was, given that we lived in a border state, to cross the border into Colombia. The Venezuelan authorities do not have the proper technology to process the migratory information (at the borders) of who leaves and enters the country quickly enough to stop or question anyone from leaving.

Once in Colombia, we took an airplane to Bogota to later travel to Mexico and start our immigration process for the United States formally. In order to take that airplane, we needed to have proof of entry to Colom-

bia, so we had to stop at the Venezuelan immigration checkpoint so we could have our passport stamped. It took us around an hour to get them stamped. It seemed as though they tried to delay the process for everybody. We were nervous and scared.

Two days later, we departed Bogota. We were heading to Cancun, Mexico. We wanted to start our Political Asylum Process at the Mexico-US border. We traveled from Cancun to Monterrey, and then from Monterrey to Nuevo Laredo (which borders the city of Laredo, TX). On June 1, 2019, we arrived at the border at Nuevo Laredo. We headed to the International Bridge right away. Then the American Authorities informed us of the very new process we had to follow in order to seek political asylum. We needed to go back to Mexico's Immigration Checkpoint to enlist on a waiting list of people seeking Asylum. But there was a problem. The city of Nuevo Laredo is considered one of the most dangerous cities not only in Mexico, but in the world. It is a very perilous city especially for immigrants. The Mafia Groups (best known as the Northwest Cartel) kidnap immigrants in the city to steal information from their phones. They know that immigrants are likely to have family or friends in the United States who are willing to pay enormous amounts of money for them to release their loved ones. That is how they operate, but we did not know it at the time. After getting back to the Mexican Immigration Checkpoint, they told us that they were not in charge of the waiting list anymore, and we needed to find a shelter that had one of the lists. We walked through Nuevo Laredo streets, completely defenseless of anything that could happen to us. We went to a shelter/church that is close to the International Bridge, but they were not accepting anybody. We felt hopeless. We felt as though we had swam and swam, just to have drowned at the shore. I remember my mom breaking down at the church. We looked at each other, doubtful, crying as well. Yet, we knew we could not give up."

Miraculously, the overcrowded shelter eventually let Alessandro and his family in that day. For several weeks, Alessandro spent hours inside the shelter, contacting immigration attorneys. It fell on him because he was the only family member who had sharpened his English—from listening to songs by Katy Perry of all things. He could never have looked for attorneys in Venezuela safely, but even at the border it was difficult, as their phones had restricted use, only given back to them for a certain amount of time per day. The shelter held these rules as a safety measure. They believed that the so-called "Coyotes" (people that work smuggling people across the border) could possibly be infiltrated in the shelter and could be taking pictures of immigrants to send them to their mafia-group bosses to kidnap them. Alessandro spent every minute he could pleading for someone to take his case, sending emails to all the contacts he could find through the Google web pages and making phone calls. Weeks went by without a word. It crushed Alessandro. The shelter was filling up, and he was running out of options.

It was at this time, July 2019, that Alessandro and I met at the shelter. I had traveled with my Aunt Nancy to the border to donate socks to those in need. I was traveling from shelter to shelter, learning the stories of the people waiting for asylum and searching for a better life. When I happened across Alessandro, I was mesmerized by his story and passion for freedom. I was particularly impressed that he did not simply want to flee a country he was afraid of to get to America but that he wanted to get to America safely in order to get the education and background necessary to fight the oppression of his home country in the right way. He wanted to better himself in order to better his country. But after hearing his difficulties with finding an immigration attorney, I started to feel very sorry for him. In fact, it was more than that. This boy and his family deserved a chance, and I felt a responsibility. Alessandro was just sixteen years old at this time, and his sister Camila was only fifteen. I was able to establish a connection with him through WhatsApp and, after returning home to Atlanta, I began searching for an attorney as best as I could. I updated Alessandro along the way.

Alessandro and his family meanwhile knew there was no reason to stay at the dangerous shelter near the border, so he and his family sought temporary safety in Monterrey, Mexico, two hours south of the border. While they waited there, I spent the little time that I could dedicate to this venture searching for an attorney. I was recommended through an acquaintance to contact Charles Kuck, an immigration attorney based in Atlanta. Charles had been adjunct professor of law at Emory University and the University of Georgia, as well as the former National President of the American Immigration Lawyers Association. He was the real deal and a globally recognized immigration attorney, and he made time to meet with me to discuss Alessandro and his family. From there, Charles put me in touch with Juan Ángel Gómez, an immigration attorney on the border. I urged Juan to take the case, but he had to regretfully decline the request, as traveling down to the border as an immigration attorney is a very dangerous task. Between the Mexican border patrol, who can be corrupt, and the Coyotes, who are known to kill, it was a gamble every time an attorney traveled there. Up until the recent law changes, asylum cases were the only types of cases Juan accepted, but now that asylum seekers were forced to stay inside Mexico versus the United States, this was the issue with finding an attorney in the world that could take the case. It could mean death to those trying to defend the immigrants themselves. It seemed that there wasn't an attorney in the world that would take on an asylum case with the new law of asylum seekers staying inside the walls of Mexico. So what was one to do, I wondered. I then pleaded with Juan to help me find an attorney out there to take Alessandro's case.

It took a lot of discussion between Charles, Juan, and me, but eventually they found Bertha A. Zuniga. It was a miracle to find someone like her who would be willing to cross over the border. This was unprecedented. It was never something immigration attorneys did, but Bertha went out on a limb to help the Cavedoni family after hearing their amazing story. In her words, this special family had a "bright future." Luckily, Bertha, who was also a former immigration judge, was the perfect fit for representing this family. Finally there was light at the end of this dark tunnel.

By September of that year, the family had a court case set for mid-November. Bertha traveled to Monterrey, Mexico, and worked with them to help make their case. The trial, however, was not easy. The family was placed in what is essentially a holding cell, where no cell phones or contact with the outside world is allowed. There was a moment during the trial where Alessandro's mother was allowed to speak for her family. She stood up and defended her family's right to freedom.

Though the journey was long and the trial was arduous, the family was granted asylum in the United States, rather quickly from start to finish, on November 15, 2019. It was an amazing day for them, but after the trial was over, the family was returned to the cell to wait for release. They did not know how long they would be locked inside the cell with no contact. They were told that it could be days. Luckily, after waiting for several hours, they were taken out of the holding cell area and released into the United States.

The family took up shelter in Houston, Texas, in a small apartment just big enough for a family of four to have a roof over their heads. From this small world, the Cavedoni's celebrated with joyful hearts and began a new life. It just so happened that they moved into their first American apartment in Houston on November 24th, Thanksgiving Day, the same day Alessandro turned seventeen. "Funny," he thought as they moved into their new home on free land, "now *we* are the settlers."

Only five months of settling went by before the brewing storm known as COVID-19 began to sweep through Texas and the rest of the world. By that time, Alessandro was in his junior year of high school with the intention of studying Political Science at Texas A&M in the Fall of 2021. There were talks of green cards coming in the next six months, as well as a house instead of the apartment they were renting. Their lives were much better, but they still had a long way to go. Although the Cavedoni parents no longer had the stimulating careers that they once had, they still worked just as hard as a housekeeper and construction worker in the United States as they improved upon their English to obtain better positions.

When the news began breaking of this novel virus that wrapped itself around the lives of people everywhere, the whole family could feel the tension mounting.

Most immigrants know that when something bad happens, they are not the first group to receive help. It typically means even more hard work for the migrant families to receive unemployment, even if they are always the first wave of people to be fired or "furloughed" from the only jobs they could acquire. The Cavedoni family felt fear again for the first time in months, and Alessandro knew this could only mean more hard work. The one silver lining he and the rest of the family turned to was that, at the very least, they were not stuck in Venezuela when the virus swept through there. Even if they were scared of the virus, they were no longer terrified of being chopped up.

And so, in mid-March of 2020, the quarantine phase of everyone's life began. It was a long time indoors. In the early days of the quarantine, Houston implemented a curfew for all residents. Only essential workers were allowed to travel past the set hours of this new curfew. Police monitored the streets, simply looking for wandering pedestrians that were outside. Luckily, both Doris and Roberth were considered essential, as she worked at a hotel and Roberth worked in construction as a laborer. Even still, their hours were cut back enough that the family dollar had to be stretched even further. During that time, both Alessandro and Camila began schooling virtually, which compounded the difficulty of learning in a second language. Despite that, he and Camila were able to maintain high scores throughout. School helped both of them stay focused and calm regardless of being indoors all day. It was not until the summer began that the panic set in for Alessandro.

During the hot Texas summer hours, stuck inside an apartment all day long, Alessandro began to feel trapped and scared. This new virus was not part of his plan for a better life. He began to experience serious panic attacks and was quick to anger much more than he ever had felt before. He needed an outlet, a way to experience real life to the best of his ability. In July 2020, he decided to get a job. He applied and was hired as a cashier at a Burger King. He was later promoted to shift manager. This extra income helped relieve his family's economic pressure.

Unlike some American families where the children are kept at bay from the parents' finances, most immigrant families are well aware of how expensive life really is, and the communications about money are more out in the open. Although the extra money was great, when school started back up in September, his grades suffered because of the time spent at work instead of on his homework. He did his best to balance both, but his commitment to good grades and high marks forced him to quit his job at Burger King and focus solely on school in December 2020.

Over those five months, while the world watched in unison as the virus spread, Alessandro saw a world he had only just begun to learn change right before his eyes. When asked how it affected him, he had this to say: "The pandemic taught me that everything could change overnight. One day you can have many things: stability, family, friends, but no one knows for how long. Still, the pandemic was not an obstacle but a lesson that many of us had to go through. I always say that I never look at what lessons like these take away from me but what they improve in my life for me and my family." Instead of cowering in the wake of another disaster, Alessandro used the vitality he acquired back in Venezuela to combat the feelings brought on by this new unknown. He worked hard to work with the pandemic rather than to hide from it.

But there was something lacking inside of him, something that had brought him so much peace and joy in his life no matter the circumstances. His violin. When they had fled Venezuela, he was forced to leave it behind. Now, almost a year later, he knew he needed it back. So in early 2021, Alessandro used some of his savings to purchase a brand new violin.

"Ever since I got my new violin, I have been playing and relieving my stress and anxiety through music. It was difficult for me to control my feelings of frustration without playing the violin, and when I finally had it, it was as though every negative emotion dissipated."

By early 2021, prior to the general public getting vaccinated, the American lifestyle had begun to do its best to resume the former way of life. Of course, nothing was as it had been, and Corona was certainly still a threat. Alessandro watched a strict Texas city slowly regress back to old ways. Social distancing and mask laws were still upheld at this point, but all the curfews relaxed significantly. Watching the Americans react was an eye-opener for Alessandro to see how differently Americans listened to power compared to how Venezuelans do. Sure, there were protests in Venezuela, but only as a demand for basic necessities. Americans did not even protest for their rights back; they just took them. It was something Alessandro, a year into this new way of life, was dumbfounded by.

But it was not just about his safety or even about only his family's. For Alessandro, he was worried for everyone. "I think of (the people) now, and I worry about them. I worry about those whose immune systems cannot fight the virus. I worry about the elderly, about the kids. I worry about the homeless, who are highly defenseless, about immigrants, about those who do not have access to healthcare insurance. I worry about the doctors that face this enemy daily and fight endlessly to save other lives. I worry not only about me but about every person that lives in this world."

Because that is who Alessandro is, a champion for the people. He uses his voice for the people, for those who have no voice, or think they have no voice.

He uses his music for himself, a way to cope and heal from life's hard trials. Sure, the beautiful melodies might sound like they are for a crowd, and maybe you might hear him and be entranced. But don't be fooled. He is playing to calm his soul, something he has done since he was a little boy. He saves his voice for the crowds. And don't worry, he won't stop anytime soon. He has big plans. But in the meantime, he will simply play the notes and pray for peace. You'll know when he begins to speak because it will change the world.

---

1. David Robson, "A simple mathematical mistake may explain why many people underestimate the dangers of coronavirus, shunning social distancing, masks and hand-washing," BCC, August 12, 2020, https://www.bbc.com/future/article/20200812-exponential-growth-bias-the-numerical-error-behind-covid-19 (accessed September 3, 2020).
2. "US Republican Senator Calls for Coup in Venezuela," teleSUR, February 9, 2018, https://www.telesurenglish.net/news/US-Republican-Senator-Calls-for-Coup-in-Venezuela-20180209-0015.html (accessed October 26, 2021).

2

"PEACOCK!"

The trip to Florida was nice, but sooner or later I knew I had to come home. My sister and I agreed that she and her family would stay with us once back in Atlanta during the quarantine, at least for a little while. I was happy to include her, but I slightly worried what life may be like back at home with seven kids and nowhere to go. I also was a bit concerned about what wild, hairbrained ideas I might come up with. And I'll be honest, I even surprised myself a bit.

On March 21st, after returning home from our getaway to Florida, my best friend Ashleigh and I took a trip to the local tractor supply store, and I purchased everything one would need to start a chicken farm. The thought had occurred to me in a conversation I had with Ashleigh on the drive back from Florida. My rationale was twofold. One, I knew that the kids would need hands-on experience since they wouldn't have any at school, so I would bring the school to them. And two, I knew that my local community, neighbors and friends and even the people I work with, could benefit. What's better than fresh eggs, right?

Over the course of the next week, we built a chicken farm

from scratch. And it turns out that this is one hell of a process if you're not a real farmer. I wanted to throw my hat in that ring, but alas, I learned that I am not made for the job of building a fence and chicken coops. I did however have a very interesting time putting it together. The kids all helped construct it. We put fences up all around the edge of a patch of field just beyond the pool area. We built a large, three section chicken coop on the left and put mulch down on the ground for the chickens to have. The coop was multilayered. They could hatch and use the restroom all in one very large man-made facility. We even put string decorations around the fenced area and bought three Easy-Fill Drinkers for water, pulling the hose up from the side of the house and connecting it to all three. Once the farm was complete, I ordered thirty hens and two roosters. When they arrived a few days later, the kids and I decided to name the roosters Tom and Jerry.

Over the course of a couple weeks with my husband, our four kids, my sister Stefanie, her husband, their three kids, Aunt Judi, and me all in one house, things were becoming hectic, minute by minute. We were attempting to homeschool seven children under the age of nine. I decided that we needed a system. So I implemented two very fruitful systems in the house. The first was "The Bell System" where if one person saw any other person doing something nice, they rang a tiny bell that sat in the kitchen. Everyone in the house would have to freeze, and the person who rang the bell could tell everyone else the nice thing that they saw. This system was a way to positively reward kindness in the house, and push the kids to be nicer and stop fighting, so they could be bragged about for their kindness by their siblings/cousins. It actually worked quite well.

The next system was simply called "Peacock," and this was for the adults only. There were seven young children in the house and only five adults, all of whom had to multitask between supervising, feeding, and educating kids and doing their own, grown-up jobs in the same house. So the rule was that at any time, in the middle of any situation, if an adult had become so overwhelmed or exhausted, they could just yell "Peacock," and they automatically got a two hour break from everything, no questions asked. Usually they would either nap or just watch TV, but it was a way to unwind and actually focus on something else, even if it was getting their own work done in peace and quiet. I came up with that random word when looking at a peacock painting we had on the wall. The system worked out well and no one abused the privilege. Some of us used it more than others but not to an unfair amount. By the end of it all, it had proven to be a great tool that most of us took advantage of every day or so.

It was around the time we were finally getting a bit of order into the home that I did something crazy. Probably the craziest thing I did the entire quarantine and quite possibly in my entire life. I bought some pocket pets. I purchased a guinea pig (we owned two already), five hamsters, and fourteen mice. The idea at the beginning was a good idea, I swear. Dr. Jonathan Glass is the Head Researcher at the Emory ALS Center in Atlanta, and he spends $10,000 a month on mice for research purposes. Since I already donate money to them on a regular basis, I figured that I would just raise mice for them, save them money, and create value at home by giving my kids something fun to do.

That was the idea.

It quickly scurried out of control faster than a cage of mice.

When I bought the mice, there were fourteen. I thought they would just run around in their cage all day and be dumb and happy. It turns out they are much more complex than we imagine. At first, the baby mice were as cute as I had hoped. They were tiny and very fun to watch. My kids even favored the baby mice over the other new pets, and they managed to get one mouse to dangle from their finger by its tail, a common practice if you can train it right. But like all animals, they grow. Not only did they grow but a few ended up getting pregnant. And once they get pregnant and have babies, they get vicious. Before I could stop it, the entire project, like an action scene in a movie, blew up in my face in slow motion. First off, I didn't have enough food. The mice just ate all day long and left their little "pellets" everywhere in the cage. Once they ran out of food, they wasted no time in eating each other. We also had to fill their water container three times a day because there were so many of them, and they were all so thirsty. Within a couple of weeks, they became a burden to manage. By the end of this epic tale, the pregnant mice had given birth to a grand total (no exaggeration here) of seventy-eight new baby mice. I know this because I returned them all to the pet store and they counted every last one of them. Because of the cannibalism and pregnancies, I returned eleven of the original mice, seventy-eight new babies, and two of the original were still pregnant and more babies were on the way.

Suffice it to say, I was not sentimental about returning them to the experts. As I drove home from the pet store, I was glad for them to be gone and could not help but laugh at myself. I admit that I went in with blinders on. I thought, "How hard could it be, really?" I see now that I truly underestimated the task of caring for some simple mice. We all moved on from the whole affair with my cheeks just slightly redder. I learned then and still remind myself now that just because you think you are doing something nice for your kids, it should never mean it drives you crazy. And the kids didn't care. They still had plenty of guinea pigs and hamsters to play with.

The evening I returned the mice, I was so tired by this point I could barely think. Sure the mice were out of my hair, but I still had a house full of kids, dogs, cats, hens and roosters, five hamsters and three guinea pigs running around, and a real estate company where most of the contracts were being terminated by people who thought it was the end of the world. As I neared my home, I agreed with my clients that maybe it was the end. And then that other thought came back to me. That nagging thought about what other people around the world might be up to around this time. I let the thought fester as I walked inside. I was so tired as I opened the door to my house that before I even got two steps inside I immediately called out, "Peacock!"

Caleb Ambudoss: A Story on Preparation

Tamil Nadu lies on the southernmost part of India, bordered by the union territory of Puducherry and shares a maritime border with the nation of Sri Lanka. The most common languages are Tamil (Thamizh) and English. It is one of the wealthier parts of the country of India and ranks eleventh among all Indian states in the human development index. It is most known for its beautiful architecture, food, and rich culture such as dance and Carnatic music. It is here where Caleb Ambudoss, his wife, Anita, and two daughters left for America twenty-three years ago. They settled down in Marietta, Georgia, and became U.S. Citizens ten years later. Both Caleb and Anita work as computer engineers and their two daughters attend Georgia State University. Life was as normal as they had always dreamed it could be until the fateful date of March 13, 2020. Then things rapidly began to change. Luckily Caleb had been paying attention, and unlike some, he was ready. The biggest task that lay ahead of him was preparing everyone else he loves.

Caleb has always believed in the idea that whatever can go wrong will go wrong. He is happy when he turns out to be, well, wrong, but he does not bet highly on the positive. For him, life means preparing for the hard times. And when a worldwide virus shut down life as we knew it, he knew this was the ultimate test. The first thing he made sure to do was to start stockpiling food. He began buying large quantities of non-perishable items that could last his family for at least three months, six at the most. He also bought sanitary materials and began cleaning surfaces thoroughly and often. But it wasn't enough to take care of the present-day issue. Caleb was already looking way ahead into the future, a future he very well may not be a part of. Caleb was not afraid of dying, but he was afraid of leaving his family with nothing. In preparation for such an event, he took out a life insurance policy on himself with the idea that his daughters could continue school and his wife would not need to take on an extra job. Then it came time for the next task that lay ahead: his daughters.

Because his daughters grew up most of their lives in America, they had American friends and went to an American school. Not to mention that when it comes to mindsets, America and India are very similar. Most citizens don't want to be told what to do, and rarely do they believe the "lies" the government is telling them. Caleb was lucky to at least live in America, where even if the mindset was to not believe what they were being told, at least they were being informed. In India, most of the citizens did not even know what was going on with COVID-19 as the leaders of their government tried to cover it up. But Caleb was not going to let his daughters go uninformed. He gathered them together at the very beginning of the pandemic, his wife by his side, and told them what was going on and how serious it all really was. They had been relying on their friends at school for information and did not think it was as serious as Caleb believed it to be, but he slowly and heartily worked to show them the truth: that this was not just going to "blow over." Luckily they took this advice to heart. Their family grew stronger by learning to stay safe together.

After his daughters slowly began to get the message and internalize the reality, Caleb and his wife moved onto family members in India. They discovered that not only was India as a country very uninformed due to their government but also that most people in the country cannot work from home. A lot of Indians are day laborers and need to stay at their job in order to do it. This caused for less of a quarantine than was needed, despite a twenty-one day lockdown in May.

Caleb was one of the first people to tell his family in India about the serious nature of the virus, and the ways in which they could prevent getting it. This went on for several months, with Caleb being the enforcer of cleanliness and health. He was lucky to have the support of his loving wife and the understanding of his daughters. The hardest part was convincing family members halfway across the world about a virus that they were, at first, being told wasn't a big deal.

However, after the death rates in India began to skyrocket, Caleb was not the only person telling India's citizens just how dangerous the virus really was. In September 2020, *CBS News* released an article that made Caleb's skin crawl. The title alone was shocking to see: "India's coronavirus crisis is catching up to the U.S.-it may already be worse."[1] By then, the only silver lining was that the government officials in India began to take the proper precautions. According to Caleb, they even invaded cell phone signals. Instead of a typical ringtone that you might hear when calling a friend or loved one, you would hear a government-mandated statement regarding the wearing of masks and the importance of staying in-doors and avoiding large crowds. They may have delayed their reactions, but eventually India caught on to the real fatality this virus had brought to the world at large.

On November 15, 2020, usnews.com reported that India had just registered over 30,000 new Coronavirus cases.[2] By then, India was fighting back and doing their best to ward off the threats of this deadly disease. According to the site, "To tackle the rise in infections, India's home ministry said it will airlift doctors from other regions to the capital, double the current testing numbers and provide 300 additional intensive care unit beds to fight the spread of the virus,"(Associated Press, 2020). It was what Caleb had feared all along, and he was glad to have his homeland responding in the right way, pushing hard to head themselves in the right and safe direction.

Back at home in America, things remained steady. He and his wife worked from home most of the year while his two daughters schooled virtually from their apartment right off campus. He still continued to check in with his daughters and family in India; things began to look up as the months went by. As the year 2020 came to a close, Caleb was able to reflect back on what he had done to prepare and how important it was to teach others the same ideals he carries with him. When asked about what this year taught him, he reflected: "Nothing is dependable. Life is so fragile and we need to help friends and family and the community. We should be proactive. We need to have a fallback plan. We need to be economical and realistic in life."

Caleb does not think it is smart to assume everything will be okay. He has a drive inside him to prepare for the worst, no matter what. When it comes to the future of the world as we know it, this virus was a teaching moment for him. He learned how unprepared he really had been, despite thinking he had covered all his bases at the beginning. He knows that if a virus like this can happen once, it can happen again. America, nor the rest of the world, is out of the woods by any stretch.

In the spring of 2021, the cases of COVID-19 were still rising rapidly in India. According to a CNN report in late April, India's major areas were dealing with mass burials for the lives lost due to the virus.[3] Given the excruciatingly large number of deaths, most victims' bodies were being burned to cut down on cost and waste in the country. Caleb reflected that more than a year after the pandemic froze the world, in places like India, the disease was far from over. It may never be over. But Caleb knows that, and he knows he must continue to do his part to protect himself and the ones he loves.

The most important thing is to prepare, to know that life is not meant to be easy, and the better prepared you are, the easier it can be. But you have to work for that ease. Therefore, he will work for himself, for his wife, for his daughters, and for the family in India that he loves and worries about. Nothing is more important to him than that, and he will fight for those things because he knows that is what is required of him. He doesn't mind, as long as those he loves, near or far, are safe when the next hard time comes along. Just be prepared, because life does not care if you are or not, so it comes down to you and how much effort you're willing to put towards the safety you need. But sometimes how hard you can physically, emotionally, and mentally work at being prepared, can boil down to how much sleep you can get.

---

1. Arshad R Zargar, "India's coronavirus crisis is catching up to the U.S. - it may already be worse," CBS News, September 7, 2020, https://www.cbsnews.com/news/india-covid-cases-coronavirus-catching-up-to-us-expert-says-may-already-be-worse-schools-stay-closed/ (accessed January 11, 2021).

2. Associated Press, "The Latest: India Registers Over 30,000 New Virus Cases," U.S. News,
Nov. 15, 2020, https://www.usnews.com/news/health-news/articles/2020-11-15/the-latest-india-reports-another-41-000-coronavirus-cases (accessed January 9, 2021).
3. Jessie Yeung, Clarissa Ward, Rishabh Pratap and Scott McWhinnie, "As India's crematoriums overflow with Covid victims, pyres burn through the night," CNN, May 1, 2021, https://www.cnn.com/2021/04/29/india/india-covid-deaths-crematoriums-intl-hnk-dst/index.html (accessed May 14, 2021).

3

SLEEPLESS

Nearing the end of March, sleep had become a distant illusion. The tension in my world and the world around me seemed to increase day-by-day. There was a constant flood of emails, text messages, and updates about the virus. When I tried to stay updated on the current news, it was like trying to mop up water from an overflowing bathtub. On top of that, there were four kids who needed help with this new virtual schooling thing. Instead of raising their hands and calling for a teacher, they were running up to me with a laptop or workbook open, asking me what this means and what that means. In total honesty, it made me feel more overwhelmed than my own work. I can do my own work, even if it is crazy. But I had not trained to be a teacher, so what was I supposed to tell them? Every time one of the kids came up to me with questions, I imagined a game of Russian roulette: how many more right answers were left in the chamber before I gave them a wrong answer?

In between responding to business messages and helping my kids with school, I swiped through dozens and dozens of news articles about the virus all day long. I could feel myself growing addicted, not to the pain, but to the unprecedented nature of this new world order. For what felt like the first time in my life, I was living through a historic moment. I wanted to absorb every bit of it.

It was, however, very hard to zero in on the news because it was so overwhelming. I had a lot to focus on for work. Contracts on houses we had listed continued to terminate. Messages of positivity were being sent out amongst team members of our company, but no one could really say for certain what was going on. We were losing money every day; my husband and I were scrambling to reorganize the business according to this new work-from-home model. We also had to decide which of our staff to keep on while bracing ourselves for the loss of those employees we had to let go. It was a hard time, and sleep was becoming the least of my concerns.

The thought of reaching out to others only increased. I spent my waking hours late at night wondering what it must be like in China, in Japan, in Germany, in India, etc. I began to make a list in my head of people I knew from different states and different countries. Who could I talk to? Who would respond? Should I do it all at once, or should I make a big group chat? And for what purpose? Just to vent, or for something more? I knew one thing for sure: whatever was going on was becoming everyone's story. Then I saw a video on Facebook that made everything click.

In the video, a man played a live keyboard rendition of the Titanic theme song, "My Heart will Go On" from his open-air apartment balcony in Italy. During a verse of the song, from another balcony a separate man began playing his saxophone along to the melody created by the piano. Several people in other balconies watched and clapped at the end.

Now, of course, this social experiment had been done before a number of times, but this one felt different. It was an example of the power of community, despite worry and pain. But there was something that struck me as new, something original. For the first time ever, we could connect, but not in person. That had never really happened before. Here were all these people separated but yearning for connection. I thought about all those people in different countries. Were they too yearning for connection amidst all this separation? Maybe I could create a connection for people to tell their story. I knew then that I had to learn all the stories I could so that I could put them together. But first, I had to start a conversation that could *become* a story.

It was late one night that the itch I had developed all the way back in Florida began to take shape. The kids were upstairs, fast asleep, and I was sitting in my basement with Aunt Judi. A movie played in the background, but to this day I don't remember what it was. I was so distracted with this idea. It had grabbed a hold of me like a thief in the night and would not let me go. So finally, at 1:24 a.m. on March 24, 2020, in my tired, maddening haste, I pulled up WhatsApp on my phone and began a group chat. The initial group consisted of sixteen people, all friends of mine that I had met from world travels. I introduced myself and listed out the sixteen names, where each person was from, and how I knew them. My goal was to create a platform for everyone to share news articles from their countries and to also share their experiences, thoughts, and feelings regarding the pandemic. I wanted them to see just how comforting it can be to have a community, even with people you don't know. It was created as a safe space for those around the world to share their experiences in this unprecedented time.

I knew my social experiment could fail. I knew it could get two responses and then be forgotten. But I was happy. I had created the idea that had been growing inside of me. Now it was just about waiting, hoping that someone would reach out and share their experience. I did not expect much, but I went to bed happy and satisfied with what I had started. That night, for the first time in several days, I fell asleep soundly. I had no idea what would come of the group chat. But peace greeted me then as I finally closed my eyes and drifted off. As I slept that night, I began to dream of a land down under.

Australia:
A Story on Perspective

The 2019-2020 Australian bushfire season was one of the worst ones that the country had seen in many years. It was so bad, in fact, that the season came to be known as "black summer." The fires burned their way through nearly nineteen million hectares, with thirty-four direct deaths, and 445 indirect deaths, most of them the result of smoke inhalation. The resulting cost of the fires hit over 103 billion USD. It destroyed 3,500 homes and 5,852 other buildings, including stores, warehouses, and apartments.[1] [2] It was so catastrophic and long that the citizens living in and around the country were exhausted from it. It didn't matter the ages, state of life, or place lived, all Aussies wished so badly for things to go back to normal. But in March 2020, just two months after "black summer" ended, normal was nowhere near close for the people of Australia.

Darwin is the capital city of the Northern Territory, Australia. It is considered the hottest, wettest, and most northerly of the Australian capital cities and consists of more residents than the rest of the Northern Territory, which is otherwise considered sparse. It is a coastal city, lying on the Timor Sea and is flanked by Frances Bay to the east and Cullen Bay to the west. It is here where Fiona McManus always planned on retiring, and when she finally did, she was happy. So much happier than she expected, in fact, that nothing was going to get in the way of that. She thought she could handle the fires. She made it through, and by the time those were over, she knew she could deal with Coronavirus.

Fiona worked for the Northern Territory Government for several years before she hung up her work clothes and grabbed her sailing gear. Her choice of yacht to sail on is called a Tasar, a small, two-crew boat with a large red and white sail. Prior to COVID-19, Fiona was able to participate in sailing regattas around Australia and internationally. And the races are not just a niche for some, more than 140 yachts compete in regattas. The ages range from ten year olds to sixty and seventy year olds. However, there was no race in 2020. In fact, there was nothing in 2020.

It was heartbreaking for Fiona and her fellow sailors around the nation, as their passion had essentially been canceled. Fiona says she cannot remember a time in her life when she had not had an international vacation during the year. And to her, retirement was her ultimate holiday. She had no idea she would be locked down during it. But alas, Fiona found ways to keep busy. She focused on minor home renovation projects, gardening, and exploring by road parts of the Northern Territory she had never seen, as she camped out along the way.

Over in Sydney, nearly 2,500 miles away, Hannah Mason had her plans put on hold, but they had nothing to do with retirement. Hannah Mason is the General Manager for the Sydney Philharmonia Choirs, typically held inside the infamous Sydney Opera House. At the time of COVID-19, Hannah's role was to oversee all logistics surrounding the choir, from rehearsal times, to live performance dates, to budget concerns. She was the go-to for all questions about the operations that make the shows happen. So when quarantine began in that part of the world and some people may not have been ready for the challenge, Hannah was the right person for that job. She had completely changed her life more than once before and was much more ready than most to take on such a large challenge.

Hannah is originally from the U.K. When she was in her mid-twenties, she was backpacking through Australia with a friend, and after seeing the sights, they decided to stay there for just a little bit longer. After Australia they were supposed to hike through Asia, but she loved Australia so much that she put her bag down in Sydney and never left. Sydney is the capital city of the state of New South Wales, and the most populous city in Australia and Oceania. It is on the east coast side of the country and is made up of 658 suburbs and spread across thirty-three local government areas. It is one of the most expensive cities there, as well as one of the most well-known due in part to the Sydney Opera House that sits right on the Sydney Harbour, just underneath the Sydney Harbour Bridge. Hannah's immediate love for Sydney kept her there, and her talent for singing gave her a place to work and thrive there as well.

Just before COVID-19 hit the country, 2020 was going to be a big year for Hannah and her place of work for an entirely different reason. It was the year that the Sydney Philharmonia Choirs turned 100 years old. Because of this, dozens of concerts, a series of commissioned works, and three international tours that had been planned months in advance were on the books. Everything was quickly canceled. The lockdowns happened all at once, and the plans for the centennial had to change quickly. One way to help make up for the loss of concerts was to rearrange their performance layout. Zoom became the tool for everyone involved in the choir. Hannah arranged different Zoom concerts, with people singing from home on their laptops, and then the separate pieces were edited together for one large Zoom concert. It's not how Hannah or any of the other members of the choir ever saw themselves performing, but it was a way to sing.

In her personal life, Hannah is married and has two daughters. Her wife's business was affected just as heavily, and she also started working from home. Their kids were nearing the end of elementary school, and she feels that their age helped them deal with virtual schooling a bit better than those young ones that might need more guidance. Not to mention the quarantine in Australia only lasted two months for the kids, and then they were able to transition back into school again. During those two months, however, they made sure to get out of the house, go for walks, ride bikes, and stay active as a family. "It was quite nice in a weird way," said Hannah later. But she, of course, was happy for the girls to go back to school when it was safe.

During her own career lockdown, things were a bit hard. Her whole job relied on crowds and social gatherings, so to have all of that canceled overnight was tough. Her hours were cut down significantly as well, which hurt her financially. She knew it was not going to go on forever, and she did her best to work through the troubles they faced. They did what they could and waited it out. The good thing about Australia is that the country as a whole took the virus very seriously, and that stopped the spread faster than many other countries around the world.

After about two or three months, life began to return to normal. The choir held small, outdoor concerts for people in Sydney, and everyone socially distanced and masked. After a few months of smaller concerts, the venue and crowds were allowed to be larger. It took some time, but eventually Hannah was able to regain a sense of normalcy by the end of 2020. She felt lucky and knew that not everyone had as short of a time with lockdowns as she did in 2020.

For Joanne "Jo" Warr, lockdowns were still happening into 2021. At the time COVID-19 became a pandemic, Jo was working as a primary school teacher in Melbourne, nearly 600 miles away from Sydney. The age range of her students ran from five years old to twelve years old. She is the physical education instructor for the school as well as the school chaplain. The first lockdown lasted six weeks. Melbourne was hit by far the hardest over other areas of Australia, such as Sydney. This is believed to have been because of demographic differences. Melbourne has a much younger demographic than Sydney, for instance, and possibly that translates to the people of Melbourne taking the virus less seriously. Jo herself was impacted greatly as well. Some things worked out for the better, and other changes made her life much harder. When the first lockdown occurred, the entire school was sent home and Jo became a remote teacher. This required her to design an entirely different lesson plan for her P.E. class. After that time, Melbourne did come out of lockdown, but as soon as cases began to rise again, just weeks later, another sixteen week lockdown was set in place.

"That was another, more horrendous lockdown," said Jo, reflecting back on 2020.

Her role this time around was to supervise the children of some of the essential working parents whose children attended the school before COVID-19. They opened one of the classrooms back up, and all the children were put in one class. It did not work out well, as some of the kids were suddenly going to school with their younger or older siblings, creating more fights during lessons. The school had a policy where the classroom teachers would hold a Zoom meeting with their online students twice a day; initially it was three times a day. The first meeting was done at the beginning of the day, where the children would be given a literacy lesson. And the next meeting would happen at noon, where the teachers taught the children mathematics virtually. Jo knew that this type of schooling would be challenging for some children, and their learning may suffer compared to attending school in the flesh where they could socialize and learn directly. Luckily the only class Jo had to worry about teaching was her P.E. class. So she began to set up lesson assignments for her virtual classes to complete at home that were fun and enjoyable, freeing the children from screen time.

In her personal life, Jo is a mother of four grown children. She had her husband, Peter, and daughter Jacquie with her throughout the lockdowns, which she greatly enjoyed. During the lockdowns, two of Jo's other daughters were pregnant, Georgie and Jessie. Georgie went into labor at the end of the second lockdown. She was able to deliver a healthy baby girl at the local hospital on September 23, 2020, but because of COVID-19, she was discharged after twenty-four hours. Luckily, Georgie was able to bring the baby back to Jo's home where she helped care for the new mother and her baby. Georgie's own house was being renovated, so she, her husband, and their dog, all came to stay with Jo.

"It worked out well, quite fun!," says Jo about that time. "The relationships flourished during that time." Just three weeks later, Jessie gave birth on the 15th of October to the first grandson.

As for her friends, Jo did her best to stay connected to them, hosting virtual bridge games and participating in trivia over Zoom every Saturday night throughout the first two lockdowns.

The second lockdown luckily did stop at the end of October 2020. And slowly, things began to go back to normal. Not everything in Melbourne is as it was. But for the most part Jo has made sure to stay connected and stay safe. As of February 14, 2021, Melbourne had a quick, five day lockdown due to a few reported cases in the area. At the end of the day, when things like this happen, Jo is used to it and does her best to stay positive. Because that is who she is, a positive person who sees her grown daughters as friends, their husbands as friends, and her grandkids as precious little babies who need all the care in the world. She knows that Melbourne is not done walking back up the mountain, but Jo Warr can see the top from where she is now.

Throughout the pandemic, Australia was listed among the lowest rated countries in the world for the recorded number of COVID-19 cases. The country approached the pandemic much more aggressively than many other places around the world. For Fiona, Hannah, and Jo, their worlds within the same country seem quite different, their lives are not the same, but their country is healthy, and that is equated by them because of the people in charge doing what is right and the citizens doing what is asked of them. Each one of these women had their lives turned upside down in one way or another. They all had just gotten over large bush fires spreading throughout their country just as the entire world was locked down. They are strong, they are brave, and they know how to put their best foot forward.

Fiona McManus just wants to do her best to stay positive and to stay afloat. Literally. She knows that while some of the regattas are still on hold, she can at least enjoy the open seas with herself or with a few friends. This next year for her may not seem much different on the outside than last year, but her worldview has shown her that the life you expected after all your years of hard work may not be as pleasant right away as you might've imagined it to be. Life takes its time before you get to.

Hannah Mason looks forward to the next few years and hopes that she can take the lessons of hard work she learned during quarantine of how to adapt and keep her head up with her into the future. She wound up in Australia almost by accident but fell in love with it because of the originality, the beauty, and the opportunity. She got her start singing and transformed it into a career with one of the best choir groups in the world. Now she just wants to continue down that path, raise her kids, and continue being a good partner to the woman she married.

Jo Warr always tries to be a positive person. Sure, she had her days during 2020 when she cursed under her breath or got down for a little bit. But she has just entered a phase of life where her family matters more than just about anything else. Her family is what keeps her going, and it is her family that narrowed her focus and gave her a filter with which to view the recent scary times. The bush fires were scary, the pandemic was scary, learning how to teach school virtually was scary. But holding two grandchildren in her arms just weeks apart was nothing short of wonderful. Jo had heard worry within Australia that between the fires and COVID-19 that the world was ending. That is not true. This world is not over, not by a long shot. If it was, then her grandchildren would not be put on this earth to smile up at her when she held them. And she plans to hold her grandkids for many years to come before everything is said and done.

. . .

At the time of writing this, Australia is considered to have one of the lowest COVID-19 rates at number 1 (lowest). That is much lower than what Americans saw throughout the year of 2020.

---

1. Meheryar Khan, "How Much We Lost in 2020," Age of Awareness, May 17, 2021, https://medium.com/age-of-awareness/how-much-we-lost-in-2020-ef9adcea2171 (accessed June 2, 2021).
2. Paul Read and Richard Denniss. "With costs approaching $100 billion, the fires are Australia's costliest natural disaster," The Conversation, January 16, 2020, https://theconversation.com/with-costs-approaching-100-billion-the-fires-are-australias-costliest-natural-disaster-129433 (accessed June 2nd, 2021).

4

438,749

It's 1:30 a.m. on March 26th. I am alone in my real estate office, my computer humming in the quiet that surrounds me. It's dark, save for the blue and white of the illuminated screen. I feel exhausted, spent, alone. It is like a maze I can't seem to find my way out of. I feel I've been trapped in this cycle of a new life for years and years. But it's only the first month. Not even the end of the first two weeks. The suits on the news say it could go on for years. God help us. Maybe He will, but He certainly won't drive me home at this late hour. No, that I have to do myself.

As I climb into my car, my body aching and my mind pulsing like a small animal's heartbeat, I cannot believe what has happened. My streamlined, "runs like a steamship," company has been hit with a tidal wave of pressure. They say this new virus attacked tourism first. Yeah right, try real estate. People are pulling out of contracts, my agents are getting sacked left and right, and money is evaporating like steam in summer. I try to shrug off those thoughts as I turn the key, but then I stop. I let go of the key. I sit back. I think.

It is my greatest asset and my most fatalist of flaws. "You

think too much," said many people in my life. That's right. And it's gotten me here. But where are we now? Sure, now I'm in my car. It's late and my kids are asleep in a home without their mommy. But mommy has to work, mommy has to think, mommy has to pray for absolution.

Not all things are bad, of course. This week has been quite good. The WhatsApp group message is getting a lot of responses from around the world; my five-year-old daughter got into kindergarten at the school her two older sisters attend; my best friend's nana turned 100 and I got to FaceTime her; I also helped a friend of mine, Dr. Good, make a promo trailer for his YouTube series. Not to mention, I got into canning. And yes, all of that is good. But then there are the constant, addicting, COVID-19 updates I flock to. Yesterday I saw that the U.S. is up to 65,797 confirmed cases. That brings the worldwide total to 438,749 confirmed cases.[1] [2] And it's only the first month. So is this the end of the world or just a dark section in future history books? I turn the key and let the car engine answer the question. It growls back at me.

As I turn onto the major road back to my house, the streets are empty. Normally the city is full of traffic filled with angry drivers, during the day at least. But now there is not a headlight in sight. That is new. That is rare. Maybe they're at home, praying for health and happiness. Or maybe they're just asleep. Because it is almost 2:00 a.m. now. The green lights don't redden as I pass through intersections on the way back home. My headlights cut through barren back roads and dense, dewy fog. I drive slowly as I near my home, where my family slumbers. I try my best to not think about the numbers of confirmed cases, or the number of lost incomes, or the number of fired employees. I try my best to think about the good things in the last few days. The things that, as we keep getting told, are most important. The little things. But right now, I cannot think of the little things. Because the numbers are irrefutable. Because 438,749 is not little, I think to myself. No, I decide, it is not.

A few days later, On March 29th, my family and I celebrated Easter Sunday as best we could. My sister and her family joined mine for a big egg hunt in the backyard. I decided to go all out this year. Why not? I had the time since Easter Sunday church service was canceled. That seemed otherworldly. I got 400 eggs and one golden egg. I hid them all over the yard and divided up the hunt between "under five years old," and "five and older." It was fun and a good way to get everyone together for a happy occasion. The weather was warm and the kids looked adorable in their bright Easter clothes. But while my heart was on my sleeve that day, my mind was on many other things. I considered a dozen times that day to sneak upstairs and check on the news or emails from work. But I didn't. I couldn't. I was in the moment, outside under the warm sun, watching young children shove chocolate eggs into their mouths. A child's innocent joy never ceases to make me smile. I was lucky that the rest of the week continued to make me smile just as much.

The next morning, after working outside on my farm, I wrote to my old boss from Morgan Stanley. His name is Phil Tague, and he has been a mentor to me since I was twenty-three years old. My life trajectory is undoubtedly on a different path because of the opportunities he entrusted me with in my role at Morgan Stanley, and where those paths took me helped set me up for success and the courage to eventually start my own business. I am forever grateful.

I look forward to when, once or twice a year, Michael and I can meet with him and catch up, as well as the letters we send to each other. I told him briefly how I had built a farm and how well it was doing. He simply wrote back, "That's right out of your playbook." From the moment I read that, I could not stop thinking about it. It may seem like a passing comment, but it spoke to me on many levels. It was similar to if you had taken a chance on a new wardrobe choice and someone in line behind you at the grocery store complimented you. In all the chaos of the present, it was nice to know that someone out there believed I was doing the right thing. It did then, and still does, validate the mini-farm my family and I built.

Midday, the last day of March, the office was deserted because of the "stay-at-home" orders. Michael and I received a call from a neighbor that a homeless man was living on the property where our office is located. I called the police to report, and then Michael and I decided to leave the kids with my sister and drive over together. We arrived to find a gentleman, mid-fifties, wearing cargo pants and a long, drab green shirt. He had been camping out in the back of our property, in a fenced-in area of the back parking lot, where we store our "For Sale" lawn signs. He had completely moved in—a knife and food on the table, bags of clothes beside it. He had even been using the trash can as a bathroom. Two local Cobb County Police Officers spoke with the man while Michael and I tried to assist.

The scene went on for some time; he pleaded to stay on our property. He couldn't stay, though, because it posed danger to our agents who randomly needed access to the office. Unfortunately, due to the new COVID-19 lockdown orders, the police officers were not allowed to take him anywhere. They could not even put him in their car. It was early enough in the pandemic that the officers were on strict orders as far as physical contact was concerned between them and the public, but yet none of us were wearing masks yet either. Suffice it to say, it was a confusing time for everyone involved.

I asked the man if he had any other place he could stay, but he did not. I tried to find a few facilities where he could go for shelter. All the shelters I had called for him were closed to anyone new entering because of the pandemic. So, with no solutions, I provided him with a brand new cell phone I just so happened to have laying in my office and worked out a way to have minutes put on the phone. He was apprehensive of my help, but he took it nonetheless. We all watched in silence as he picked up trash bags filled with his belongings and walked off our property and down to the street corner. Once he was safely off the property and taken care of to the best of our ability, Michael and I got back in the car to drive home. That's when I began to wonder. I wondered where the man would sleep that night and I wondered what circumstances brought him to this place. I wondered how, of all the fenced areas in Atlanta, he ended up in mine, during the most chaotic moment of my life.

Was this some sort of sign, or was this just a homeless man who needed a hiding spot? Did I do the right thing, or should I have done more? These questions swam through my mind. And then I thought about the number. The 438,749 confirmed cases. That many people could die. People with families, with mortgages, with pets who needed to be fed. And here was this man, maskless, homeless, friendless. And then I was reminded of the group messages, the people from all over the world who must be experiencing such similar, otherworldly chaos.

As we neared the house on that last day of March, the crest of April coming over the horizon, I wondered if these people from around the globe could participate in answering this new question in my head. How does all of this work together so haphazardly? How can I throw a beautiful Easter egg hunt one day and two days later I'm chasing a homeless man off the same property that has my name on the door? I suddenly could not wait to hop back on the app and tell everyone my story. I could feel that itch flare up inside me again, the gravitational pull inside me to lunge for my phone and read more stories from this chaotic, messy, beautiful world.

If only then I had an inkling of the kinds of stories I would come to learn about so well. Like how sacred life is, both at the beginning and at the end.

Benjamin Elbracht:
A Story on Life

Life in Bremen, Germany, was like living anywhere else you can imagine, and Benjamin Elbracht liked it that way. He was your typical family man: fun, loud, with a big smile on his face, and a hearty laugh that comes from a soft place. Before the world changed, Benjamin worked in the wholesale brewery business, traveling throughout the major parts of Germany as the middle man between breweries and their distributors, such as bars and grocery stores. He'd been working in a job that allowed him to live comfortably and engage in his social, gregarious nature. Then the Coronavirus brought the entire known world to a screeching halt. And suddenly, life became very different for Benjamin and his family, but it did not become any quieter.

From flying all over his home country to suddenly being locked down in his home with his wife and young daughter, Benjamin knew things would not go back to normal for a while. The first thing he noticed was the impact on bars and believe it or not, many grocery stores being closed down. He quickly saw the business he had made a living from for more than a decade begin to crumble. Suddenly, the typical beer and wine companies were not comfortable producing new products, and the expensive products took a big hit financially. What many people don't know is that people mostly consume high end products like Grey Goose and Maker's Mark when they go to the bar and buy cheap beverages when they go to the grocery store. And in a country like Germany, beer is one of the top industries. Who could've predicted that a time would come to this world where nice liquor would go untouched? But it did. And it strained the brewery business that Benjamin was a part of.

This strain on this industry forced Benjamin to draw back from his work life. By the second month of quarantine, he was working twenty percent of the time he used to work, and he could not travel. Like most people around the world, it became all about family time with card games and Netflix. But there was a wrench in the works for the Elbracht family that only grew bigger by the day. Benjamin's wife, Annika, was pregnant before the pandemic began, and by July of 2020, she was at her nine month mark. Before they knew it, it was time for another child to come into the world. As much as they had been preparing in the months prior, they knew this birth would be like nothing they'd ever experienced.

By this point, however, surprises and hospitals went hand-in-hand for Benjamin. The year before, in August 2019, Benjamin's father, Roland, was diagnosed with Stage 4 Lung Cancer while traveling through the south of France with his whole family. They had spent the rest of the trip in the best spirits they could. A few months before the lockdown, in January of 2020, Roland underwent a surgery to get rid of the cancer as best as the doctors could remove it. He spent a little over a week in the hospital after the surgery. Once back home, he continued with his chemo.

Then in March when the virus hit, it made everything more difficult. Little things began to change about the regular way that Roland had been receiving his treatment. Instead of his usual taxi ride, Benjamin's mother had to drive his dad to his chemo appointments. Then she had to wait outside the hospital while Roland did the rounds by himself. Later in the month, Roland started immunotherapy to kill the remaining cancer cells. That exercise did not work out as well. But in June of 2020, they did a test again to see if any cancer cells were left. The doctors couldn't detect anything. So they went to another doctor for another opinion and more testing. Again, no cancer cells were said to remain. As far as they knew, Roland was in the clear. But by that point, Annika was just beginning her hospital adventures.

In July 2020, when Benjamin and his pregnant wife arrived at the hospital, the first thing the hospital staff told Benjamin and Annika was that she would be required to give birth alone and he would have to wait outside the hospital. He informed the well-meaning staff that by no means would he leave his wife to fend for herself during this. The next best solution was a COVID-19 test for both of them. They each gladly took it, then had to wait for the tests to come back negative. Once both of them were approved, they were ushered into the delivery room where they were told to stay for the next twelve hours. And the real kicker? Neither of them were allowed to leave under any circumstances. Now both Benjamin and his wife were used to a stressful birth. Their first child, a daughter, was born by C-Section given her position in the womb. But this was a different situation entirely. He described these twelve hours as feeling "frightened." As the doctors came in temporarily, Benjamin became more and more antsy. At the time, he was a smoker and was not allowed to have a single smoke break the entire half a day that they were kept in the room.

Finally the birth commenced and the baby boy came out healthy and ready to take on the world. No C-Section required. The birth created a new problem though because now Benjamin was forced into a room alone and had to wait for permission to see his new son after he was taken away to be cleaned. After some time, when the doctors finally approached him alone, he was informed of two things: he would have to get into a lot of hazmat gear, and he would only be given twenty minutes with his son, then he had to leave. It confused him, why could he be in the delivery if he'd tested negative for COVID-19, but not be allowed to see his son without such precautions? The doctors told them that the baby and mother were being kept in a separate room by themselves, so as to lower the risk of infection. As a compromise, they would bring the baby to him individually, but only for those twenty minutes.

"Whatever," thought Benjamin, "at this point, I'll take what I can get."

He donned the gear and enjoyed the limited time with his son, holding the new boy in his arms for the full twenty minutes. And for the next week, that was how it went. His wife remained in the hospital for a full week with the baby. This extra stay in the hospital was in case of any exposure to COVID-19 that either the mother or baby received. It was the hospital's mandated quarantine. The logic was that babies are fragile enough for the first few weeks, so it was obviously best to keep them free from exposure and in a hospital for any urgent needs during a worldwide pandemic. All seven days, Benjamin was allowed into the hospital, given a COVID-19 test, forced to wait until it came back negative, then given the right clothing to wear, and was provided access to his son for twenty minutes. After that it was another twenty four hours until he could do it again. He says without hesitancy that he would have done it for a year if that's what it took to hold his son in his arms.

Luckily, the week ended and he was able to bring his wife and son home. The ride back to the house was a relief to both of them. They could resume their life in lockdown with the whole family. The week prior had been difficult for Benjamin, as he longed for his wife, missed his son, and did his best to help his daughter through those long days. Not to mention he still worried about his father. Despite not being able to travel, the birth and the rules surrounding it gave him a new outlook on family time. He felt that nothing was more important than being surrounded by those you love, especially those as young as a newborn. What Benjamin didn't know is just how close he was to losing someone only months after welcoming a new person into the world.

A few months went by as normal as they introduced the baby to their home and the rest of Benjamin and Annika's family. In September of 2020, they went to a small island in Germany called Wangerooge for a vacation. The entire family rented a house, and they noticed very quickly how remarkably well Roland was doing. He began smoking again, drinking on the beach, and really seemed to be back to his old self. They left the trip with a positive outlook, and Benjamin felt that perhaps his father had made it over the hill of this long, scary battle. Maybe his father had beat the cancer.

That all changed within weeks when, at the end of September 2020, Roland began experiencing a shortness of breath and had trouble with something as simple as walking his dog. After a few days, the issue still had not gone away on its own. Benjamin's mother called an ambulance, which was a challenge in and of itself with all the new questions and screening they had to do for each person before emergency services could enter the home. Finally they made it inside, carried Roland out, and rushed him to the hospital. He was only there a few days before deciding on his own, contrary to doctor orders, that he wanted to go home.

"He was always stubborn like that," Benjamin recalled fondly of his father.

His father stayed in bed for the majority of the next three

weeks. They quickly were able to determine that the shortness of breath was due to a lung infection, a side effect of most patients who have lung cancer. Nevertheless, Roland did his best to stick it out, hoping that the infection would pass. He did recover just a little bit, enough that on October 26, 2020, he was able to go and visit Benjamin and Annika and the new baby. But while he was there, he requested an ambulance, which was out of character for a man like Roland. Benjamin could tell right away something was wrong. They called for the ambulance, and after the same screening as before, they rushed Roland to the hospital alone. He was placed in a section of the hospital for new patients who have not yet tested negative for COVID-19. Each patient generally waits in that section of the hospital for up to three days before being taken to the right area. So there Roland was, alone, with shortness of breath, unable to have his family by his side.

To quell his own anxiety, Benjamin called his father and spoke with him, but Roland was having such difficulty even breathing, that talking was limited to a twenty second phone call. Benjamin waited a little bit before calling back several hours later. Roland didn't answer that time. Before assuming the worst, Benjamin held his head high, figuring his father had just fallen asleep. He drove to his mother's house, and that is where they both received the phone call that his father had passed away.

They immediately began asking when they could visit him, how soon it could be, how many people could go into the room at the same time. The hospital staff put up a fight against visitors, especially in the COVID-19 screening ward. But nonetheless, Benjamin and his family persisted and were granted visitation rights to say goodbye to Roland. It was as much unlike a movie moment as one could imagine. Each one of the family members who came to visit had to wear a mask and suit, they could enter one at a time, and they could not stay in the room for more than a few minutes.

It was a very trying time for the family, all dealing with such a great loss in their own way.

Even the funeral, as nice as it looked, was a difficult affair. It was held at a small local chapel on November 6, 2020. Only eighteen to twenty people from the immediate family were allowed to attend the actual ceremony. They all wore masks inside while the rest of the friends and family remained outside. It was a very emotional time for Benjamin, whose year had been fraught with lots of hospitals and more than one person's normal range of emotions. He could have never predicted that in just one year, the year 2020, all of this could have happened. But that is the problem with trying to predict anything — you never really know what's waiting for you.

These times in the post-COVID-19 outbreak have changed him as a man in many ways. Benjamin was always the vivacious guy who loved to host cookouts and invite loads of people over for a party in his big backyard. The year indoors, he admits, made him quieter. The loss of his father made him contemplate life as he raises his son without his father's guidance. Despite the loss of someone so important, because of the addition of new life, Benjamin looks to the future optimistically. He's seen how quickly life can change, in good and bad ways at the same time. He hopes that no matter what happens in the future, he can take this new appreciation for new life to its fullest extent possible. He wants to show his son what being a great dad can look like, and lead by example. Life is about the endings as well as the beginnings.

Interestingly enough, on the other side of the pond, at the very same time, there is a story of incredible success within the same industry, simply because of how the approach was taken.

It worked; it also would have never been allowed in Germany in the year of the pandemic.

Jeff Coyle: A Story on Versatility

For a man with a lot on his plate during the time of a worldwide pandemic, nobody expected to find success in opening a micro-brewery during lockdown. But that was exactly the right time to do it. At least that's what Jeff Coyle thought.

At the start of the pandemic, Jeff was working remotely in St. Simons Island, Georgia, for a software company based in Boston called MarketMuse. He was and still is the co-founder and Chief Strategy Officer for this high-level content intelligence platform. MarketMuse hit the ground running back in 2015, and at the time it was Jeff's passion project to help create content and market strategies for businesses around America. He worked alongside his other co-founder, Aki Balogh, to help all sorts of old and new businesses get their best products out in the most interesting and commercially stimulating way. But when COVID-19 hit the world, most of those businesses were shut down, and the ones that were left were petrified. It quickly occurred to Jeff and Aki that they could help steer a lot of the ships left out at sea, so to speak, due to the lockdowns. So, in the spirit of their "empathy" mission statement, they battened down the hatches and began rolling out a new way to do business.

The COVID-19 pandemic created a lot of uncertainty in the marketing world. Nobody knew what to do with their marketing strategy as everything had to be considered through the lens of COVID-19. From Jeff's perspective, the goal for MarketMuse was to dramatically change people's marketing strategy. As their mission statement had always been, MarketMuse focused on empathy and generosity for their customers. The pandemic was when people needed empathy and a leg up more than ever. They had a way to help out where most people could not.

One of the major ways they helped their customers was by making a new platform completely free to their lower level customers. MarketMuse Pro was created to focus on small or medium range businesses who needed help getting their brand out there. What would have cost each company around $500.00 a month suddenly cost them nothing. It was a promotion from MarketMuse that ran from March 15th—July 2020.

By the end of July, Jeff estimated that they had more than ten thousand people using MarketMuse Pro for free. This created a very kind and generous public image for MarketMuse, a place where businesses could feel they trusted their marketers. Whereas most businesses shut down and saved every penny they could, Jeff and his team did the exact opposite, they completely opened their doors and had the confidence in their customers to know their generosity would win out in the end.

Jeff's entrepreneurial spirit did not stop there. In fact, he had a secret passion that he and three other people had shared for more than a decade. It was a passion that had actually been in the planning stages for at least half that decade already before COVID-19 hit. The passion was in none other than the niche world of micro-breweries.

For five years, Jeff, his brother, Kevin Coyle, and their friends from St. Simons Island, Ally and Chris Moline, had all been working on the side to open a microbrewery in a nearby town, Brunswick, Georgia. In order to first make it happen, they pooled their money and purchased an entire city block in Brunswick, Georgia, and built the microbrewery there from scratch. They had been working for a long time on this project, and the official opening had been set for late 2019. In fact, for a few months before their projected opening, they had a sign out front that read: "Pouring in 2019." But as the saying goes in business, if you are starting a new one, everything takes twice as long and costs twice as much. Soon January was upon them and the business was getting closer but had still not opened. Little did they know what they had in store for them come March.

When COVID-19 first hit, Jeff got caught up with MarketMuse and his partners got busy picking up the pieces of their own jobs; nobody had time to open the brewery. But in late June of 2020, things began to calm down and the brewery was set to open. They had debated whether an in-person business was worth opening at all, given the lockdowns, but they pushed ahead in hopes their potential customers saw it differently. In order to be approved for their grand opening in July, the four-member team had a few more hoops to jump through thanks to the virus. The first was to get approved for COVID-19 Restriction Protocols for people to come inside. They luckily had a beer garden out back, so this helped their case. The second hoop was distribution. That would be turned on its head by Jeff and his team before anyone could blink.

When it came to brewery distribution before Covid, most microbreweries would only start delivering their brews after a few months, once they had built up their brands and sales from inside the store. Much like Benjamin Elbracht's distribution problems in Germany, after COVID-19 hit the world, distribution companies in the United States took big hits because no salespeople were out pushing products, therefore there was no need for distribution in the first place.

So those two, one old and one new precedent, stood in the way of Jeff's new microbrewery opening. But Jeff saw an opportunity that not many people would have seen, sort of a "you scratch my back, I'll scratch yours." What he decided was that, unlike microbreweries in the past, Jeff's brewery would start distribution the day of the grand opening. He saw it as a way to immediately get his name out there by also helping out a local distribution company who needed the work. It was very similar to the way MarketMuse had handled their COVID-19-related issues. Help someone else out, and it can also help your business public image.

So with the COVID-19 protocols in place, indoor social distancing worked out, and distribution all ready to go, the Silver Bluff Brewing Company opened its doors on July 1, 2020, right smack dab in a time when most hadn't even be out to get a haircut, let alone go get a drink. But for those who were worried this might have had a bad ending, have no fear. The microbrewery instantly became a local hit. Everyone in the Brunswick area and beyond flocked to it quickly.

When asked about the immediate success, Jeff said, "In our area, it seemed like what everyone was waiting for. People wanted a place to go outside of their house and have a beer." And that is exactly what they did. Within just a few months, the new place became one of the top five fastest growing breweries in Georgia. But it didn't stop there.

They also decided to try their hand at the International Beer Competitions that happen throughout the year. Although most of them had been canceled for the entirety of 2020, a few were still planned, and they decided to participate. One of those was the U.S. Open Beer Championship. Jeff and his team submitted their top-selling beer, their Mexican Lager and won a silver medal. It was almost unheard of to come out of the saloon gates swinging that hard, but they did it nonetheless. And there is even more success. They began partnering with local, failing restaurants and allowed people to bring food from the restaurants (where no one was allowed to sit inside) and sit out in the beer garden to have their food. Local food trucks were later allowed to park outside the brewery and sell food that way as well. The summer was gangbusters for Jeff and team, and they could not have been more proud.

Despite all the success, the question still remains, how did they do it? The simple answer is that they had confidence and just used good old fashioned courage. When most people saw a world about to end, Jeff saw a market completely open for a new business to jump onto. Much like the way his other company used their platforms to help smaller companies during a hard time, Jeff saw an opportunity to unleash a new place for people to come to during a scary time. He played by the COVID-19 rules and did his part to keep his patrons safe, and then he just did what no one else was willing to try.

That is who Jeff Coyle is, a man of acute confidence, not only in himself, but in his fellow man. He, alongside the people he chooses to do business with, see opportunities that others can't. He knew that in the middle of a lockdown all that the average Joe wanted was a place to sit back and crack open a beer. And so Jeff used the passion for micro-brewery he'd been carrying for a decade, and planning for half that time, and put it into action. Because he could hear the world around him silently calling out for exactly what he was building. He took chances and he supported everyone he could along the way. He did not undermine anybody but instead lifted up the men, women, and businesses around him that were in need and did his part to lend a hand. And in return he was awarded a successful business that is still growing and thriving today. Sometimes, when everyone else can only see that the world is about to end, some people can see that the world is actually about to change, and they do what they can to be on the right side of that once-in-a-generation, cataclysmic shift.

In 2020, that someone was Jeff Coyle.

1. Sydney Jennings, "COVID-19 Update: Global Confirmed Cases as of March 25, 2020," Patient Care, March 25, 2020, https://www.patientcareonline.-com/view/covid-19-update-global-confirmed-cases-march-25-2020 (accessed March 26, 2020).
2. Coronavirus USA: total cases and deaths - 25 March 2020, Other Sports, March 25, 2020, https://en.as.com/en/2020/03/25/other_s-ports/1585144255_092364.html (accessed April 15, 2020).

5

EARTH

On the first of April, at 6:30 a.m., the first thing I did was look at the updates for COVID-19. The number for confirmed cases in the U.S. was standing tall at 188,592.[1] The deaths totaled 4,064. The total confirmed cases worldwide came out to 878,368. I scoffed at the sight of those astonishing numbers. Whoever thought this would all "blow over" by the end of March were fools, in my opinion. I closed my phone and got out of bed. That's when I had a sinking feeling hit my gut: this can only end badly for some. For the ones that live, it may never end. Then my mind cleared at the sound of my husband waking the groggy kids up. At least being a mother will never truly end either. I will always be needed in some capacity by my children, no matter what their age is.

The rest of the day was just as busy as the ones before it. I stayed downstairs for most of the morning to help the kids adjust more to their new virtual school routines. I had four upturned plastic boxes, one for each of them. They all had little iPads, different colored rubber cases around the edge. I oversaw the arts and crafts and made sure they got help when needed, as their teacher could do no more than repeat instructions for the thousandth time. It was a controlled chaos down there for most of the morning, not to mention the incessant noise from all four different iPads blaring the teachers' voice from the tiny speakers. I eventually got a bit smarter and bought headsets for everyone. All the voices blending together were making me feel crazy and also making it harder for me to hear the voices in my head. And I certainly had my own voices to listen to.

My company was under siege, or so it felt. Agents were still doing their best to hold on to worried clients, the market seemed to be drying up, and money was draining through the cracks in my once tight ship from the storm this virus was. And yet I was not just a regular employee. I couldn't take my "furlough" letter and show it to an unemployment office. I had to keep my business afloat. Luckily, my business was about community, and I knew people needed that more than ever right now. So after the virtual schooling was wrapped up, I headed over to the office and began setting up for an offering to help support clients, friends, and neighbors. Only I knew how much it also greatly supported myself. If the business with my name on the door went under, so did I.

Before we left Florida a couple weeks prior, I made sure to grab all the inventory supplies I could from Bayshore, including toilet paper, paper towels, cleaning supplies, etc. We laid out all of these things on different stations along the front porch of the cottage-style building where our office is located. We also had other stations with fun things people could take home, as a gift in these trying times, including books and Girl Scout Cookies. We made sure to get the word out by advertising it on our social media sites. Since our building sits on the corner of a major road in Marietta, we were able to attract passerby, neighbors, as well as clients that followed us on Instagram and Facebook. It was a way to spread joy and reassurance during a collective hysteria. I also believe, looking back, that it helped our clients stay positive about our commitment to the community. Even if they didn't show up for a free book or some toilet paper, they saw the photos on the websites and would know we were doing all we could.

The next day, I noticed how little the virtual schooling was helping my kids. While one of them would try to focus on getting the assignment presented well to her teacher, two more would run around like crazy people right underneath her. My home was quickly becoming a madhouse. In the same moment, while I tiredly did my best to keep the kids under control, I checked the news and saw another numerical update. Instead of death, this one was about unemployment.

As of that day, there was an increase in unemployment of 1,100%, the most claims ever filed in one week in Georgia history.[2] When I looked back at my kids, one running around in their princess costume while the other tried to be a good student, I breathed a sigh of relief. I was instantly glad they were young. I would rather them learn math through the computer than live jobless during this time. You have to pick your battles and you have to pick your smiles. I smiled big at the girls and continued my battle to get them under control. In all of this controlled chaos, I heard the chime of the doorbell.

When I opened the door I found toilet paper fresh off the truck that I had ordered several weeks back from whogivesacrap.com. They sell recycled toilet paper and wrap them in fun tissue colors. The girls always get excited when we get this delivery because they love to build castles with them. Today was especially exciting not just since toilet paper was hard to come by, but also because it was a form of entertainment for the kids who so desperately were seeking things to keep themselves occupied.

On April 3rd, the "stay in place" orders were issued for the state of Georgia, and by April 5th, our new floral print masks had arrived. I also made sure to send out masks to all of our agents still working with clients and showing houses. Wearing masks was new as up to this point, people weren't wearing them in public. At first, it was odd to wear them and very surreal to see the kids wearing them. Later on it became normal, mundane, and ordinary.

A little over a week later, on April 11th, my sister, Stefanie, turned thirty-seven. Stefanie and her family came over to my house and we celebrated (they had returned home to live about two weeks earlier so we could all attempt to focus on virtual schooling). Michael made a cake and we had a great time. The kids swam. I remained distracted, though, as was a common theme these days. I thought about the incoming messages from the WhatsApp group chat. So many people were writing in, talking about their stories, their lives, their hopes and fears for the present and for the future. So many people were living in the "now" when all I could think about was the future. What would it be like for these young people ten, fifteen, even twenty years from now?

On April 14th, a couple of French Mermaids arrived on my front porch. They were polite enough to ring the doorbell, I guess their mama taught them well. Earlier that morning, my two youngest girls dressed up as mermaids for a school project. They dressed in secret and then decided to surprise me by running around the side of the house, unseen, and ringing the doorbell. They were adorable, and I was glad to see them having fun. Of course when you have two out of four girls dress as mermaids, the rest shall follow. By that night, all four of my little girls dressed up, planned, rehearsed, practiced, and then performed a musical for Michael, Aunt Judi, and me. It was incredible to watch these girls, in the middle of a worldwide pandemic, not lose their spirit but use it collectively to create something magical, if not a bit chaotic.

The next day we had another kind of animal arrival. This time it was another live pet to add to our farm. A few weeks prior, all of us visited a local farmer who was raising bantam chickens, or as I like to call them, miniature chickens because they are so small compared to all other breeds. I was able to bring home one of the baby eggs for the girls, but like most things, it was not as simple as it sounded. In order to keep the egg warm on the drive home I purchased a child's size french fry from McDonald's and placed the egg inside of it until we arrived back at our house where I could place it in an incubator. A typical egg takes 21 days of incubation before it hatches, and that day was its birthday. The girls and I were able to watch for the first time as a baby chick came out of its shell. I saw the glee in their eyes as the chick greeted the world.

At that moment, as crazy as it seemed in the beginning to build a chicken farm, I was even more pleased that I had taken the chance on doing it. Not only had I already been able to provide friends and family with eggs, but I was able to show the girls nature up close. Perhaps they would have seen something similar on a field trip a few years from then, but that day they got to witness the miracle of nature right before their very eyes, in the comfort of their own home. Maybe there is a silver lining to these "stay at home" orders.

The next day, we removed the baby chick from the incubator and put it under a heat lamp. Moments later, as I scrolled through my phone for a moment, I saw a headline stating that the president of the United States had pulled funding from the World Health Organization (WHO). My jaw dropped. Really? In the middle of a pandemic? The article stated that the president said it was a waste of money in the prevention of the new virus.[3] It was astounding to watch how the administration was handling something so novel and scary to so many people. It worried me for the future of my country, but I could not change that, I could only use the nervous energy from what I had read to make my life better. I was glad that the girls and I could bond over a new life like this. We spent a few minutes transitioning the baby chicken into a new environment. How odd, I thought, that the people in charge did not seem to care about keeping a country of people safe, but these little girls could take such care in keeping just one little baby chicken safe.

On April 18th, with a small group of family and friends, we celebrated my second oldest daughter's birthday. It was a wonderful experience to see some of the faces I had not seen for a while. We threw a pool party and the kids got to do some scuba diving in the deep end of the pool. My daughter got her wish of a hoverboard, a toy that she and the other girls enjoy a lot. Thanks to the "stay at home" orders, our local church's parking lot was vacant, so we decided to take it there for practice. The girls were able to play on the hoverboard in the open space. And I must say they got quite good at riding it.

Several days later, on April 21st, we received white baby chickens, (called silkies) for the farm. These chickens are quite unique. They are shaggy all over with long feathers that look like flippers on their feet and cover their eyes much like a shaggy dog. The girls instantly fell in love with them. It was tons of fun to watch the girls play with them and to help the girls name them. On that same day, I read more interesting news. This time about the oil industry. The price of oil dropped to rock bottom, making April 21, 2020 the worst day for the oil market in modern history.[4] So here I was, a mother of four girls playing with four new baby chickens, and the country's oil industry might be out of business like a Kmart. Once again, how could the world be so enriching and so alarming all at once, I wondered as my babies held their babies.

Wednesday, April 22, 2020, was a day I had been looking forward to for several months. It was the fiftieth anniversary of Earth Day. As a self-proclaimed animal and humanitarian activist, I was so excited to celebrate the day of Earth with my girls. I had decided months earlier to spread the joy that day for my company and community. We hung a banner outside our office that simply said, "We are in this TOGETHER." I wanted people to know in my community that they were not alone. When you are a part of a community, and part of a world so fragile, it helps to know that there are others out there. For my girls, for my husband, and for my team members, I wanted to be that person as best as I could.

I knew that the number of COVID-19 cases were rising, I knew that the oil industry might explode like someone put a match to it, and that old and young people were dying from a disease that even the president of the United States didn't seem to care about or believe in. But I cared.

I may not have the loudest voice, but for those who cared, who wanted to listen, who needed a champion, I wanted to be there for them. I have a soft spot in my heart for the preservation of living things, be it plants, animals, or humans. And here was a time of life when all of those were in jeopardy. This new virus had started a chain reaction of negative impacts. I wanted to highlight the positive impacts already out there and create those that were not yet available. In times of worry and suffering, nothing is better than to say, "I am here." And that is all I wanted to be. Even for people outside of my community. Because I knew the world was suffering, I knew the earth was in peril. If I could do my part, I would. And I was not the only one wanting to do their part for their community.

Anne Marie:
A Story on Fulfillment

Imagine New York City, the biggest city in the United States—the Big Apple—filled with millions of people. A completely overcrowded city. Imagine the hospitals overrun with patients and their families. Imagine there being too many patients and not enough beds. Imagine a gunshot victim being ushered in, a pregnant woman halfway through labor and their spouse demanding a private room, a young boy who fell off his bike with a bone poking out of his elbow, a young NYU student that got hit by a taxi and her cheek crushed and nose mangled, and an elderly man with dementia who was brought in by a frantic wife after she found him overdosing on the wrong medication. The halls were crowded and the people were louder. It was January 2020, just a short time before the world changed. Now imagine this constant chaos, and then on top of it, a virus sweeping its way through the streets and homes of the largest city in America, infecting rich and poor, young and old. What would happen to those hospitals then? That was exactly the question on Dr. Anne Marie's mind as she left her Brooklyn apartment to head in for a double shift. But as she locked her door, mask already on, she felt a baby's kick in her stomach and smiled.

Anne Marie works at a hospital in Brooklyn, New York. She is the Attending Physician, part of the Core Faculty, and as of March of 2020, she had worked there nearly two years. At that time, when the virus hit, she was more concerned about the city itself than her pregnancy. She had a wonderful husband, a loving family, and more than one back up plan to make sure her child came into the world safely. Being a medical professional, her eyes were on the world around her, and she was well aware a massive amount of people could wind up in her hospital, just weeks after the pandemic made landfall in New York. In her words, New York City was "slower to quarantine than we should have." One of the reasons for the city to be so hesitant was due to the role schools play in the City, especially all the after school programs offered to families with two working parents. "Some families live in a one bedroom with three kids and have no access to computers for the kids to learn virtually." Not to mention the fact that no one, not even the most seasoned doctor, truly knew what the virus would look like.

The doctors did know one thing for certain. This new virus was described as the flu but worse. The flu alone impacts hospitals every winter, making it very difficult at times for doctors to do their jobs. Young people come in very sick, crowding the ER, causing the wait times for beds to go up. And that is a growing issue every time another sick, pregnant, or dying person comes in. That was something hospitals expected and planned for every year. They already knew enough about the novel virus making its way around the world to know that COVID-19 would be worse than that. The question for her hospital was, "What does that mean?" They began by sketching out scenarios: how many patients would they have? when were they going to come in? how bad would the surge be? how many ventilators were they going to need? and so forth. The hospital is modeled for a specific number of beds, with the winter flu uptick only taking up half of those beds. They knew most of the COVID-19 cases would be sent to the ICU. Their main concern, because of this, was when (not if) they would run out of ventilators, how to best allocate more, and when to begin that process. This was critical, specifically to a hospital in the United States.

In most developing nations, you are given all necessary items that a hospital provides (ventilators, medicine, a bed), only if you have a chance of survival. If you are going to die, the logic in those lower-income countries is why waste the materials on someone who will not ultimately benefit? It is the exact opposite in America. You, as a citizen of the country, have a right to every possible procedure and the items a hospital can provide, no matter your chance of survival. This created some dilemmas for the hospital. Morally and ethically, Anne Marie and her team had to ask some tough questions: Who gets the right supplies? How do we determine who gets the best help? etc. Things changed even more once the patients began to arrive.

The most fundamental problem the staff had was that they did not know how to treat the virus. They had never seen anything like this before, and right away they realized that the ventilators did not seem to be helping people. So now they had to change their perspective from a ventilator question to a treatment issue. The doctors realized that they had to maximize life support methods of oxygenation. "It changed the game in a lot of ways," said Anne, reflecting back on that first wave. This crisis management was not something new to any of the doctors, including Anne Marie, but it still took its toll on her. She found herself working at an upwards of fifty hours a week during the last trimester of pregnancy. Luckily, she was able to bring those hours down closer to the end as she began to get too big for comfort.

She was uncomfortable, but so was everyone else. "The entire hospital staff was uncomfortable. We did not have as many masks as we needed," she says of those early days. It did not help when, first a large quantity of the regular surgical masks were stolen from the hospital, then the N95 masks were stolen after that. Many of the doctors did their best to use the same masks as consecutively as possible. Anne Marie used the same surgical mask for two weeks at one point during the peak season of the surge. And that was only one of the ways she protected herself. Very soon she stopped touching patients altogether, unless she had to examine them. That became common practice among many staff members as well, eventually to the point of standing farther away from them than usual. "We just had to have that distance." She says, because the truth was, nobody knew how to stop it from spreading. But she went on to say, "It felt like it was going to spread no matter what we did."

This fear did not just lie with the frontline health care industry. All of New York City felt frightened. Suddenly a city known for its crowded subways and busy parks became an old western ghost town. The famous Bull in the middle of Wall Street stood alone while inside the walls of the Financial District, the New York Stock Exchange hit its lowest point since 1987.[5] The ferries for rides to the Statue of Liberty were docked, and the sales for tours anywhere in the city plummeted. The restaurants and nightlife dwindled in popularity as everyone huddled behind closed doors to wait out the surge. With the streets bare and the rumors flying, most in New York City didn't feel safe. This power of fear drove Andrew Cuomo, the Governor of New York, to host a series of fireside chats that gained him notoriety (and a handful of memes).[6] They were significant, as they harkened America back to the 1930s when, from 1933 to 1936, Franklin

D. Roosevelt became the first televised president and hosted thirty fireside chats to talk the people through the war and the depression. History was repeating itself. The economy was on the brink of another depression and the People's War was raging. But this war was different. It was inside our bodies, attacking our hearts and lungs until we died. It fell on people like Dr. Anne Marie to fight for us.

As the next few weeks turned into months, the doctor hit the end of her pregnancy. Anne Marie had to decide whether she wanted to have her baby in Brooklyn, at the same hospital she'd been working at or if she wanted to get away for a bit and deliver her baby closer to her family that lived in the Southeastern part of the United States. Luckily, because of her experience in the field itself, even so far as having delivered many babies before, she knew exactly how she wanted to do it. She was able to pick the hospital she wanted to deliver at. It was a hospital in Atlanta, Georgia, that she used to work at. She knew the staff there and she knew their capabilities. Add to the fact that during the early days of the pandemic, New York City had taken extra precautions when it came to patient visits and labor and delivery. In New York, women were delivering with no loved ones by their side. This scared her because Anne Marie knew the data. Studies have shown that without someone with you during the delivery, there are greater health risks to both the baby and mother. The pain in the mother takes over your entire body, and you need a significant other or family member to be your voice and coach you through the pain and trauma of delivery. Knowing this, she did not want to take any chances.

Anne Marie and her husband Simon left for Atlanta, GA. The delivery went very well, easier than expected, and they chose the name Magnolia for their new little girl. After that, for the next six weeks, it was Anne Marie, her husband, his mom, her two parents, and her brother, all living in a five bedroom house, with two dogs and a baby. Anne said it worked out "shockingly well." Everyone inside the home was able to meet the baby, be together, and reduce the risk of exposing themselves or the new baby to the virus. After enough time, however, it was time for Anne Marie's husband to get back to work.

Simon runs a research lab at an Ivy League university and mentors fellowship students studying there. Although he had been working from home during the six weeks in Atlanta, he needed to get back to work in person. By that time, the "shelter in place" laws were relaxing enough for him to return safely. This was fine with Anne Marie because she was ready to get back to work too. She needed to be back in the environment she felt most comfortable, a place where she could take up the mantle again of being in charge.

"I was the bossy older sister," said Anne Marie, describing what she loves about her job. It is a place where a person can definitely excel if that person is a little bit brash and a little bit loud. At her job, she can tell people like it is, and be more blunt than in some other career paths.

For Anne Marie, she can get her "little fiefdom" out of her system, then she can go home and not have it follow her. She also believes in the heart and soul of her job. She can connect and help people, even in a small way. To her, that feeling is really meaningful.

By December of 2020, as questions began to be answered and a sense that a new chapter was turning, Anne Marie was able to look back on the year and see how this all impacted her. "It's not over yet," she said, but the air around her felt better. She could not say when the end date would be, but she knew, as a front-line, medical professional, that this would come to an end. When looking to the future, she looks forward to Magnolia playing with other kids, running around outside, and not being stuck in front of a screen all day for school. Anne Marie counts her blessings.

---

1. Bill Bostock, "Fauci said it will take 12 to 18 months to get a coronavirus vaccine in the US. Experts say a quick approval could be risky.," Insider, April 1, 2020, https://www.businessinsider.com/coronavirus-vaccine-quest-18-months-fauci-experts-flag-dangers-testing-2020-4(accessed May 12, 2020)
2. Jonathan Raymond, "As Georgia unemployment claims spike 1,100%, Emory expert says we could see 20-25% unemployment," 11Alive, April 2, 2020, https://www.11alive.com/article/news/health/coronavirus/georgia-unemployment-could-reach-20-25-percent/85-fd1acb2e-92d0-4e70-ab82-214a6eb4eea7 (accessed May 12,2020)
3. Berkeley Lovelace Jr, Noah Higgins-Dunn, "Trump halts US funding for World Health Organization as it conducts coronavirus review," CNBC, April 6, 2020, https://www.cnbc.com/2020/04/14/trump-calls-for-halt-to-us-funding-for-world-health-organization-amid-coronavirus-outbreak.html (accessed April 10, 2020).
4. Matt Egan, "Oil prices turned negative. Hundreds of US oil companies could go bankrupt,"CNN, April 20, 2020, https://www.cnn.com/2020/04/20/business/oil-price-crash-bankruptcy/index.html (accessed October 26, 2021).
5. Stan Choe, Damian J. Troise, "US stock market tumbles to worst finish since 1987,"Times of Israel, March 17, 2020, https://www.timesofisrael.com/us-stock-market-tumbles-to-worst-finish-since-1987/ (accessed March 30, 2020).
6. "Cuomo's fireside chats conclude," Niagara Frontier Publications, June 19, 2020, https://www.wnypapers.com/news/article/current/2020/06/19/142045/cuomos-fireside-chats-conclude (accessed October 26, 2020).

6

THE WAR WAGES ON

The end of April 2020, was met with the reminder of death and the forging of new life. On the 25th, we threw Maddie her third birthday party. It was a small affair but joyous because my family was still safe, happy, and together. My life by this point had not settled down, but there were small routines being formed and worked out. We were able to figure out the best way to do virtual schooling, and we had the girls doing different chores around the house. I was so focused on a million different things, both inside my home and outside in the world where my business was in limbo. We were not profitable, and my conscience ached for the employees we had to let go. It was so chaotic, only dealt with day by day, that I was not shocked to discover rodents nesting in my ghost town vacant office building. I had been in fix-it mode, and it took me no time at all to come up with a solution to that problem. Something that would take less effort and cost nothing compared to an exterminator. We adopted two orange cats, brother and sister, and let them live in the office. There, at least one problem was solved. And by the way, it really did solve the problem. After the summer ended and our office reopened, we brought the cats back to my house, and I am happy to report that even over a year later we have had no further issues with rodents at our office.

A few days after the birthday party, I woke up to the alarm blasting from the speakers on my phone. I turned over to check the time and froze when I saw the date.

April 29th.

Could it have come around this soon? In the middle of my busy life, I had not expected to see it crop up so suddenly. I leaned my head back on my pillow and held the phone over my face. I couldn't pull my eyes off the date. For a few minutes, anytime the screen went black, I tapped it again and continued to stare at it. It was only when my husband stirred and asked me what time it was that I was able to snap out of it. But even as we rose out of bed, poured the coffee, made the kids some breakfast, got the laptops booted up, and opened the coloring books to a fresh page, I still had the date blinking in my mind's eye.

April 29, 2020.

It was the fifth anniversary of my dad's death.

Fred Seidell was born in Indianapolis, Indiana, on November 5, 1947. He served as an airplane mechanic for the Air Force during Vietnam. He passed away on April 29, 2015 at the age of sixty-seven from ALS. He died in my mother's arms on what also just happened to be their thirty-seventh wedding anniversary. It was a tragic time, and one I will never forget.

As I watched the girls settle in for another day at home with mom and dad, I wondered what my father would have to say about this virus? It makes me wonder about how many things can happen in one lifetime. I can never picture going to Vietnam. So many young men died there, and for those who didn't, they probably still felt like it was the end of the world. It was wartime; a scary war with burned flesh and bullet-ridden bodies. My dad heard all sorts of stories like that, even witnessed a few scary things himself. And yet, life moved on for him, and he died many years later in his wife's arms. If a man like that, who saw what he saw, could move on from what others might've called the end of the world, could his daughter do the same thing? Could his granddaughters?

That was a real war, with real people and real enemies, and yet, what happened then was similar in so many ways to the war we were facing. The enemies were not hiding in the jungle with machine guns. The enemy was infected in the phlegm and mucus of a coughing man nearby. The world had certainly moved on, but would my father have seen parallels if he was still here? I wondered if years from now if people would have flashbacks the way that war heroes do?

What I was reading in WhatsApp and in the news made me feel that this was war time. It was not a combat war, no, but something else. It was a war between people and a deadly virus. It was a war fought by people with people. It hit me as I took my last sip of coffee that morning and headed to work on my computer that there might be a name for this time. A title for this time in the world's history: The People's War.

The next day, as April came to a close and summer danced in the air like winter wind off the growing green trees, I thought about that concept of war again. On the morning of April 30th, I read a news article that said, another 3.8 million Americans had lost jobs and that the U.S. unemployment continued to grow, while people had yet to receive benefits to compensate for lowered income[1]. Talk about a battle.

Though I was not bloody, I didn't carry a gun, I was well fed, and I got to sleep in my own bed every night, I was still hunkered down behind enemy lines, waiting until the threat of death passed by. How long would this invisible war for our health continue? How many more would have to die before the antibody treaty is signed? This concept stayed with me, clouding my busy mind piled high with thousands of other ideas.

The first of May brought sweet memories flooding back through my heart like warm water you can soak in for hours. The girls began enjoying the freedoms that the "stay at home" order had gifted them. They could stay up a little later and sleep a little later. They could almost literally roll out of bed, run a brush (or hand) through their hair, and snack on a breakfast bar while the teacher over Zoom recited the Pledge of Allegiance. The fight for them to get to bed on time had been removed, as well as the frustration of dragging them out of bed every weekday morning for a cold ride to school. This new set of childhood rules provided both the kids, and Michael and me, a chance to enjoy more late night adventures, like movies or a round of card games.

On one particular early May night, we were watching one of my daughter's favorite's, *Zootopia*. She was only three weeks into being eight years old, so this new freedom of late night movies was revolutionary for her. She sat happily in the center of our couch, snacking on single pieces of popcorn, her eyes glued to the screen. Halfway through the movie, I slipped away to grab some more popcorn for the mostly empty bowl. I passed by a bookshelf that I had passed by dozens of times in the last month alone. That night I stopped and looked at the top shelf. Sitting off to the side was a present that she made for me in preschool when she was three years old. Inside the beautiful jewelry box was a poem she wrote that I had not read in almost five years. I set the popcorn bowl aside and opened the box to read the tiny poem, scratched out on a paper in her beautiful, childlike handwriting. The poem read:

"Mommy. Here's a trinket box that I made just for you. You said that it is very small, but I am that small too! Little treasures we will keep inside just for you to see. They will help us to remember, this was made when I was 3."

I was surprised to have forgotten I was raising a young Walt Whitman, but even more so, I was brought to tears and goosebumps rippled over the tops of my arms. Here was the most beautiful poem in the world, talking about the past. I thought about my dad, how the time for him must have flashed by in a second. He was a young man fixing airplanes, next he was marrying my mother, next he was holding me in his arms, and next he was on his deathbed the same year that my daughter wrote me a love poem. Five years had gone by, and she was eight years old, and the world was at war with the health of its inhabitants. Perhaps, I pondered, life is The People's War, and the time of COVID-19 and masks and lockdowns was just a battle. As a younger man, my father held up the weapons and fought. At sixty-seven, he let down his weapons and died peacefully. And at three-years-old, my daughter held up her weapons and wrote a ballad to encapsulate the very thing we were in this war to fight for: Love.

As I gathered the popcorn and walked back to the couch, I didn't say a word. I let the movie play and the little girl next to me just enjoyed life. Those were the quiet moments in this war of ours. I knew that tomorrow she would rise again, brush her hair, and fight another day. It may not be bloody or loud, but it would be no less valiant. We must fight to stay alive and to preserve little girls, so they may write the pure poems to be read again and again, for the years of battle to come. And not all battles are fought alone, some are fought with the people you love right by your side.

Mike Stiles:
A Story on Acceptance

Life in the Stiles household meant you did not whine. Mike and his wife, Kim, both had this in common. They were not complainers. It is not because they don't care about life or think they're invincible. On the contrary, they know that whatever might happen can happen. In other words, you take what life throws at you and move on. So then why is it when neither of them had been worried about the cold season or swine flu rumors years before, did they take such notice of this new virus before lockdowns even began? In a post Mike wrote that went viral—no pun intended—he describes his unconscious reasons for such early preparations. "For as much as the public mission was to convey a sense of confidence and a plan in motion based on data, it grew clearer to me that there were far more unknowns and uncertainties than anyone cared to admit."[2] So he looked for the basic solution: sanitation.

In early winter of 2019, while everyone only saw the word "Coronavirus" on news updates and National Geographic magazines, Mike began wiping everything down. A trip to the grocery store meant wiping down the credit card after swiping it, wiping down the bags before placing them in the kitchen to unload, wiping the handle of the car you touched after carrying the bags from the cart to your trunk. And of course, washing your hands before and after this whole ordeal. This was still when the CDC rumors said that only old people and babies could be in danger. Mike was fifty-six at the time, he technically didn't have to worry, right? But something told him to keep sanitizing and putting the mask on anywhere he went. In the end his worst, underlying fears came true. On March 16, 2020, Kim began showing symptoms.

It began with dry mouth, body aches, and exhaustion. The

missing clue to label it COVID-19, the smoking gun, was a fever. Kim never went above the average healthy temperature. They both knew that if Kim went to the hospital without a fever, she would be sent home and told to rest. They decided to heed that advice ahead of time and wait it out. Luckily, besides a few tough days, Kim's symptoms subsided. The only lingering side effect was the cough. They felt relief wash through them after that. Maybe that's all it was. Little did Mike know what was waiting around the corner for him. If his wife was missing the smoking gun, he was in for a fire fight.

While he had done his best to keep a distance from his loving wife during her time—sleeping in the guest room and eating at separate times after cleaning up after each other—a house with one contagious person typically leaves no survivors. By March 23rd, Mike began experiencing his own symptoms. This time, he could feel something terrible was coming. For him, it began slowly. First it was digestive issues and joint pains. Okay, he thought, I'm over the hump of middle age, maybe this is normal. Come on, these feelings are a coincidence with the COVID-19 timing. Given this rationale, and his "power through" dogma, he didn't let these issues stop him. Then the gun fired its first shot.

On March 27, 2020, Mike felt a fever coming on. In his later reflection piece, Mike described the fever as a good thing. "They're an indication your body is well-engaged in the fight against the invading virus. And I had all the confidence in the world that my body could handle that little cage match."[3] But still the fevers began to climb day by day: 100 . . . 101 . . . 102. . . . What began as just "small pains" turned into a battle. He was "zonked" for up to 20 hours a day. He would wake up only to find himself once again drenched in freezing cold sweats. But still, during the peaceful moments in between battles, he would wonder to no one in particular, "Am I winning?"

It was only days later that the hallucinations began. They were small at first, little bits of childhood flashbacks as he rocked himself to sleep in the sweaty sheets stuck to his skin from the sopping wet bed. On March 31st, a large storm of straight-line winds ripped through the Atlanta, GA, area where he and his wife live. Now there was no power, no AC, no clock on the mantelpiece to tell him the time. Everything was dark, out of time, and sweaty. The only thing he could see was a single candle flickering next to his bed. He began to imagine that he was stuck in colonial times, a wounded soldier on the verge of death. Sounds of gunfire (thunder) and cries of agony (wind) raged outside his dark tent (bedroom). Was this some sort of time travel purgatory? Would he actually die covered in sweat, stuck in another realm not his own?

By the middle of that same night, Kim managed to stick a thermometer under her husband's tongue. When the analog numbers blinked 104 degrees, she took matters into her own hands. By this point, Mike was aware, but he was too weak to fight against the idea of going to the hospital. He knew even then that it was the only option. Kim drove him to Piedmont Newnan Hospital near Atlanta. As Kim pulled up outside the ER, doctors met her at the passenger door with a wheelchair. As they lowered Mike into the seat, they strapped a mask over his mouth. The feverish time travel must have gotten to him, as he immediately puked into the mask. Despite his groggy state of mind, Mike remembers this moment as a trigger. Before that point, there had been no nausea to speak of. Maybe this was more real than the skeptics had said. And yet, his pragmatism lingered like a song lyric playing on repeat in his mind. "They'll probably send me home to rest up." Not by a long shot. As they wheeled him into the ER, he wanted to turn back and wave goodbye, but he could not. He was whisked inside before he had the chance. Not only would he not be sent home the next day,

Mike would in fact not see his wife, or any loved ones, for a week.

He was laid in a bed and informed that immediate X-Rays were necessary for treatment. As they took these, his wife filled out paperwork in their car in the hospital parking lot. For most of the night, Mike remembers being impressed by the doctors' speed, but he does not remember much else. He was too drowsy and sick to have enough strength for loneliness, and he just needed rest. Of course he would have liked to have been surrounded by loved ones, but he knew that was impossible.

"You don't sit in the room with your loved one. You don't hold their hand. You don't get to talk to the doctors when they come in because they're too busy, and they want to limit the time in a room with a COVID-19 patient." For now it was just Mike and the doctors against the world.

The battle had begun.

From the X-Rays, the doctors could tell very quickly that Mike had the classic look of a COVID-19 patient. "Shredded glass" was how the doctors described his lungs. This surprised him greatly, as he did not think his breathing had been impaired too much during the last few days. He was then admitted to his own private room. What Mike did not know at this time, and something he learned later on, was just how close he was to septic shock. As he sat in the hospital room, the fever declining by the minute, he primed his ears for the word "ventilator." He'd read up on these recently. He knew they were in low supply. The last thing he wanted was to hoard one for himself when someone else could use it to stay alive, and he did not want to be hooked up to a machine. Besides, he'd already made peace with dying in a tent during the Revolutionary War. What could be harder than that?

He caught a lucky break when, in the hospital haze of that night, he uttered the phrase, "Let's avoid a vent," and somebody listened. He was moved to the ICU unit for non-vent patients. From that bed, he watched the reality of what he'd been reading about hit home. The typical hospital stay looked nothing like an ICU stay for COVID-19 patients. Every time someone enters the room of a COVID-19 patient, there is a long and specific procedure. This includes double masking, a face shield, a gown, a cap, gloves, and booties. Afterward, everything but the face shield is disposed of, which is washed thoroughly for reuse, as there was a short supply at the time. "I was so sympathetic to what was required for someone to enter my room, I literally never once hit the call button with a need," said Mike later on. "If you're not a jerk, you consolidate what you need then get it all done during the nurse's visit."

The next few nights followed a similar pattern. He was kept under a strict lockdown and was monitored quite heavily by doctors and nurses. The fevers continued during these early ICU days, but they declined as his other vitals were brought back up. He was lucky to be surrounded by friendly doctors as well as an old college friend who worked in the hospital and was able to visit with Mike often. He looks back on this time as more or less an out-of-body experience.

"These were the worst nights with regard to fevers and the accompanying disorientation and fever dreams. Several involved working intensely for hours and hours to solve some unsolvable, completely illogical problem. Keep in mind, you don't have the luxury of occasionally realizing this could be a dream. These trips were every bit as much a part of reality as any waking moment. In the most powerful way, I went to a plane of existence just above ours, where there are both beings who love us and those who are extremely angry and bitter. There was no difference between wind and music, it all flowed naturally together. And there was no difference between singing, speaking or chanting; the voices I heard all blended into something like

I've never heard on Earth. I didn't hear it with my ears, I experienced it vibrationally throughout my body. The only message I remember from my extended time in this surreal place was 'grace.'"

Eventually, after days filled with fever dreams and blood thinners, the battle waned and the opposing forces tired. He was soon able to contribute to his own recovery. He forced himself to eat, walk around the room, and answer a few text messages. He knew it must be hard for those who loved him not to hear back, but he had been in no state of mind to answer logically either way. However, once he was back to his own state of mind, it lifted his spirits to see all the loving messages of inspiration. It gave him an appreciation for the time he went through, and it showed him that when someone is in dire straits, that person does not have to hold onto hope alone.

After a week in the ICU, Mike was able to return home. He was blessed to be healthy enough again to see his wife, but the doubts that started in the ICU came back with him. He carried the weight of this experience around with him like Linus' blanket. What if I get sick again? What if I'm still contagious? How soon can I see my grown-up kids? Will I ever go back to work? Will life ever go back to normal? These questions were the first round of mental recovery from what almost killed him. But as time went on, he began to take other people into consideration and just be grateful for his own health, while he still had it. The most ingrained difference in his mental arsenal became the appreciation for healthcare workers. "Sure, we may carry them in a general, mostly silent, high regard alongside police and firefighters, and we might agree they should be called 'heroes,' but candidly, that often never rises above well-meaning lip service. I assure you, when you're lying in a room and you know for a fact that you personally are a mortal threat to health and safety, then someone suits up and comes into the room to help you anyway, it's one of the most humbling experiences you can ever have."

As the months went on Mike and Kim got back to a new sense of normal, they both experienced a humility few get to experience until they are brought to death's door. For Mike, he used to think that whatever happens is just a part of life. But now he has a new sense of duty and honor bestowed upon him by the days he almost lost his life and the people who worked tirelessly to save it. "The only thing that really matters is how many people you sincerely love and how many friends and family you have that sincerely love and care about you." And with that power comes the responsibility to fight, to survive. You cannot love and cherish if you do not fight to stay alive. The dead can't hear you when, in the afterlife, you call out their names to try and say you love them. By then, the six feet of solid earth is too deep for your voice to travel. While you can, Mike believes that you must say it now, when your voice and your body are on earth. Hug those close to you and send messages of love to those far away. And if anyone can understand that beyond Mike himself, it would be a man much older than Mike who has had a lot of experience to learn from.

Bruce "Popi" Marden: A Story of the "Simple" Man

In February 1940, in Norfolk, Virginia, two sisters were decorating the apartment of the older sister and her three-year-old son. Her name was Carol, and she was a single mother. While up on a ladder with a paint brush, Carol slipped and fell very hard. She cut her foot on the chipped wood of the ladder siding. The cut quickly became infected with gangrene, and several days later it turned into pneumonia. Just a few days later, she succumbed to her infections that had spread and passed away. Bruce was left behind. His father had walked out before he was born, and now his mother was gone. Her sister, Frances, who was there that day in the apartment, took it upon herself to raise Bruce. She raised him until he was eighteen. But that did not mean she cared for him in the traditional sense. Her parenting skills were quite different than most. According to Bruce himself, "My first memory was of my mother being lowered into a grave when I was three." He didn't record another memory until he was six years old. "Since then, I have been independent my entire life."

Nothing ever worried Bruce. He knew how to take care of himself. "The first lesson that Frances taught me: 'if you want it, go get it.'" This mentality has kept Bruce ahead of the curve, giving him the necessary mindset to manage life. He developed skills early on to deal with the problems he faced. If he wanted a new pair of pants because the boys at school picked on him for the pair he was wearing, his adopted mom told him to figure out a way to get new pants. If he wanted to go to college, he would have to get a job and really learn how much a college education was worth. And he did. Because the truth is, one way or another, he got what he needed.

When he was a younger boy, he delivered newspapers to earn his "keep." And then he discovered pool halls down the street. At sixteen, Bruce began playing for money, beating out some of the older men too headstrong to understand how good he was at the game. Their cockiness would cost them several dollar bills that went directly into Bruce's own pocket. That hustling mindset bled over into school as well. In high school, a friend of his came and asked him if he could take his final exams because the boy was failing and would be sent to military school if he did not pass his courses. Bruce agreed and got the kid a B+

because an A, the boy said, would have given away that he cheated. He knew he could have been expelled from the high school, but he risked it anyway. It was a way to get by, and that was his greatest asset.

At eighteen, when it came time to go to college, Bruce scrounged together the funds and headed off to the University of Miami in Florida. He got as far as medical school before discovering he did not want to be around sick people. In his mind, he had worked hard all of his life to live a good one, he did not want to spend it all day with people in an infirmary. "I wanted to be around vibrant people." And he got more than he could have meant by that statement when he met Josephine. She was five years his junior, but that didn't deter him from asking her out. They fell in love and married and have been together ever since.

Together the two of them lived in Miami. Later on they had a son, Jason, and moved to Georgia. Bruce opened an art gallery in Atlanta and sold his and other artist's paintings. From there his life did not turn out exactly the way he thought it would go. When Jason was in college, he met a woman and she got pregnant, giving birth to two girls two years apart. Being so young, they were unable to handle raising the kids. So life, as it does, circled back around, and it now fell on Bruce to take an unexpected child into his home, just like his aunt did for him all those years before, except this time there were two of them. He and Josephine legally adopted the two girls when they were seven and five years old and raised them until they left for college. To this day, despite how unplanned it was at the time, Bruce is thankful he had a hand in raising his granddaughters to be the women they are today.

As the years progressed and Bruce aged, he spent more time focusing on his true passion: painting. Maybe it was because of what his mother was doing when she died-even he could not be sure of that Freudian reasoning-but he loves the freedom it allows. It's not only a job, but a special hobby. When he passes on, he plans to give away the rest of his paintings to his family. "They will be a gift to them, that's all. When the paintings are theirs, they can do whatever they want with them."

Now, being in the mid 80's, his life is as simple as one's can be, even in the time of COVID-19. Of course, he knows the world has changed, but he has not. Bruce says that when you pass the eighty year limit, you mostly stop going out. The news of the Coronavirus did not impact Josephine and him; the "stay at home" orders didn't force either Bruce or Josephine to do anything different. The truth is that before COVID-19, the two of them had arranged a retirement lifestyle that suited their needs perfectly.

The only impact the virus began to have on them was less trips to the store and a lot more sanitizer. Oh, and of course, the addition of the cane. When out in the real world during this time of COVID-19, Bruce began to carry his cane around whenever he went. Whether it be the doctor's office or at the gas station buying lottery tickets, if anybody came too close to him or Josephine, he would stick the cane out and politely tell them to "Back the fuck off." He learned quickly that with his age the general response was, "I'm sorry, sir," which made him feel relaxed, because he felt he had handled the situation appropriately.

"I'm not afraid of anything," says Bruce of his personal health and safety because he knew he was taking the virus very seriously. What he feared for was the world around him. For as long as he has lived, Bruce has watched America get through hard times. America has won several wars, overcome 9/11, and fixed a busted economy on more than one occasion. In the mindset of a nation like America, Bruce says a virus cannot stop them, not after all they've been through. He does not have to worry about his own mortality when it comes to the virus because he says he is going to be gone soon, and he is okay with that. But he isn't sure most people would feel the same way if they knew the kind of death sentence they're signing by not taking COVID-19 seriously.

In December 2020, the virus in America was almost as bad, if not worse than it was when it first hit. Yes, Bruce's life had not changed, but he could see the world around him changing, and he didn't entirely like what he saw. "Every minute counts towards the end of my life." That is a true fact for everyone, but Bruce feels that only the elderly seem to understand it. Because they can see the light calling them closer and closer to home, out of this world. For those who cannot see that light, it does not mean it isn't close. For some, that light is closer than they realize. Like the light that shined on his mother in her early age, striking her from this planet and robbing her of the years she thought she was promised with her little baby.

He may paint for hours in his free time but Bruce says that he does not have much of a fantasy life in his head. He lives in this world and only this world. During times of deep thought and contemplation, he does not think of magical lands or things he wishes he could do now, or should have done when he had more time and ability. He paints for his own enjoyment and spends the rest of his thoughts on things like the future for the people he loves, including his wife, his children, his grandchildren, and his new great-grandchild, Neil.

"I don't have much time left," he says of his final days. "I know that." He just prays that for those who cannot see the light, that they walk as carefully around in the dark as they can.

Reflecting back on his complicated, beautiful, and yet, at the same time, simple life, Bruce thinks back to a time he had with his son. His son was having a bad day one day when he was about nine or ten years old. And so Bruce took him out to the edge of the property by a creek. Lying on the creek bed was a large stone, and Bruce asked his son what he saw.

"A stone," said Jason.

"What's on it?" asked Bruce.

"Some dirt, some moss."

"What do you think is on the other side?"

His son shrugged his shoulders.

"Turn over the stone," said Bruce.

Using both of his small hands, Jason turned the stone over and looked underneath.

"Now what do you see?" asked Bruce.

His son studied it for a moment, then looked back at his father. "There is some more dirt, sand, some water stains. And there are a few bugs."

"But you didn't know about all that until you turned it over, did you?" asked Bruce.

Jason shook his head slowly. Bruce watched his son soak in what he was saying before he spoke again. "That's life, son. You never know what someone's life is like until you turn over the other side of their stone. It's the same for you as well. You have to take time to turn over your stone and see what's lying underneath you."

That is what Bruce spends his time doing now. With the time he has left, much like the advice he gave to his son so many years ago, he is turning over his own stone. He'd like to see both sides of his hard, weather-worn stone before he passes on. This time of the Coronavirus has only provided him more time to study both sides of his stone. By doing so, he is able to ask questions of himself.

That is his advice to anyone today. "With the quiet time this pandemic has offered us, take the silence to reflect, to turn your stone over, and really look at what lies beneath. We only have a limited number of days left on this earth to find out what lies beneath the surface of ourselves. I think about what I'm doing, who I talk to, what I say, how I treat Josephine, how I do not treat Josephine. What can I do about it? At this time of my life, I will not worry about changing things that I cannot control. I can only think about them and use the power I do have to improve the things that I can change." Like the saying goes, "*God, grant me the serenity to accept the things I cannot change, courage to change the things I can, and wisdom to know the difference.*" If there is anything Bruce can say about the world post COVID-19, it would be to be a good person and take care of what you love because you never really know when it will be gone.

In March 2021, Bruce was happy to report that he was given both vaccine shots to combat COVID-19. He was lucky to receive the shots early on, because of his age. With the first shot, Bruce reported: "I was not apprehensive at all. Everything went well with those giving the vaccine. A little pain in the arm and after a short while I felt a small degree of euphoria, like a hit on a joint. Then I was very relaxed and took a nap." When he received the second shot, he spoke about the slight difference: "I had no reaction other than relief that I finally got the shots. Physically I felt great, mentally I'm still a little apprehensive (about two percent) because there is always a chance that I might still get the virus. So, I'm staying safe."

He went on to add a simple word of advice from his perspective when it comes to all of this stuff. In some ways it is his bottom line, despite everything he and his family have been through. He said, "Take care of yourself and particularly your children." Because that is who Bruce Marden is, a man of simple words with deep impacts. He knows life can get complicated and he knows it can become unbearable, but staying true to who you are is the best way to combat anything life may throw at you. In order to do that, you must surrender yourself to the flow of life's changing course.

1. Charisse Jones, "Jobless claims climb to 30 million in six weeks as COVID-19 layoffs continue to rise,". USA Today, April 30, 2020.https://www.usatoday.com/story/money/2020/04/30/unemployment-benefits-3-8-million-file-jobless-claims-amid-pandemic/3046759001/ (accessed May 1, 2020).
2. Mike Stiles, "Lessons from My COVID-19 Journey," LinkedIn, April 12, 2020, https://www.linkedin.com/pulse/lessons-from-my-covid-19-journey-mike-stiles (accessed October 25, 2021).
3. Ibid.

7

SURRENDER TO THE FLOW

Just before the start of May, I had begun to look up the idea of mantras. Those idioms and dogmatic phrases people say to help their mindset. It felt silly to me, something only people in AA or other support groups say together. It did not seem like something I would do. I get my stress and worry out by working harder, maybe taking on a new project. But as we entered into the third month of lockdown, I was running out of things to do. So, what could I say? On May 4, 2020, I spent an hour on Google looking up mantras, wondering which ones work best, how often they are repeated, and if there were Christian ones. According to Dictionary.com, Mantras are defined as: *Hinduism*. 1. a word or formula, as from the Veda, chanted or sung as an incantation or prayer. 2. an often repeated word, formula, or phrase, often a truism.

The other thing I found out was that mantras are divided up by the part of your body you most want to focus on: body, mind, spirit. The last option seemed most appropriate to me, and I began to research which ones work best under the third category. I found the perfect one:

"I surrender to the flow and have faith in the ultimate good."

It spoke to exactly what I needed to do, how I needed to think, and what I needed to instill in my girls. The flow in my life had been determined by me for about as long as I could remember. And now the flow had sped up and slowed down all at once, and I had no control. I felt like I was standing in the middle of a hurricane, the world around me ripping through the air, torn asunder by storms and thunder. But inside the hurricane cone, I was safe, without a clue of how long this would go on for. How long it would last until the waves broke.

I read it several times in silence. Then, alone in the bedroom, the door closed, I stood up. I faced my computer, the mantra nearly memorized, and said it out loud. Despite my best intentions, the words came out in a scared little girl's voice. I coughed, stood up straighter, closed my eyes, and said it again. Then again. And then again. By the fifth time, my voice was clear and I actually believed it. I left the bedroom with the words swimming through my mind, sitting on the tip of my tongue.

I walked out of my bedroom to find the girls in their pajamas, gathering cereal bowls and arguing over milk. I took charge of the milk pouring duties and looked over at Michael. He was sitting at the bar on the other side of the island, the iPad in his hands. His eyes were glued to the screen, his lips shut tight. I know this look well. It means only bad things. When my husband is truly scared, truly stressed, or truly pissed, he does not let it out. Instead, he sucks everything in like one of those spaceship vacuum bags sealed tight so the food is packed in completely.

"What is it, babe?" I asked him, while one of my daughter's was tapping my leg for me to pour the milk into her bowl.

Michael remained quiet for a moment until she got her

desired amount of milk and then sat back down. He sucked in even more air and turned the iPad over to me. On the screen was a one page release from the Governor's office in Florida. I read it over and felt my insides tremble.

"Shit," I said not so softly.

"Mommy!" yelled my oldest daughter from the table, a spoon halfway to her mouth.

"Eat, girls," said Michael, his voice stiff.

I could barely hear them. My hands on the iPad stiffened against the metal corners. The one page brief spelled out how Florida would remain locked down for sixty more days, with no bars or restaurants opening, and only gyms and libraries opened at twenty-five percent capacity. It certainly was not the end of the world by any means, but it meant the end of our vacation home rental business, at least for the time being. And on one hand, I felt like the decision made sense and was the right move for the Florida government to keep a handle on the virus in their state, and on the other, I worried about the lost business. Nobody rented a beach house in Florida just to sit inside it all day. And this was the beginning of the busy time for us. Soon it would be June and July, August after that. How in the hell were we supposed to make a dime off of these "stay at home" orders? I wondered. And that's when the mantra came dancing its way through my frontal lobe again: *"I surrender to the flow and have faith in the ultimate good."*

"Oh shut up," I mumbled to no one.

"What?" asked Michael, getting up from the island.

"Nothing."

The next day, as financial matters battled with the new manta in my mind, I found something awful with one of the hens out back. She had developed what is known as wry neck, when a chicken or hen's neck is twisted at an odd angle from the rest of its body, making it difficult to breathe, eat, or sleep. This can be caused by an injury, a birthing problem, or vitamin B deficiency with the muscles. I tried my best to keep the girls away from the trauma, but I quickly found they were not scared of the pain the hen was in, only determined to help it. I called a friend of mine to see if she could help with the issue. She came soon, bringing the vitamin B shots. It was hard to watch the poor hen try and recover. She was calm, as much as her kind can be with humans and unexplained injuries. My friend did such a great job, and we placed the hen in her own cage to stay safe. We prayed for her and did our best to move on with our day. I got back to helping the girls with their virtual school. All throughout the day I continued to look out and check on the poor hen. If I had to go with the flow, so be it. But I would at least keep an eye on the direction the flow chose to go.

That evening, after a long day of number crunches and client-broker phone and zoom calls, I was exhausted. As the night came down and darkened our backyard, the girls and I went outside to check on the hen. The girls took turns petting her gently, and then we spent some time with the silkies. The four little babies were so eager to see us, like genuine pets. I was glad to have a moment with my girls, the dark of the night made us stand closer together, the early May air keeping us warm as they used their tiny, delicate fingers to stroke the backs of the tiny, delicate silkies. The next morning we awoke to find the wry neck chicken had died. Surrender to the flow.

The rest of the week went pretty much like that one. I would wake up, say the little mantra, then exit my bedroom to catch up on how the world had fallen apart even more while I was asleep. For instance, on May 7th, I read an article over breakfast about how Airbnb laid off twenty-five percent of its workforce, equating to nearly 1,900 people.[1] Great, I thought sarcastically as I sipped my coffee. I couldn't say I was any better than them. We'd had layoffs and agents who gave up the practice. It was just hard to see even major companies doing this, as well as the small independent companies.

Nearly a week later, after all the endless cycles of work and worry that ran through our sedentary days, I woke up on one of my favorite days of the year. May 12, 2020: Mother's Day. I walked into the kitchen to find the girls were surrounded by a breakfast cake that Michael, instead of worrying over his iPad and spreadsheets first thing, had woken up early to bake for me. I kissed him, then each one of the girls, and thanked them all. I sat down as Michael cut a piece for me, the cake smell still wafting through the kitchen from its heat in the oven. My second oldest daughter came to my side and presented a card written out to me. The writing was childlike and friendly. The message was real and hit me hard:

Dear Mommy,

I wanted you to know that I love you so much. You're the best mom I could ask for. Happy Mother's Day. I don't want you to stress no more, I got you.

It was like God himself had spoken through my daughter, using her hands to write out a message from Him. It was as though he was showing me how great my life was, and how wonderful and important my girls were. I knew that already, of course, but don't we all think we know it? The more I thought about that card, the more I knew it was His way of saying, "No really, you are okay. Look at your children's faces and you will see peace." I thought about the mantra I had forgotten to say that day. Surrender to the flow. How much clearer can that message be made to you than your eight year old daughter writing it out to you in crayon?

The next few days were spent with more work and more eggs. The girls and I had regularly begun to gather the eggs from the chicken coops and come up with different places and people to send them to. Around this time, despite all the other work we had on our plates, Michael and I had begun discussing a possible trip. We had always wanted to take the girls on a trip around the country. We had put it off, deciding to wait until they were older. But now we had nothing holding us back. Everyone in our office was working from home. Our nanny was still practicing lockdown orders, and Vacation Bible School was canceled. We had to find something for these kids to do all summer. The moment that swim team was officially canceled, we decided to go for it. Our plan was to eat and sleep in the RV and to visit National Parks everywhere. We figured we could be just as safe, if not safer, traveling the country, than staying in Atlanta. We began looking at RVs to buy. On May 14th, the girls and I collected another batch of eggs from the coop and Michael spent the morning contacting RV salesmen. As I collected the last handful of eggs, I noticed a rather tricky issue with my breathing. And my nose began to run. I chalked it up to the cold morning air and rushed with the girls back inside.

Michael finalized the details of our trip to go see the RV we were interested in while I got the girls ready. I could feel my nose swelling up a bit as I put on a little bit of makeup. When I leaned in close to the mirror, I saw that my eyes were a bit red as well. I stared at them for a long time, thinking, debating. I knew what it could be, but I almost didn't want to believe it. I just could not accept what it might be. I thought about the second part of that mantra I'd memorized a week and a half earlier: " . . . have faith in the ultimate good." I decided that I would do that instead of worrying about what I feared it was. I looked away from the mirror and shut the bathroom lights off. Then, I quickly forgot about it.

Michael and I got the girls loaded into the car and we drove out to the RV park. It was quite a long drive, and I could tell that Michael noticed my silence. I am usually the energetic one on car trips, happy to keep the girls entertained while Michael keeps his focus on the road. Luckily the girls were so excited about the prospect of a new home on wheels that their excitement rose without my turning any dials.

The salesman was waiting outside for us when we arrived. He was a big man with short work sleeves and a wide tie. His pants were dirty and his clipboard had seen better days. He waved us down and greeted the girls cheerfully, bumping their elbows playfully in lieu of high fives and handshakes. He walked us graciously over to our chosen RV and opened it up. The girls went from excited to ecstatic just at the mere motion of the automatic stairs. We climbed inside together and took in all the features. I did my best to listen to both the girls and the salesman who went on a long rant about all the new features and gadgets of this particular model. But, despite my brave face, five minutes into the tour of the vehicle, I had to leave. I could feel a heated forehead and nausea hitting me hard.

I stumbled back to our car and climbed into the seat. The dirt and the outside air, not to mention all the movement, made my fever skyrocket. I leaned the seat back and put a chilly, wet palm over my burning forehead. I used the bottom half of my hand to hide my eyes from the sun that scorched its way through the hot glass of the car windshield. No mantra played in my head, no mention of faith or flow or flapjacks talked to me. Just the thought of death. I thought, as dramatically as I could in that moment, that I might die. I knew I was being dramatic, like a diva on a 1930s movie set. And the thought of these dramatic antics, the back of my arm placed lazily over my head, made me laugh. But I truly felt so weak and sick I could barely stand it. I realized when I tried to chuckle that it was more out of hysteria than hilarity. I remember thinking, this was how I was going to die: in the middle of Nowhere, Georgia, laughing myself into an early grave.

Turns out that it wasn't hysteria, just a fever dream. I barely remember the rushed drive home, Michael turning the car's AC on full blast as he sped towards our front door. The girls, I later learned, watched in silent fear as their mom was walked inside by their dad, her eyes lolling half open. He laid me gently on our bed and pulled the covers over me and then turned the fan on. The rest of my memory drops off at this point. I just slept a lot and only woke up to suck down a water bottle that my loving husband always managed to keep constantly refilled. I don't remember my dreams of those first two days or the things I said. On the third day, I remembered one important thing and my heart sank.

That was the day of Jane's Kindergarten graduation. The entire affair was socially distanced, but I knew a sick person in the middle of a pandemic couldn't waltz right in. My COVID-19 test had come back negative, but that didn't mean it was accurate, and I wasn't about to take any chances—plus I couldn't even if I wanted to. I was too physically weak to leave my bed. So, I stayed in bed while Michael and the girls attended. Of course, I saw the videos and the pictures. But it wasn't the same. I remember lying in bed on that day, more frustrated than I had been in a long time. Why now? I thought. Why can't I just be a part of this important event instead of being stuck in this bed? How is it fair that I cannot attend a major milestone in my daughter's life? And that is when I had a moment of pure clarity. A voice began to speak to me from inside me. Call it God, Buddha, or Oprah, I don't know. But the voice began to call out to me. And it was not gentle:

"You still have not surrendered to the flow, Megan. You say it, sure, but you will not do it. Your girls do it, all the time. Maybe you have to learn from them as they learn from you. Life is a cycle, and so are relationships. We interact with our loved ones in a circular fashion, doing the things they teach us, and teaching them things in response. It is never obvious but it always happens. Your girls wake up and enjoy breakfast. They may dread another day of online school, maybe one will worry about a test they would have done better on if the lesson was taught in-person. But they go with the flow more than you know. You do not. That is why you are sick. It is not just a physical sickness, it is emotional, mental, spiritual. You are trying to control your world. But you must wake up. You must see that the world you want so badly to control and run your way does not work like that. You cannot solely have faith until you first surrender to the flow of the world where faith is required. Words are written by the order of logic. '*I surrender to the flow and have faith in the ultimate good.*' Do you see? 'I surrender to the flow, *therefore*, I *can* have faith in the ultimate good.' You cannot do one without first doing the other. Ever. Your girls instinctively know this. It is in the heart of a child to go with the flow. They do not know yet what it means to take control. You do, but you must unlearn it if you are to survive the walk down this new path you find yourself on. Always remember: Faith always follows Surrender."

I sat with those thoughts for several days after. And as I rose out of the depths of this sickness, I began to see clearly what I needed to do. I had to surrender, fair and square. And as the number of days towards the RV trip approached, my health got better. How fitting, I thought nearly five days after nearly collapsing in Nowhere, Georgia, that I can put my new mantra to the test. Because we all know that there is no better way to experience surrender than to go out on the open road. But it takes faith to start out on an open road like that.

Frazier Keitt:
A Story on Faith

Life was all about movement and change for Frazier Keitt before the world was shut down and the doors were closed. But either indoors or out on the road, she knew that the life she led was guided by the hand of God. She was always taught from an early age about the power of prayer and belief. She believed that nothing can get you farther than what you ask the Lord to provide for you. Matthew 7:7-8 says, "Ask, and it will be given to you. Seek, and you will find. Knock, and it will be opened for you. For everyone who asks, receives. He who seeks finds. To him who knocks it will be opened." This was her worldview, and if a great flood could not keep Noah from believing in God, then a pandemic could not break Frazier's faith. If it is God's will, then it shall come to pass.

Frazier works as an Internal Medicine and Sports Medicine Trained Physician in Atlanta, Georgia. This job took a long road to get to where she is now. In the past five years, before COVID-19 hit, Frazier had lived in eight cities across the country. It began with her undergrad in Boston College, then to a Master's program at Hampton University that allowed her to do research. From there she went to Virginia College of Osteopathic Medical School, then transitioned to South Carolina for the second half of medical school. After that she went to Ohio for her residency, followed by Philadelphia for a fellowship, and finally ending with Atlanta for her career. At the time of all the moving, she did not love it. The travel was hard on her and the changing destinations made her feel uneasy. Then COVID-19 hit and she found herself bound to Atlanta. Looking back, she was glad she had traveled so much, knowing she may not be able to for a while.

At the time of the virus outbreak, Frazier was working at Emory University School of Medicine at Grady Memorial Hospital in Atlanta. She had been working in an outpatient clinic with patients who had non-operative orthopedic issues and sports injuries. She also moonlighted with the internal medicine group for the hospital once per month. This allowed her to get comfortable with the needs arising in this department. But with her belief in God, she knew it was more than medicine that healed people. It was a power far greater than we as humans can comprehend. But still, Frazier admits that she, nor most of the other staff, really knew what to expect with COVID-19. Her feelings aligned more with confusion than fear. She relied internally on her faith and externally on the hospital directors to tell her what to do. The only change she initially made was to begin working more in-patient schedules, admitting patients to the hospital, and checking up on them during her rounds. She began dealing with COVID-19 patients, admitting them upon arrival and treating them, as well as her usual orthopedic patients that came in.

The only exterior challenge that Frazier initially seemed faced with was that she was living with her parents. She had moved back to Atlanta and into her old house to save up for her own place to live. When the pandemic began, she was worried that working at the hospital all day was going to put her parents in danger when she came home from one of her shifts. But to her surprise, both of her parents were not very concerned. By that point, her mom was fully retired. She was on the couch enjoying retirement. So was her dad. They had done their time and didn't have to go out of the house, virus or not. She describes them as very religious, and they held a peace that everything was going to be okay. Despite being a grown woman, Frazier looked to her parents for guidance. "I swear my mom has a direct line to the man upstairs," says Frazier of her mother's beliefs. "If she's not rattled, I'm not rattled." This helped quell her worries about her home life, but as the months marched on, her fears turned to the world around her.

Her life remained the same as the virus worked its way into the collective conscience, but not everyone listened to their conscience when it came to the severity of the new disease. She began to notice the lack of responsibility people take when lives are at risk. Beginning around December 2020, she was beginning to notice more and more people in stores without a face mask on. It made her more mad than worried. How, at this point, could someone still not be getting the message? Whereas most other countries had curfews and day passes, Americans worked more on an honor system. She also began to notice a common mantra among many Americans. When someone spouts the term "healthcare hero" with reverence, and then turns around and does not wash their hands after going to the bathroom in a grocery store, it shows a lack of awareness that is detrimental to the future health of America itself. To put it simply, Frazier describes it as, "Completely and utterly ignorant, selfish, and frankly stupid that you even say that." Healthcare workers should be the last line of defense during a pandemic, not frontline heroes. If you are healthy enough to do so, then take care of yourself, and don't potentially endanger those who cannot.

In order to combat the daily issues she saw in real life, she balanced this out by watching worldwide news every day. She wanted to compare and contrast America to other countries. She also kept up with the American news media daily. It downed her spirits even more to witness how politicized everything became, in America at least. Frazier felt it was devastating that a worldwide pandemic broke out in the last year of a hard-headed President's first term. She felt that he used the media to lash out against false medical claims to try and expose himself as the true knower of all things COVID-19, when all he did was stand in the way of medical professionals handling a problem.

She also saw how the news highlighted the very concerning racism and classism in America. She says that no matter how much she thought she knew, "It is way worse than I thought . . . and not an isolated issue, definitely global." But at the end of the day, Frazier knew the only thing she could do was to stay focused, go to work, turn her efforts to her family and friends, and when she could find private time, turn her prayers to God.

From a career perspective, she knew that her job was to take care of patients. Her work in healthcare taught her how to compartmentalize. A lot of the COVID-19 patients needed a friend, someone to help them get through this tough time on a personal level, not just someone to administer medicine. This need from patients brought Frazier to a helpful, healthy mindset. She would take care of those in need and provide a better, more positive worldview for them.

From a personal perspective, Frazier was able to end 2020 on a slightly more positive note. This virus ripped families apart, teaching her to appreciate the family she has. She wants to be there for her sister and for her mom and dad. She learned that, as the saying goes, "Our tomorrow is never guaranteed." She was able to learn resilience and to trust her own strength through faith in God. To watch the world bring itself back from near annihilation shocked her, but to watch her mom remain cool, calm, and collected through all of it inspired her. She knows that her parents have faith in God. And she was given the gift of being their child, inheriting their strong will and fortitude, but the year she spent on the frontline of healthcare gave her a newfound hope in God that not even her parents could have done for her. When asked about what the experience taught her most, Frazier Keitt said, "I am a firm believer in God, and I believe that He only puts me where I need to be. And if my faith was ever to be tested, it is with this." And faith can be tested in so many ways, both at home and on the go.

---

1. Deirdre Bosa and Salvador Rodriguez, "Airbnb to lay off nearly 1,900 people, 25% of company," CNBC, May 5, 2020, https://www.cnbc.com/2020/05/05/airbnb-to-lay-off-nearly-1900-people-25percent-of-company.html (accessed May 7, 2020).

8

CROSS-COUNTRY FOR BEGINNERS

May 22, 2020. We had been on the road for five days. Michael was driving, I was sitting shotgun, and the girls, Jonah-their cousin who we brought with us-and Luna, our dog, were relaxing in the back of the RV, except for our second oldest daughter who was practicing playing "Phantom of the Opera" on her keyboard. The open room of the camper we bought provided enough space that they didn't feel "strapped in." It had been an incredible adventure so far, and we were still on the East Coast. We had already visited the little town of Helen, Georgia, my Aunt Nancy in Charlotte, North Carolina, and stayed a night at our first campground of the trip in Virginia.

We drove through Kentucky on our way to Sunbury, Ohio. There was a campground I couldn't wait for us to stay at. The pool area with the awesome slide was closed, but that was okay. They had gold mining onsite. I pinched myself that we were actually doing this trip, and I was thankful to have a husband brave enough to drive the behemoth we bought while pulling our minivan behind us.

As we crossed over the bridges that run through I-71, I took in the beauty of the East Coast. The changing landscapes offered picturesque moments no matter which direction you turn. As I clutched the guidebook, I was so grateful to have this moment. After only a couple months in doors and in fear, I felt liberated.

Halfway through the state of Kentucky, we stopped outside Fleming County, the local Amish community in the area. We thought that "Amish sightings" would be rare birds. But five minutes into our drive through the area, we spotted two horse-drawn carriages riding along the side of the road. The girls watched with wide eyes as the people that believed in the simpler times of yesteryear trotted beside our new age moving home on their way to the farms and fields. We continued on past them and found a local county market called The Dinner Bell.

The porches outside were wide and flat, offering comfortable deck chairs, much like a Cracker Barrel. Inside we found some fresh blueberry Amish pies for the girls and a special new Amish style metal cup and bowl set for our outdoor meals (that metal set served us well on that trip and afterwards we began using it in our kitchen at home; whenever our guests use these special blue and white bowls and plates they always ask us where they can buy them and I tell them to drive to Amish country). We pushed our cart to the front of the store, and an Amish dressed woman checked out our stuff. Funnily enough, they still took credit cards. Before taking off, we sat down and dug into our pies.

We climbed back into the RV, Michael behind the wheel, and drove through Maysville, Kentucky. The architecture was beautiful. Historic houses lined the road, packed tightly together like paper dolls cut in sequence. We made it through Kentucky with stomachs full of pie and heads full of beautiful scenery. As we transitioned into the lands of Ohio, the tight houses gave way to wide open fields with a single barn or home every few hundred acres.

We made it to Sunbury, Ohio, and drove through a convenience store drive-thru for some dinner and drinks to get us by for the next day or so. The drive-thru was like driving through a car wash. I had never seen anything like it before and never have since. It was indeed a converted car wash to liquor store with refrigerators with glass fronts lining the insides of the walls to the left and to the right as you drive your car through. It was easy to slowly drive through, see what was available, and pick what you want. They would gladly load your trunk with the booze, while you pay from your car window, and never had to leave the vehicle. It was raining when we made it to the campground, so we opened the outside awning, watched a movie, and went to bed early.

After a great night's sleep, we woke to another rainy day. This time it was only drizzling. The girls were able to participate in the onsite gold mine which included stones, shark teeth, and gold, and at midday we climbed back into the RV and traveled to St. Joseph on Lake Michigan. The area was a bit brighter. We swapped the mud and wet grass for a view of a large lake and some sand. I had the girls sit under a large sculpture that had been raised high above the lake and I took their picture.

Michael and I walked with our crew onto a pier that headed toward the middle of the lake. We took in the vast beauty of the water. The kids played on the playground, we picked up pizza, and the kids were able to freely ride their bikes all over the campground. The night ended with a small campfire and s'mores. It was so idyllic we decided to stay another night. I found myself more relaxed than I typically am. I remembered the days of my sickness. "Surrender."

Indiana Dunes State Park in Chesterton, Indiana, is a beautiful place. Half turn-of-the-century Gothic architecture, half beach resort, the entire park has something to offer for everyone. The kids were excited to get their bathing suits on and jump into the lake. Albeit chilly, it won out over the same living room and virtual classes they'd been subjected to for the last couple of months. We spent the day burying each other in sand, laying out on towels underneath the shiny sun peeking out from over the tops of the clouds, running around to get all the saved up energy from the RV ride out of our systems, and best of all, we slid down the large sandhills for hours.

Every parent knows how much little children can reignite the childish spark gone dark in all of us. To see my hardworking husband, who's head usually remains crammed with numbers, names, and dates, get to run around acting as silly as his five-year-old daughter was a blessing. We had hit day seven, one week on the road, and I was already thanking God for the miracle this trip was to us. And of course, as soon as I did thank him, he winked back at me by dropping a monsoon of a rainstorm down onto us on our way into Chicago.

The rain followed us all the way to the campground just outside of Chicago. We arrived to learn that there was actually a tornado watch, and we were quickly ushered inside the laundry room as we waited it out. Once that subsided, the kids grabbed their bikes and rode around in the large, twelve inch deep puddles at the campground. Our dog Luna enjoyed running through the puddles, too. The very next day, we hit the road again and set out for Wisconsin in search of cheese! And boy did we find some . . .

The cheese in Wisconsin is no joke. Sure they have the University, the observatory, and there are more reported ghosts per square mile than any other state[1], but they don't call it "Dairyland" for nothing. We stopped at a store called Ehlenbach's Cheese Chalet. We got all sorts of cheese, including some flavors I'd never heard of. We bought sweeter cheeses like raspberry cheddar, and more savory cheeses like garlic dill. We bought balls of cheese, string cheese, and cheese rings. We had so much fun buying cheese!

Next stop was Madison, the capital of Wisconsin. Due to COVID-19, what normally would have been a busy downtown area felt more like a ghost town. Buses were not driving through the city, there were plenty of parking spaces, and the lines for busy downtown food stops were almost nonexistent. It was a nice change of pace to walk among a different landscape, look at a city up-close, and see it for what it was. We wandered around for a few hours taking in the buildings near the capitol, the University architecture, and the sights of the nearby lake and we finished off the day enjoying ice cream.

The next day we visited a museum called "The House on the Rock." You have to stop reading this for a second and Google image this place. It is by far the most bizarre museum I have ever visited. Its claim to fame is that it is home to the largest carousel in the world. The rest of the museum had just about every odd and unreal collection you can imagine.

"During the 1940s, a man named Alex Jordan saw a 60-foot chimney of rock in the beautiful Wyoming Valley. It was here that he decided to build a house on the sandstone formation called Deer Shelter Rock.

Jordan built the house as a weekend retreat and never intended it to be a tourist attraction. However, people kept coming to see the architectural wonder they had heard about. Jordan eventually started asking for 50-cent donations. That was only the beginning. The 14-room house is the original structure of what is now a complex of many buildings, exhibits, and garden displays.

It can take many hours to walk through the House on the

Rock, and it's nearly impossible to see it all in one day. Among the collections within is the world's largest carousel, boasting 269 carousel animals, 182 lanterns, more than 20,000 lights, and hundreds of mannequin angels hanging from the ceiling all around it." [2]

Inside we saw everything from a room full of stained glass colored lamps, to a room full of old and bizarre guns, to a hallway lined with hand carved wooden objects. We also saw antique lighters of every shape, and a room full of vintage cars. All of that was before we got to the world's largest carousel filled with creepy dolls, and mannequin-esque figures populating the seats and poles around the entire ride. By the time we found the last exit door and walked out into the sunlight, I thought my head would explode. That evening, our family was content to find a campsite and relax to a movie and s'mores before going to bed early. Next stop on the list was Minnesota. I was glad to be getting much-needed rest and saving my strength for the journey. I learned that from an unlikely girl once, her name was Jenna Holton.

Jenna Holton:
A Story on Strength

Imagine your Senior year of high school, whether it's in the past or something coming up in your future. You're probably picturing final exams, college acceptance letters, prom night, the infamous senior spring break and graduation. That is the kind of life Jenna Holton was living, give or take the dozens of extracurricular hours she signed up for with the little time she had to spare. But all of that came to a sudden, full stop on the fateful day of March 13, 2020. Like everyone else, when the news first began to hit the airwaves, she had no concept of what it would be like. For her, she thought maybe it would blow over soon. "I give it two or three weeks," she thought. Besides, she had no other choice, she had a high school career to finish and a college career to get started on.

Jenna was born and raised in Atlanta, Georgia. At the time COVID-19 first hit, she was attending Sprayberry High School, in the city of Marietta. She was top of her class, student body president, and on track to attend Emory University, a college she had dreamed of attending for years. Her final months of high school were no slouch either. Maybe for some it's the ride down the roller coaster after all the flips and sudden jerky turns. But for Jenna, she was still full of ups and downs, and she was at the front of the roller coaster. She was juggling a lot and managing more than just her own set of expectations. She was well aware nothing could stop this roller coaster as it sped down the final hill, nothing at all.

Right?

Like most people's assumptions, Jenna was proven wrong and sent home along with the rest of the students and faculty for what the news and others were calling "virtual schooling." Fine. But, like she had envisioned, it would only go on for a few weeks. She kept her head up and did her best to stay positive for her whole graduating class. Given her ranking in the hierarchy of her class, as student body president and class president, she was given the high responsibility to confer between the teachers and principal and translate to the rest of the school. She kept her eye on her duties and kept spirits high. It was only at the tail end of the third week that the first inkling of fear crept in. By the end of week four, there was no word of returning back to school. Pretty soon the year had been canceled. "But that can't be true," thought Jenna instinctively, although she knew deep down that it was.

Her next few days were spent in utter turmoil. This wasn't supposed to happen. She had a plan. She always had a plan. It's how she became SGA President, how she made last year's Junior-Senior prom such a success, how she would give the Valedictorian speech at her graduation, a ceremony that had been put on an indefinite hold. This was all wrong and yet she still had to have a brave face, not only for her friends and family, but for the girl that looked back at her in the mirror every morning and every night. Luckily, Jenna does not give up, and this virus would not stand in her way.

Over the next month, the plans for the end of the year changed drastically. While the traditional graduation plans were on hold, a "Senior Parade" was planned. In order to end the year, the school faculty arranged a short drive by graduation parade that began at a local church near their school and ended in the school parking lot. The students were instructed to wear the formal cap and gown, including all the cords they had earned over the year. The community came out to support them (socially distanced, of course) and the teachers came in their cars to cheer them on as the students all drove through a little pathway in the school parking lot. Among the items given out as treats, besides the typical senior year T-shirt and candy, were two other amusing gifts: a roll of toilet paper and a sock that could be used as material for the students to make their own mask. While any other year these gifts would have come off as extremely odd, this year they fit perfectly with the theme of keeping a smile on during the pandemic panic. They ended the parade by calling each student's name and then everyone drove off. It was a sweet and heartfelt farewell. It may not have been what anyone planned, but the staff and faculty came together to try and give their graduating students something to remember. And for Jenna, that is what mattered most.

Later, at the closing of the school year, another surprise

parade came to Jenna's front door. But, for all of her contacts at the school, she had no clue this would happen. It began with a very odd request by her mother, calling her downstairs to take the dog for a walk outside. At the time, Jenna remembers feeling quite confused. At the beginning of the year, Jenna had signed up for all AP (Advanced Placement) classes and that day she had one of those exams scheduled in the late afternoon. It was a particularly stressful day of studying in prep for the exam. The last thing on her mind was to drop everything and take the dog outside. But nonetheless, she thought a study break might be nice. So she grabbed the leash, got the dog's harness secured, and walked outside.

"Also," called her mom from the kitchen, "don't go too far." If it weren't for the pressure of that day's upcoming exam, Jenna would have known something was up. But that day, she just thought her mom was being weird.

When Jenna did finally step out into the May air, she slowly realized what was going on. Written out in chalk on her driveway were congratulatory messages from all her teachers. When she looked up, Jenna noticed a car coming down the road. It wasn't until one of the school administrators pulled up very close to the driveway that she began to understand what was happening. And that's when the rest of the cars followed behind, each one with a different teacher of Jenna's from the past four years. As they all leaned out their windows to congratulate her from a distance, Jenna learned that she had won a National Semi-Finalist for the National Honors Society and had won a full ride scholarship to Emory University. She also learned that six of her other closest friends had been named finalists in the National Honors Society, which was the first time a single person from her school had made the list in several years, much less seven people. She was overjoyed and incredibly humbled at the news. But there was just one catch: she couldn't call her friends and congratulate them all at once. As it were, the band of traveling school faculty could not be in two places at once, and Jenna's was the first house they came to. So Jenna had to wait until the teachers made the rounds for all other six students. Luckily, in the meantime, she could enjoy the bag of goodies the faculty brought to her, including a beach towel and a pool donut float, all with the intention that now the students could finally relax.

"If only they knew how stressed I was at that moment," said Jenna upon reflection.

The good news is that, by the time her exam was over, her friends had all been told and she was able to celebrate over Zoom with everyone.

Then there was another home car parade. During the second one, Jenna was recognized as a member of the Senior Elite for her class. This award recognized her community service and leadership roles throughout high school as class president and swim & dive team captain. It happened on the day of her AP Microeconomics Exam, so she was a tad stressed, but nevertheless, she was overjoyed. In a normal year, the entire class would have had a large ceremony in the gym, where a teacher or coach of your choice taps you with a rose to earn the award. However, since they weren't in school, they did a separate drive-by car parade. During this one, Jenna's swim coach from all four years of high school brought a rose, a yard sign with balloons, a certificate, and a T-shirt. She handed these all to Jenna with a smile. It was another good day in the midst of a stressful few months, and there were a few more good days to come.

The school quickly learned how to handle COVID-19 and changed their official graduation to accommodate the health concerns. In past years, the school held their graduation at the Kennesaw State University's Convocation Center, but as that was indoor seating, they moved it to McEachern High School's football field. There were, of course, some rules for both students and family. The seating was socially distanced, as expected. But the unexpected was that each student, instead of being given eight tickets for friends and family, only received four and no one could buy extras. This limited many people to only bringing their parents and maybe a sibling or two. Jenna only has one older brother that could not make it, and her grandparents were high-risk. So, in keeping with the unexpected nature of things, Jenna's divorced parents came to support her, sitting socially distanced because of a whole other kind of pandemic. However, the day still went well for the most part. There was only one remaining factor left for Jenna personally. The speeches.

Jenna was in the rare position of having to give two speeches at the graduation. She would have to give a welcome speech as senior class president, and a valedictory address as the class valedictorian. Both of these would be given to the entire crowd. And, even though it would be half the size of a typical graduation, she still felt the pressure. On top of that, she would be doing it at a high school she was not familiar with. And, for the pièce de résistance, there would be no rehearsal. A typical ceremony of any size, big or small, with any crowd, will have a rehearsal. It is a simple way to know where everyone will sit, stand, and how to move. Not to mention *when* to move. But none of that would be available to them. Not only that, but Jenna would also not be able to practice her speech on the real stage. So, in order to combat this worry, Jenna, a naturally introverted person, walked onto the football field during off hours with one of her best friends and practiced her speech on the deserted stage to an empty crowd. She was fully prepared to leave if asked, but she was able to practice in enough time. She later reflected. "It felt silly, but it worked." Luckily, the next day everything came together, and the class was able to say goodbye with some semblance of closure.

Jenna's life in academia is nowhere near over. As the summer came to a close, the transition to college was pretty anticlimactic. She did not get a new bed set, new clothes, or select a new meal plan. The reason is that, to ensure safety, she chose to begin her freshman year at Emory University studying English and Psychology virtually. "I pretty much stayed in one of two rooms in my house all day long," said Jenna of her past year. It wasn't easy, but it was what she had to do.

Jenna has always stayed positive and determined to make the most of her situation. It is what got her to the top of her class, what won her student body president four years in a row, and what got her through a very unprecedented senior year, and it was what had to get her through the beginning of a new phase in her life.

In reflecting on the first year of the pandemic, Jenna looks back with gratitude. Yes, it is not what she expected, and that is how everyone feels. She is grateful that despite the unexpected changes, she was surrounded by great friends and hardworking teachers who made the ending of that chapter in her life memorable, in a different way than ever before. Now, in her future as a college student, Jenna wants to remain relentlessly appreciative. She may not have had a typical transition, but Jenna knows that how she reacts and handles what she is given is what will define who she becomes.

It is clear that Jenna is a self-disciplined and tenacious person. She is more determined than ever to remain this way, as she pursues her hopes and dreams. Ultimately, Jenna arose from the year of the pandemic with a better mindset and even more appreciation for life. All it took was strength.

1. Chad Lewis, "Wisconsin's 10 most haunted places," Milwaukee Journal Sentinel, October 18, 2013, https://www.jsonline.com/story/travel/wisconsin/2013/10/18/wisconsins-10-most-haunted-places/87625180/ (accessed June 4, 2020).
2. Dylan Thuras, "House on the Rock," Atlas Obscura, https://www.atlasobscura.com/places/house-rock (accessed June 17th, 2020).

9

THE WORD HEARD 'ROUND THE WORLD

In late May of 2020, two and a half months into the world being shut down, Michael, our four daughters, one nephew, and I found ourselves walking along the Stone Arch Bridge in Minneapolis Minnesota, overlooking the massive Mississippi River. According to the plaques on either end, it is the only arched bridge made entirely of stone found across the entire length of the River. From end to end, it spans 2,100 feet and took two years to build; construction began in 1881 and was completed in 1883. As the day crept along, we slowly transitioned our way from the bridge to a historical neighborhood just outside the city. The houses that lined the road were all unique. A few were Victorian in design, others Colonial; all of the homes were spotless in upkeep. Some, I'm sure, could very well date back to before the Arch Bridge was first conceived. Therefore, in a way, I was traveling back through time. And for anyone who has traveled across America, you cannot stop the clock that winds backwards the deeper you dig into this young country's rich past.

I tried to fathom that concept as we made our way to the end of the neighborhood. And, as is the universe's custom, the last house on the corner was a Colonial two-story with a plaque stating the construction date as: August 4, 1777. The kids were tired. They were incessantly complaining of their aching feet and their bored heads. Even Michael was ready to head back, albeit slightly less obvious with his whining. I could barely hear them as I stared at the house. I tried to imagine the settlers who possibly came to this land in 1775, just two years prior, constructing their house in the middle of the war. Can you imagine — they not only came to America but made their way to MINNESOTA!? No infrastructure, no planes, no IKEA/Walmart/Target upon arrival to help get their home furnished or Home Depot to build it. Wow! I thought about how much our country had changed, evolved, devolved, lost older morals and found new ones. And then I remembered the old phrase I'd learned in grade school, the saying that set off the Revolutionary War. It was, "The shot heard 'round the world." My breath caught in my throat and my eyes filled with tears.

For the past two months, I'd heard the same word everywhere I turned and every place I looked. From China, to Australia, to America, to Sweden, "COVID" was the word heard around the world. No, it was not a shot, but it was a distress signal. It shut the world down, it crippled the moving economy, and tied up the flow of the human race. The planet was suspended in a sort of limbo. I had not really fathomed it as much until the moment I saw that house. It was mundane to some, boring even to the likes of my exhausted daughters. But it was a reminder of just how much a single act, a single phrase, a single word, or a single organism, can seemingly stop the world from spinning on its axis.

I turned back, and smiled. "What's the next stop?"

"Mall of America!" the girls shouted in unison.

I laughed and sniffled at the same time. "Of course it is."

We made our way to the shutdown mall for a picture in front of the sign.

A few days later we drove into South Dakota to visit the Badlands National Park. The sights were barren and beautiful. Large desert mountains made of cracked dirt and sand that overlooked dried brown grass flowing in the hot winds. It was a sight to see and a breath of hot, fresh air. I was happy to see the girls still excited by the changing scenery, and it felt good for all of us to be out of the house. I found myself still thinking about that house back in Minnesota. I thought about the WhatsApp messages, the kind words and scary stories filling up my phone's home screen every five minutes. The idea of people from around the world sharing their stories had really taken hold, and I itched more now than I did before we left to read each and every message with rapt attention. I could slightly relate to them more, and I had more to offer. I had set up connections with people from every part of the world, and now I was traveling the entire width of my own country. I felt more connected to those in other countries, if only slightly. Because the middle of the South Dakota Badlands looks nothing like Marietta, Georgia, I'll tell you that.

We left the Badlands and drove through South Dakota to Mount Calvary Cemetery in Rapid City. I was there, not to dig deeper into America's history, but into my own. My great-great-grandparents, William and Mae Seidell, were buried there many years ago. It was a sight I had longed to see all my life, and the chance to show it to my own children brought me an even deeper peace of mind. We walked through the bright green grass cut short for visibility of the graves. Big trees lined the pathways between the gravestones, and beyond that were large, rolling hills off in the distance. We came to the middle of the field and found the name: Seidell etched into a large stone, with Mae's nameplate on one side and William's on the other. I wondered where their spirits were now. I wondered where the spirits go of all those who come before us. Did they reincarnate, or had they passed on to another plane of existence only reserved for the buried? I thought the latter might be true for human souls but not for the soul and spirit of the nation itself. That soul, the one created by foreigners to be called "America," is always being reincarnated. It changes with the seasons like the leaves pinned to the trees above me. Once, it was infantile, fought for by its forefathers. Now, with its current incarnation, its citizens were calling out for help because of an invisible monster plaguing its walls. But as I left the cemetery, my daughter's hand in mine, I realized that the other citizens of this world were yearning for help and praying for safety. The response to the word "COVID"' was "help." But the response to the word "help" was what?

It was sixty-six degrees Fahrenheit when we arrived at the Mount Rushmore National Memorial in Keystone, South Dakota. The sky was clear, the wind was mild, and the faces on the mountain of those aforementioned forefathers never looked so crisp. I had heard for years of their magnitude, but in person, I was astounded at the mere height and stature of them.

My girls loved it, too, and Michael thought it was marvelous. My youngest spotted the sign for Thomas Jefferson Ice Cream on the way in, and I knew she was mostly thinking of that, as we had promised her we would get some before we left. Nobody in our group was bored. There are some places in the world that take you outside of yourself. The eyes of those great men look down on you and you cannot think of much else. Even my thoughts of America's history were laid to rest as I simply just looked up. But it felt nice, it felt right, it felt better just to look nowhere but up.

We ended the trip to Mount Rushmore with the promised

scoop of ice cream, and then headed over to Bear Country, U.S.A. where we drove down a long path and marveled wide-eyed at elk, deer, goats, and of course, bears. It was a good way to end the day, but I could not leave South Dakota. Some people dismiss the middle of America as something to overlook, one of the states where you sit in one of their airports for an hour during a layover between coasts. There is even the phrase "middle of America," meaning you are bland or have no character. I found it the complete opposite. For me, the longer I stayed in South Dakota, the more I came to appreciate its beauty, and we decided to stay another night.

The next day we traveled from our campsite to an old Bishop's home in Rapid City where Helene M. Duhamel, my great-great-great-Aunt Helen's granddaughter, the State Senator for South Dakota, lives with her family. We spent the next couple of days together, and I got to learn all about this fascinating great-great-great aunt of mine. Among many accomplishments, her shrewd business skills brought the local area news to three different states (these states previously had no local news coverage). She was also the only woman amongst one hundred men from around the country to attend the National Broadcaster's annual conference meeting. The story goes that the meeting kept getting postponed because the announcer was calling for all the wives to leave the room. Helen did not leave because, unbeknownst to the announcer, she was a part of the meeting. At Helene's house, I was able to go through old photographs and garner incredibly inspiring stories and visual memories from her posthumous collection.

After the history lesson for myself in the morning, we traveled to Rapid City's Storybook Island where the kids could run around and enjoy all the displays from classic children's tales. There was the *Wizard of Oz* display, the Dalmatian display, the Dr. Seuss display, and so many more. We then topped the day off with a quick trip to Dinosaur Park, which the kids loved but not as much as pretending to ride Cinderella's carriage at the previous park. We ended the day with a trip to Mount Rushmore Resort and Lodge. We found a place to park the RV and took the rest of the evening to unwind. This was my favorite RV Park of the entire trip because it offered more for the kids to do than any other RV park.

As the day came to an end and the next day's trip loomed over us, I was happy to lay down and let the world quiet around me. I was in good spirits for a number of reasons, and I could tell that the girls had fallen asleep with smiles on their faces. But something still nagged at me. It was like living through this irony that ripped me in two. The world I'd known my whole life, the world I brought my four beautiful girls into, was changing as sure as the minutes clicked by. And yet, I was living the present days in an "old world," visiting a land left in the past. From visiting my relatives' graves, to the faces of Mount Rushmore, and the pictures of my Aunt Helene, I was existing in small increments of forgotten time. As I neared sleep that night in Rapid City, South Dakota, I wondered what it would be like to step back out of this history book I'd traveled into and live in the real world again. I didn't want to think about coming home so soon, but I also wasn't sure of what home would be like when I returned. I just had to stay positive, like my friend Marian Baltazar.

Marian Balthazar:
A Story on Positivity

With a husband and three kids, Marian Balthazar's life in the Philippines was laid out perfectly prior to March 2020. She made sure of that when she signed on to work for an American company remotely. Because of the time change, Marian became a night owl, perched over a computer screen while the world around her slept. Being a prompt, planned person, she knew she could handle it. It came at a tiresome cost, but it was worth it. "I made sure that my daily routine in the morning for my family was well planned and scheduled, even doing groceries, laundry, and preparing kids for school. I had been doing the same scheduled routine in the morning after my shift ended and made sure to finish everything right after lunch so I could go to bed to sleep before night came," Marian said of her time before the pandemic. Life is full of surprises—some offer goodness, and others offer hardships. Marian learned the hard way how to make those hardships into something good.

As we have learned, when COVID-19 peaked, every country acted differently, in part based on way of life, and in part based on the way their government handled it. Almost immediately in the Philippines, each family was issued a quarantine pass. It is not a free pass to be used whenever you feel like using it. Without this pass, you could not enter grocery stores or pharmacies. Each family had a designated day and time each week that they were allowed to use the pass. For Marian's family, their pass was scheduled for Wednesdays from 12:00 p.m. to 9:00 p.m. and on Saturdays from 1:00 p.m. to 5:00 p.m. The passes were just one of the ways that the government sanctioned her family's daily life. Curfews were also implemented, from 8:00 p.m. to 5:00 a.m. This level of monitoring was not met well by the citizens during those early days. Some people inside the country were met with violence by law enforcement when they were found outside without a pass or past the curfew. Despite the government implementations that were perceived negatively by citizens, the government also did their best to help in positive ways.

When the pandemic hit a surge and the citizens of the Philippines began losing their jobs, the government developed food relief programs and monetary assistance to provide temporary income. This helped greatly because of the level of quarantine that the Philippines was under compared to most places during much of the pandemic. Nine months into the pandemic when most governments had significantly lessened or done away with quarantines in place for its citizens, the Philippines still found themselves in quarantine. At the beginning when the virus was new and the government was not sure of its impact, they took the strictest approach possible. The citizens were put under Enhanced Community Quarantine, or ECQ. This is where the curfews and passes came into play. Over the next several months as the medical community learned more, the Philippines relaxed to a General Community Quarantine, or GCU. This gave the citizens more of their previous freedoms back, and things like the curfews and passes became less of a necessary evil.

During the GCU phase in the beginning of 2021, any person from the ages of eighteen to sixty-five was allowed to travel more freely, even entering certain malls and shopping in certain stores. Public transportation began operating again at a reduced capacity. And most businesses had opened again to fifty to seventy percent capacity. But even as businesses opened back up, there were new procedures in place to regulate the virus and track the spread, should another spike happen in the area. The most prominent of these procedures was the individual tracking by each business. At grocery stores, convenience stores like 7/11, and fast food restaurants like McDonald's, every patron who entered must fill out a card with their full name and contact number and the temperature that was recorded by the person checking temperatures at the entrance.

Back home, inside the safe walls of her home, a scary storm was brewing. Not within Marian, but within her son, David (his real name has been kept confidential at the request of Marian). By the time the lockdown began, he was ten years old. On the outside, he was a typical, rambunctious boy. But on the inside, he was dealing with mounting seizures. He'd had a history of seizures in the past. So far, they had only included minor attacks lasting no more than thirty seconds at a time. They intensified to a high level on October 9th of 2020. During these twenty to thirty seconds of terror, he had difficulty with speaking and swallowing properly. He also was having trouble with standing on his own, due in part to temporary paralysis of the body and numbness to the joints. During the attacks, he would be conscious but unable to control his movements. After witnessing the worst attack so far, Marian and her husband brought him to the hospital. He was diagnosed with Convulsive Seizure and Brain Dysfunction. When they heard this, Marian and her husband quickly grabbed hands behind the desk across from the doctor, gripping each other for the long road ahead that this would bring for both them and their son.

David was admitted to the ICU and remained there for ten days. During that time, his vitals that had dropped due to the seizures returned to normal, and he was moved to a private room for recovery. After only twenty-four hours, his vitals dropped rapidly, and he was rushed to the ICU again and was put into a medically induced coma for forty-eight hours. Those were the scariest hours of Marian's life. She didn't sleep. She used the time to pray intently, asking for a miracle. When words of prayer escaped her, Marian watched her beautiful boy sleep on the verge of a nightmare, and she silently hoped that inside his sweet body, good things were occurring and his brain was filled with happy thoughts. When David woke up two days later, Marian was relieved to hear and see him speak so normally to her, assuring her that he felt better.

After that, David began to get better. He started physical

therapy almost immediately. In the second week of November, the hospital provided lodging for Marian and David as he went through therapy three times a day. For her, despite the smile she showed David, she was frightened. The world was on lockdown, the people were dying from a super flu, but she could not pray for that. She had to put all her prayers towards her son's recovery. Due to these COVID-19 restrictions, she and David were not allowed to leave the lodging provided. It was tough to be in such a bubble during such a frightening time. For the first week of therapy, David responded very well. Marian recalls that for a span of five to seven days, David could stretch his arms and legs, the movements progressing at a healthy rate. He could not walk yet, but he could stand on his own for a short period of time. Because of this, at the end of the first week, the doctors advised that he could continue the therapy from home. First they had to take a COVID-19 test and wait for twenty-four hours to know the results. Once the results came back negative, Marian and David went back home.

At home, David continued to stay in a wheelchair most of the time while he progressed toward using a walker. The walker helped him to further his motor movements and push forward toward a new normal. But unfortunately, in mid-November just as David was at home recovering, the Philippines was hit with a category 4+ typhoon, known as Ulysses. The Balthazar home, the same sanctuary Marian had just brought her son back to, was hit hard. Their first floor was literally underwater, forcing them all to live on the second floor. From outside, Marian and her family could see parents shouting for help from their rooftops as they held children in their arms. Water waged through the streets of the neighborhoods and markets as cars and people drowned with their pets. The water remained on the first floor for over two days. Most of their attention was on David, hunched over a walker while water leaked from their windows and out their front door. It took another week for the entire house to be cleaned and restored to normal, whatever normal was anymore.

In the end, despite a scary month in the middle of the lockdown, Marian stayed positive. She describes herself as a resilient person. "I try to manage everything with a smile on my face." Because of her husband's support and her own fortitude in the face of hard times, she was able to power through her fears, put on a brave face, and embrace a life more at home with her children by her side.

Many months after this all happened, just as it seemed life was getting back to a new routine, Marian began to feel something was wrong. During the first week of March 2021, Marian and her family went to the grocery store on a Sunday. In Manila, they were still requiring every customer entering any store to fill out all their contact information on a card before they were allowed to shop or eat. The government called it "contact tracing." It meant that if someone who had been at the store at the same time you had been and within a certain window of time later tested positive for COVID-19, the government could send out health agents to your home and bring the entire family to a testing facility to make sure they did not contract the virus. And that is exactly what happened to Marian. As it turned out, one of the employees at the grocery store had COVID-19 when she and her family had been there.

When Marian woke up on Monday night for a night full of work, she felt body pains and a headache. She had experienced these symptoms before because of the odd hours that she works, so she took some painkillers and moved on with her work. However, on Tuesday morning, Marian woke up with a fever and knew it could be something bad. It continued to worsen until Thursday, when she was contacted by a medical team in charge of tracking her area. They informed her that an employee at the grocery store had been out sick on that Friday of the weekend that Marian and her family went to the grocery. Then the employee came back to work on Saturday and Sunday but went home early on Sunday because they were not feeling well. They were confirmed positive for COVID-19 the very next morning, and unfortunately had been in contact with Marian's entire family. The medical team told Marian that they would be arriving in forty-five minutes to fetch her entire family for testing.

They showed up quickly wearing PPE uniforms and said they would be taking them to a testing facility. "It was scary to have these folks in our home, but they were very nice. They explained that they had to do this for our safety," said Marian later. When they reached the testing facility, they all had to take the swab test, which was their first time being tested. The swab test results were fast, and in less than thirty minutes they got the results that Marian and her mother-in-law were both positive. Her husband and the kids were all negative so they were transferred to a separate isolation room. She took another test with a blood sample, and that confirmed that she was indeed positive. At the hospital, Marian started having an itchy throat and the food she tried eating tasted "dull." Her throat swelled so badly that they had to put a respirator on her to help her have enough oxygen. She could not do anything while waiting for the results. She could not even call her husband to see him and the kids. It was also very hot in the facility, there were four people in the same room with just two ceiling fans with plastic covers on each of the beds, which was obviously very uncomfortable. When asked about this time, all that Marian could say was, "I really don't want to go back to that situation."

After a few days of being stuck at the facility, she was released with a negative result and went home. She had no fever, no muscle pains, and her throat was slowly getting better.

The kids were okay with their father, but they were not allowed to come home because Marian had to quarantine for another seven days alone and do one more final test before the medical team would allow her family, that had been staying with her mother, to come home. Once she was cleared, then the kids and her husband returned.

Even after all the hardship, Marian still had a positive way to look back at the situation. "I consider myself blessed that I did not get this virus when Manila was hit with the typhoon or with very high numbers of positive patients. When I was there I could hear people crying for help and some died while waiting for their turn to get treated in the waiting areas. After I left the hospital, Manila went back to strict quarantine. The curfew hours tightened from 6 p.m. to 5 a.m., and we had to continue to have quarantine passes so not all family members could go out again."

The entire experience was a not-so-gentle reminder of the lingering effects that the virus still brought into different people's lives, no matter where you live or who you are. At the end of the day, when reflecting back, Marian says that before COVID-19 hit, she was already a patient person. A multitude of terrible events tested her patience over the year of quarantine, but she was able to rise above it. No matter what happened, or what will happen next, Marian just wants to hug her children tightly and keep her head held high. She knows that is all she can do to carry on with the great life she has been given. And she is not the only one who believes in staying optimistic.

Jose Martinez:
A Story on Optimism

When Jose Martinez (his real name has been kept confidential at his request) was sixteen years old, both of his parents were killed in a bus crash when returning home to Nicaragua from a work trip in Costa Rica. The bus was going too fast over a bridge, and as it came down to the end, the driver over-corrected on a turn and flipped the bus. Many people lost their lives that day, including his two parents. Jose almost lost a piece of himself when he heard about the deaths, but something else happened to him instead. He was just at the age where a boy becomes a man, the kind of time when you don't want your parents around but exactly the time when you need them the most. And then they were gone. But instead of crumbling in grief, Jose learned what lay inside him, a kind of resilience took hold in his gut that day, a tether to optimism that never swayed during the hard times. He'd never been faced with something harder, but this did not break him. He knew, even then, that if that could not bring him down, he would have the ability to bounce back from tragedy better than most. It was not until two decades later that he realized he was right.

On April 18, 2018, the president of Nicaragua had just decreed all social security reforms for the citizens, which increased taxes and lowered benefits to the bare minimum, had been set in motion.[1] This was an extreme blow to the people of Nicaragua as the second poorest nation in the Western Hemisphere, and the government is corrupt to a lethal degree. The protests began. The first protest lasted five days and caused thirty civilian deaths. After such a catastrophic response, Ortega repealed the reforms. But this did not end the protests completely. Seeing the power he wielded, the people of Nicaragua continued their protests, aimed specifically at Ortega himself. These revolutions became the deadliest civil conflict since the end of the

Nicaraguan Revolution in 1990.[2] And by March of 2020, they were nowhere near over, but that did not stop a global pandemic from bleeding its way into the country at the same time.

Jose saw this civil unrest every day from far away. He considered his own life a paradise, despite how hard he had to work each day in order to make it that way. Jose has two companies: he owns a frugal real estate company on the Nicaraguan coast, and he owns two restaurants. By March of 2020, his income was becoming more and more difficult to keep afloat. "The restaurants took a beating in those early days," says Jose. And, around this time, just as the protests began to settle down, the news from other countries and the States regarding COVID-19 brought tourism numbers to an all-time low. Tourists could not make it into the country—no flights were coming in. The borders of Nicaragua remained open, but the neighboring countries shut their borders and flights from other places halted. Jose could not bring down the rental prices of his properties because they were already at their lowest, due to the civil unrest that had been running through the country.

For the first few months of the pandemic, the government of Nicaragua provided no real information about the COVID-19 health updates. It was as though the country ignored the virus. While the rest of the world leaders addressed their countries daily in the early days of the pandemic, Ortega was nowhere to be found. Thanks to the internet, many of the citizens followed other news sites from neighboring countries, such as Costa Rica, to learn what proper precautions to take and what to do as health officials learned more. This extra information from the world wide web did not stop the Nicaraguan government from covering up the truth. For a long time they denied that the virus was even in the country, despite the lack of healthcare needed to prevent its infection. The government became so obtuse in their cover up of the pandemic, that they began to hold mass burials each night at midnight for the people who had died from COVID-19 in the hospital that very day.[3] The burials were so rushed that some family members who were called last minute to their loved one's funeral feared whether or not the box they were mourning even contained the right dead person. By May of 2020, in the middle of these mass burials, *The New York Times* reported that the Nicaraguan government insisted it had the lowest COVID-19 death toll in Central America.[4]

During the first few months, the contacts in the hospitals told the local families how serious many of these cases were. The medical community was being threatened and pressured by the government at the time to not give out any information about the virus. But if you had a friend who worked in a hospital, you could learn a little here and there. Lucky for Jose, he had a friend who told him the hard truth one day as it first erupted in March. "That was it for me. We were told by our government that everything was fine, but the rest of the world said it wasn't. My wife and I decided to bring our three young children out of school," says Jose of those early months.

The kids stayed home the next day and for the next year after that. He lives in a mountain in the jungle, just off the coast, and his kids all went to a private school at the time. This provided him and his family enough isolation from the pandemic and its impact, but they still did not want to take any chances. Soon the private schools in the country shut down—of their own volition—and a month later, after the parents had been pulling the kids out anyway, the government finally issued for the public schools to be shut down as well.

The summer months were a bit more relaxed for Jose and his family. The one plus of the Nicaraguan government's cover-up was that, although most beaches in neighboring countries like Costa Rica were closed, the beaches that Jose lived right next to were not. His family did their best to mostly stay inside, but the kids were allowed the rare outlet that most other children during the pandemic were not given: they got beach days. "I could still go surfing every day and go hiking in the mountains with my family."

Despite the intimate family time, the business side of Jose's life was getting complicated. Since there was no government mandate to close down small businesses, people in the restaurant industry were unsure of what to do. Most of the places closed down entirely after hearing what other countries were doing. Jose decided to keep his restaurant closed for indoor and outdoor seating purposes and trained his employees on the proper precautions in order to keep delivery an option. This helped his restaurant survive through the pandemic, where others failed and were left behind. The moratorium on dine-in seating did not last long at Jose's restaurant, as more and more locals got tired of being indoors. Luckily they already had open area seating, and halfway through 2020, they began opening outdoor seating again. By that point, many other restaurant choices had already been shut down and run out of business, which allowed for Jose's eatery to thrive amid the desperation and limited choices. His restaurant business began booming in success. His real estate business did not do as well.

"My 2019 was better than my 2020 because my business is selling to tourists and neighboring countries shut their borders for their citizens to enter through the year," says Jose, of his real estate ventures. "No international flights were coming into Nicaragua, because the airlines had canceled them, so we were pretty much isolated from the rest of the world." This did not bother him too much; he knew he was lucky to have one business thrive even if the other business did not do as well. He looked at what was going on that was good and put blinders on for all the negative aspects, and this was rather easy because of how he trained his mind early on.

When it came to the riots and protests of 2018, he ignored it the longer it went on, otherwise he could not focus on the things he needed to focus on. The same became true as 2020 continued.

At first, all he could do was absorb the COVID-19 updates from around the world, especially since his government was not providing the right answers. But by the summer of 2020, Jose paid less and less attention to the virus news, to the point of ignoring it completely. He had to narrow his focus on his children and his wife, and he had to focus on his two businesses and let the healthcare workers do their jobs.

A few months later, Jose's attention was again turned toward the outside world. A law was passed by the government of Nicaragua on October 26, 2020 called the 'cybercrime' law.[5] It stated that if any citizen is caught speaking out against the country or the politics, even over the internet, they will be prosecuted. A *CNN* news article published in the wake of the law stated: "President Daniel Ortega asked the Supreme Court of Justice on September 14 'to promote national reforms to national laws to penalize those who commit hate crimes with life imprisonment.'"[6] It was a jarring lesson for Nicaraguans. The entire world was indoors, and compared to Americans who could spend all day long typing about how stupid or inadequate their government was, under the First Amendment, Nicaraguans had no such luxury. They may look similar to Americans, sitting inside all day during the pandemic watching Netflix, but they certainly were not on the same plane of existence when it came to personal freedoms, including a person's right to speak freely. This made Jose very wary. Typically he had felt far removed from the deep oppression that the inner city Nicaraguans faced every day. They were always monitored, but he had never felt that way. Now this law, in some ways, called his bluff by telling the people of Nicaragua that they may think they're on their own, they may think that they're free, but think again. You really answer to us.

It seemed that despite the increased policing of free speech and stay at home orders, the citizens of Nicaragua all functioned under a similar mindset. Bad things had been happening in their country for decades. Yes, they got scared at first when another disturbing thing happened. A civil uprising almost drove their country into a civil war just two years before the pandemic hit. So, by 2020, the citizens were already on high alert, and they could handle the unrest of a pandemic better than some other countries. They certainly were not immune to health scares, but they just knew how to care for themselves, their businesses, and their loved ones even if the world around them was coming undone. "It sucks, but we're ready," said Jose of the collective Nicaraguan mindset.

"I live in paradise," said Jose. "People all over the world will learn to adapt, to get treated, and to take the right precautions. And when they do, they will come here to escape what they cannot change. People have been coming to visit this land of paradise for years before the pandemic hit. And they will come again. Covid made Nicaragua a little bit more attractive. Here, at the Nicaraguan beach, we are away from the rat race life that many live. Folks all over the world have re-examined their lives and how they want to live due to the pandemic. And the pandemic even helped change the political climate in the country of Nicaragua. To the citizens, it's no longer about political uprising, it's about quality of life." And to Jose, he knows that there is no better quality of life on the outside than a nice ocean view.

Internally, he knows people will be alright too. Yes, everyone either lost someone they loved or heard about someone they knew who did. But he knows how strong people can become in the face of the worst disasters. He rose up from the pits of despair when the two people who brought him into the world were taken from him without a moment's notice. He knows that not only are the Nicaraguan people strong but everyone else can be too. Staying optimistic is key. When life gives you lemons, just make some lemonade. That is true, even when you are miles away from home.

---

1. Caleb Diamond, "Charting a Smarter Path Forward in Nicaragua," Center for Strategic & International Studies, October 1, 2019, https://www.c-sis.org/charting-smarter-path-forward-nicaragua (accessed June 28, 2020).
2. Frances Robles, "As Nicaragua Death Toll Grows, Support for Ortega Slips," The New York Times, May 4, 2018, https://www.nytimes.-com/2018/05/04/world/americas/nicaragua-protests-ortega.html (accessed June 27, 2020).
3. Alfonso Flores Bermúdez and Frances Robles, "Coronavirus: Nicaragua's midnight burials tell of a hidden crisis," The Irish Times, June 1, 2020, https://www.irishtimes.com/news/world/coronavirus-nicaragua-s-midnight-burials-tell-of-a-hidden-crisis-1.4267891 (accessed June 4, 2020).
4. Alfonso Flores Bermúdez and Frances Robles, "Resisting Lockdown, Nicaragua Becomes a Place of Midnight Burials," The New York Times, May 31, 2020, https://www.nytimes.com/2020/05/31/world/americas/coron-avirus-nicaragua-burials.html (accessed June 4, 2020).
5. Associated Press, "Nicaragua approves 'cybercrimes' law, alarming rights groups," PBS NewsHour, October 27, 2020, https://www.pbs.org/new-shour/world/nicaragua-approves-cybercrimes-law-alarming-rights-groups (accessed November 2, 2020).
6. Mario Medrano, "Nicaraguan National Assembly approves special cyber-crime law," CNN, October 27, 2020, https://cnnespanol.cnn.-com/2020/10/27/asamblea-nacional-de-nicaragua-aprueba-ley-especial-de-ciberdelitos/ (accessed November 4, 2020).

10

THE DIVIDE

On day seventeen of our cross country tour, we arrived at Yellowstone National Park, the first National Park in the United States, and often regarded as the first National Park in the world. It was #1 for us, too. This was hands down our favorite park of the entire trip.

Yellowstone was established by the U.S. Congress and signed into law on March 1, 1872, by President Ulysses S. Grant. It is mostly located in the Northwest corner of Wyoming, extending into Montana and Idaho. Known for its vast wildlife and ecological intricacies, Yellowstone is most famous for the Old Faithful Geyser as one of the premier tourist attractions. Our route took us through Montana on the highways. Before we even got off the major roads, we spotted large Bison grazing in the wide green fields that lined the highway. As we parked the RV and stepped out, the air felt cool and the wind felt soft.

We all yawned and stretched. I glanced at Michael as he yawned with his eyes closed. I was so grateful to him for driving so much. I know he had work on his mind, the pandemic on his mind, and the hundreds of miles still to go on his mind. Despite all the things he kept juggling silently, he was still able to let them go and follow the kids out to stare wide-eyed at the wildlife and the geysers. As we walked along the designated trails and took in the sights, I pecked him on the cheek before the kids could see. He smiled back at me, and we had one of those silent "I love you" moments that only people truly connected can share.

We first connected in January of 2005, in an accounting class of all things. Some of my friends from that class and I were sitting around in the classroom one day, comparing the most recent test scores. Michael had been sitting behind me for most of the term, and I could tell he was lonely, a bit left out. I turned around to ask him how he did on the exam and he said, "Oh not so good, I got a 92." I was astounded that he thought that was a bad grade. I admired his work ethic, he didn't look half bad, and he had an accent. I asked him where he was from and when he told me Germany, I responded with the same lame response I have heard a thousand times since every time someone asks him that question, "I've been to Germany." I had, that was no lie, but what a way to win a guy's heart. Soon after that I got the gumption to ask him out. I offered to show him Atlanta since I had lived there my whole life, and he was new to the area. Our first date was March 1, 2005.

The first day at Yellowstone was spent exploring nature. We watched as the geysers spewed smoke from underneath the ground, the teal color that rose up made the girls' eyes pop. The ground there looked more like a different planet. We then drove along the highway, parallel to the Park, behind some bison that made their way wherever they needed to be. When we parked again, we found a whole forest that looked to be torn down. Typically you expect a National Forest to be pristine, but I assumed, like most things, if you look hard enough, you'll find some broken pieces. After further research we discovered that beetles were the cause of the forest destruction and that the devastation they were bringing was linked to increasing climate change.

We eventually reached Old Faithful. I highly recommend anyone reading this to add this adventure to your bucket list if it isn't already there or if you haven't already visited. In 1938, a mathematical relationship of duration and intervals was first described for this faithful geyser. It was the first geyser to be named inside the United States. A single eruption can shoot over 8,000 gallons of boiling water, and the best part is that the water shoots over one hundred feet in the air and is a miraculous site to enjoy anywhere from one and a half to five minutes. Interesting fact, the geyser was once used as a laundry machine in 1882. A man known as General Sheridan and his soldiers found that linen and cotton fabrics were kept secure despite the powerful action of the water. However, woolen clothes were torn to shreds.[1] [2]

Michael and I quickly learned that we make a great team in business and life in general. We eloped after two and a half years of dating. We built several successful businesses together and had four daughters. For the longest time, I thought I might be the one person in the world who had a perfect marriage. Until March 2020, more than fifteen years after I turned around in class to look at him.

After seeing enough of Old Faithful, we ended the day by donning our raincoats and hiking up the side of the mountain, next to a large river. It was cold and misty, the wind a bit harsher the closer you got to the top. Eventually we had the best view in the world of the Upper Falls. Despite the wind and the rain, it was worth the hike. When we eventually got back to our campsite, we changed into our pajamas for the rest of the evening as we grilled out. We had to rest up for day two. I sat next to Michael while we watched the kids scarf down hotdogs, and I held his hand. He looked back at me and we exchanged that same smile. It was comforting, but it said a lot more than the girls would ever hear.

When COVID-19 came crashing down around us, affecting our way of life in a huge way, it took a toll on both of us. Everything in our worlds changed from our businesses to suddenly managing our children 24/7 in a way we never had to before. Between feeding, schooling, and raising four children in general and dealing with multiple businesses that had to pivot, we never had a break, and suddenly, before either of us knew it, adrenal glands miserably weak, we were in a constant state of stress and we found ourselves taking it out on each other.

The next day in Yellowstone was just as magical as the day before. We all woke up early and visited Yellowstone Lake. We were able to stand over the bridge where the lake bleeds into the river. Watching the water collide was a metaphor to me on how life works. We run together, even if we do not know if we will connect with that other person. It is our predestined nature to do so. We are on a path. We don't necessarily know where we are going, but when we collide with that other person, everything begins to flow together.

By the end of April, in the year of COVID-19, it looked like a scene from a movie. Michael was standing by the door, overnight bag packed and sitting at his feet. For the first time ever in our marriage, I told him I needed some time apart. I asked him to go to the beach house in Florida. He spent less time away than I had anticipated. I decided to take the girls for a little bit to an empty home we owned in Georgia. I can still remember driving to that house, my head swimming from everything I was feeling. A plan began to form in my head. I was terrified of this time, frightened of the uncertainty with the state of the world, and of the future of our marriage.

We soaked in the beauty of Yellowstone that second day there. We spotted hundreds of bison, including dozens of "baby bison" (calves) of all sizes. Later, we saw a deer and her baby eating grass and walking along the forest together. Unlike the deer you see by the side of your road, or in your backyard, this mother and baby were calm. They were in their own territory. As I watched my girls take in the sight of the mama and baby, I wondered where the father deer was.

That night at the house, with the girls fast asleep, I began to devise a plan, something that could get us out of our rut, change up this new normal. We wouldn't only take the RV trip we had always talked about, we would leave home all summer long and just stay gone. We had been putting on happy faces to our friends and children, but it was getting worse, not better. Maybe time away for all of us, not just Michael or not just me, would work. So as the girls slept, I began to hatch the plan in all the possible details I could come up with in my head. I would have to get someone to handle our farm. I would have to organize the business to run without me physically present, which meant postdating checks and organizing an array of other administrative items like this so that everything could run smoothly in my absence. It would be a big task, and deep down I knew that it might just be the best thing for us.

. . .

One of the last stops in Yellowstone National Park was the infamous Continental Divide of the Americas. The Continental Divide was first discovered in 1891, just ten years after Old Faithful got its name. The nearby Isa Lake cuts through two bodies of water, draining into the Atlantic to the east and the Pacific to the west. We, of course, had to pose for pictures and we took plenty, happy as clams to be standing in the middle of the divide marker itself. As I snapped a photo of Michael and the girls, I was reminded again of what pushed us to do this in the first place. I was unaware of what it would cost, where we would go, and how long we would actually be gone for. I just knew it was something that might help us get better. As Michael and the girls smiled back at me for the camera, I only hoped that it would do more than just distract us from COVID-19. I hoped it would bring our attention back to what matters: each other.

When we returned to the house a few days later, the girls ran to their rooms, and Michael and I walked to our room, closing the door and locking it. He sat on the bed, and I paced back and forth. This was hard. We had the business, the house, the cars, the girls. It just felt like presently we did not have each other.

"Something has to change. So, I have an idea." I finally said.

He didn't say anything, but he didn't shake his head either. I could tell he was waiting for me to speak again.

"You, me, and the girls need to spend the entire summer on the RV trip."

I could tell he was listening. After a decade and a half, I could tell a lot about him.

"Because the girls are bored, school for them is pretty much over, and

—" I stopped. Just then he looked up at me. Our eyes met from across the room.

"You mean it would be for us?" he asked.

"Yes," I said after my own moment of silence. "For us."

Finally, he stood up from the bed and approached me. He held out his arms and wrapped them around me.

"It's a great idea," he said.

I took in his scent.

"But," he said. "There's only one thing."

"What's that?" I said, my heart beating like it was about to explode.

"I want to visit both the highest and lowest points in the United States."

We both laughed.

"Deal," I said with a smile on my face.

As we packed the next morning and waved goodbye to Yellowstone, I was amazed at the beauty of it. But even more so, as I watched the man beside me guide us to our next adventure, I was amazed by the beauty of our lives. As we passed the sign to exit the first ever National Park, I'm glad that we had gone through the divide. It was harder than any other time in our relationship, but I don't think we would be where we are now if it wasn't for that. I also don't think I could have loved him more than I did after the division we suffered together, because I knew the addition of each other to our lives again was stronger than we had before. Love is what binds us together. Just ask Matthew Whalen.

Matthew Whalen:
A Story on Love

Jumping in his car and driving all the way across the country for a girl was never in the cards for Matthew Whalen, but then again neither was a worldwide pandemic. Matthew was born and raised in North Carolina, only going out of town occasionally, but otherwise growing up as a homebody person. He didn't mind packing up and moving on but only to go as far up as the Western Carolina Mountains or as down south as the coastal Carolina shorelines. He'd loved movies since he was a kid, studied directors and writers, and knew Hollywood was something feasible. But it was out of a lack of motivation that was a product of fear that kept him from pursuing the western landscape in search of the Hollywood Walk of Fame. That was the case, of course, until he met a girl.

Her name was Camilla, and they met at just about the wrong time two people meant to fall in love could meet. They were film students at the University of North Carolina Wilmington, paired together on a senior film project in the spring semester. In other words, not the right time to start courting a potential interest. But there was luck, running like an undercurrent, pushing them together more often than they could have imagined. By graduation just a few months later, they were certain, one way or another, their relationship would stick together. There was one small problem, though, Camilla had just accepted a job as a tour guide at Warner Bros. Studio in Burbank, California. She would live with her sister who was already there, and she would live close enough to walk to work every day. All her boxes were checked. That left Matthew a little behind. But who could blame her? She had met him too late, they both knew it.

As both the newly graduated kids moved back home for the time being—Matthew back to Charlotte and Camilla back to Winston Salem—they did their best to stay connected for the last few weeks before she was going to move. They drove back and forth the hour and a half each way, spending days at a time together in between Matthew's job selling tickets at the same movie theater he'd worked at in high school. Once, when visiting his parents with Camilla before she left for California, Matthew's little brother, Brad, struck the side of Matthew's car when backing out of the driveway of their family home. It dented Matthew's car pretty badly but nothing impaired the driving. Eventually time flew by, as it always does, and Camilla boarded a plane bound for California. They were both heartbroken, devastated for the loss of the other. Neither of them were going to throw in the towel right away, but how often did two people in their position actually stay together?

The first few weeks were tough, and it only got worse when a desperate and broke Matthew quit the theater job and took a job serving at a Japanese restaurant across from the movie theater. Meanwhile, the nine-to-five job Camilla now had, plus the three hour time difference, made for a tricky FaceTime schedule. Once, after a few days of only phone calls, they connected over FaceTime and upon seeing each other's faces neither said a word. They just looked at one another, staring at the monitors projecting the other's face. It was a bittersweet moment, and Matthew knew then that he had to get to Camilla. The conviction to leave increased tenfold everyday he spent not going after her. He was miserable, there was no doubt about it. But he felt something else, something new and nauseating but nonetheless invigorating.

For the first time in his life, Matthew was lovesick.

After two months of separation, Matthew was desperate. He was living in his grandmother's spare bedroom, he was working at a job he hated, and the girl he loved was on the other side of the country. It was only on a trip to visit his dad for lunch that his luck began to change. Over an order of BBQ pork, his dad informed him that he had filed an insurance claim between his two sons, they found the little brother (Brad) at fault, and they would reward the other party (Matthew) $3,000.00 in repair costs. He could do what he wanted with it, including keep the car since it still drove just fine. Matthew could not believe it. He was serving miso soup and ginger salad on a never-ending goal to raise funds for California, and here comes his little brother's blind spot to save the day.

After rushing to leave a voicemail for Camilla that afternoon, they spent the next few weeks looking for an apartment. Between her schedule, she spent most of her free time touring local apartments while Matthew talked his college friend into moving with them as a third roommate. Eventually, Matthew's luck began to change. Slowly. Week after week went by without a word. They had a few offers out, but none of the apartments had selected them yet. Then, on a break from a particularly bad day at work, Matthew saw his phone light up with his favorite name: Camilla.

"We got Friar St.," she said. "We can move in, in a month."

Matthew immediately broke into tears, an onslaught of pent up depression and desperate urgency in his gut came pouring out. He told her he loved her, he thanked her, then after saying goodbye, he cried some more. After gathering himself, he went back to work with a spring in his step. The next day at work was his last, as he happily quit and jumped in his car to go pack. But just because he had quit, did not mean he wasn't busy. He had an even bigger job ahead of him, possibly the biggest yet.

The exit sign for Hollywood, California, was the best sight he'd seen in days. After five days, four nights, 3,000 miles, and one hundred hours of podcasts and music, the drive alone out West along I-40 was almost over. But it had been even longer than that. It had been two months of loneliness, despair, sadness, and worry. Most of that would not be solved by his girlfriend, or a new apartment, or even Hollywood. But it could be solved by a new way of life. So he put his pedal to the metal and cruised up the off-ramp towards a new journey.

Three hours later, parked outside of a Bob's Big Boy in Burbank, California, Matthew got out of the car and took a long stretch. Just past a row of planted trees along the edge of the parking lot sat the apartment Camilla had been staying in for the last two months. He took a second to stretch some more before texting her that he had arrived. He knew she'd been waiting all day for him—heck all summer—so he wanted to look good. He quickly changed into a nicer shirt, changed his shoes, and sent her a quick text: "I'm here." He knew how much more that meant than what it said.

He walked up the sidewalk, taking in the surroundings he would now call home. He was amazed at the energy one city could provide. He came to the building he had written letters to for the last two months. He stopped. Breathed. And then he saw her. She came bursting down the stairs, two and three steps at a time, rushing towards him. She flung herself into his arms and he caught her, desperate at her smell and skin and hair and hands. They kissed and laughed and hugged some more. Then he whispered in her ear a line he had not prepared, but one fitting for a Hollywood movie of their own: "Let's never do that again."

Matthew's time in Los Angeles was not all smooth sailing. The first month was hard, gathering his surroundings and learning to live in such a new environment. The depression he'd felt in Charlotte did not just disappear, but manifested itself in other ways. He eventually got a pretty cool first-L.A. job at the Barnes & Noble in The Grove shopping center, in West Hollywood. Every so often at this new workplace, he could spot a familiar famous face around the corner. It was cushy, simple, and cool on the outside. But what he really wanted, and had wanted since Camilla first got the job before they graduated, was to work for Warner Bros. as a tour guide. It was the hardest part of their relationship, the jealousy he had for her job. It seemed fun and cool and just about the most Hollywood thing you could do at his age. He had applied and not heard back yet, but he knew it could take time, so he did his best to stay calm (not easy for him) and wait it out.

After four months of living in North Hollywood, Matthew received the call he'd been hoping for. "Would you like to interview for a temporary position at Warner Bros?" asked the lady over the phone. Matthew agreed, despite knowing it would only last 30 days for the holiday season.

And, of course, the interview date was set far in advance, creating more of a wait time. It was a confusing period for him; it's hard to put excitement on hold. The days rolled by as Matthew waited with bated breath, counting off hours and minutes until eventually, on December 5, 2019, he began his first day as a tour guide. He was, after lots of driving and many months of shelving books, ecstatic to say the least.

The next month flew by as he learned the ropes of the job, learned his way around the studio lot, and did his best not to freak out every time he saw the original couch from *Friends*. But around this time, something happened that was unknowable then. Camilla began to get very sick. She was coughing non stop and always tired. She was sweaty when she should be cold and shivering under blankets. Granted, the busiest time of the year for tours was Christmas, so it was to be expected that the long hours and thousands of tourists a day could tire anyone out. This sickness felt odder than usual, but still, they just called it the flu. The holidays continued and eventually she got better. Then, before they knew it, the New

Year was upon them. 2020, the year they would always remember.

Unfortunately, his time as seasonal tour guide came to a close. He said a fun farewell, snapped a ton more pictures of his new friends and the lot itself, and returned to *Barnes & Noble*. In the span of exactly thirty days, he'd been shown the good life, then it was gone. He shelved magazines alone while he did his best to hold his head up. That intention was not always met with success, but when you have a partner in your life who loves you as much as Camilla loved Matthew, he knew everything was going to be okay. It had to be, right?

About three weeks into his less flashy stint as a bookseller, Matthew began to notice a word splashed across magazines like *Popular Science* and *National Geographic*. "Coronavirus," they called it. He wondered what it was and why everyone was talking about it. He was by no means a news junkie, but he assumed he would know that a pandemic was on the rise if it was all over the headlines. But maybe that's it, he thought, maybe it wasn't real to him because he wasn't seeing anything about it in real life. That all changed a few more weeks later when the oldest employee at the store came in wearing not only a mask but latex gloves as well. All of these rumors sparked a conversation between Matthew and Camilla. What if this new virus had infected her before anyone was talking about it? What if that awful, terrible, no good, very bad flu was something akin to this new Coronavirus? She had fully healed within a few weeks but she had been in perfect health before. Maybe sicker people were not so lucky.

By this time, however, Matthew was in talks with the human resources at Warner Bros. to come back and be a tour guide again for the spring/summer. He was elated at the chance to come back, especially after having just gotten a good grasp on the job before it ended. He was on pins and needles, counting down the days until he could return, and putting his ducks in a row to work two jobs all summer. Then, all of a sudden, in early March, a month away from entering the gates of Warner Bros. once more, Matthew received an email. Tours were being shortened, tickets were being refunded, and there was no need for an onslaught of returning tour guides. The job was canceled. The next week, to add insult to injury, Barnes and Noble called him to tell him the new magic word: "Furloughed."

Now here he was, in the middle of California, both jobs out the window, with nowhere to go, and a lease he was still held to. He turned to Camilla for comfort, and like always, she was there.

The next few months were hard for the two of them. Camilla was eventually laid off as a tour guide, but their roommate remained an "essential employee" at the Chick-Fil-A in Burbank. A lot of the California they'd grown up wishing for changed dramatically. The hundreds of movie theaters were shut down; the Griffith Observatory began to look more like a mausoleum; and downtown Burbank's nightlife looked D.O.A., day or night. The couple spent a lot of time either in their apartment or across the street at a large cemetery that began to double as a quasi-park for a lot of the locals. Thanks to government assistance, Matthew began making more money than both jobs combined would have paid him. But besides catching up on a lot of reading, he began to reassess his future in California. He and Camilla began to wonder what was left for them, how much this was all worth it. Sure, the entire world was shut down, but California was particularly locked down, and it wasn't even their home. Not that they wanted to run back to their old bedrooms, per say, but maybe familiar scenery would be nice.

They spent the last months of summer going over their options of where to live, weighing the pros and cons of each choice. They looked at Maryland, Vermont, Maine, Virginia, and

Georgia. They realized after some tough thinking that perhaps Atlanta, Georgia, might be their best bet. Not only was it Hollywood for the East Coast, but it was also called the "City of Trees" on Wikipedia. Wasn't that reason enough? They spent one more week ruminating on it before breaking the news to their roommate and began planning the trip.

By almost the year mark of first moving into the apartment, the car was packed and the gas tank was full. For the second time in one year, Matthew got behind the wheel to drive back across the country. Last year his only destination was California as quickly as possible. This time, the world might've still been shut down but nature wasn't. Their first stop, the Grand Canyon. It was a magnificent trip, with beautiful scenery and enough pictures to fill a shoebox. Nothing was better after months indoors watching Netflix and eating cheese puffs than to step back out into the world and let the surroundings fill them up like a breath of—literal—fresh air.

They spent the next five days and six nights on the road. It was a trial to drive with two people in a loaded sedan, and nothing tests a relationship more than seven months indoors together followed by seven days driving in a car together. They still got along, as the movies say, famously. It was an incredible experience for both Matthew and Camilla to cruise the highways across America, seeing the sights and experiencing the energy in the different small towns and big cities they stopped in. For Matthew, it almost felt like he had driven all the way out to California just to pick up his girlfriend and bring her back home. He was just lucky enough that she agreed to go with him.

They spent a few weeks visiting with their families in North Carolina, but pretty soon it was time for the drive to Atlanta. After only a few days in the City of Trees, they were satisfied with their choice. They liked what they saw, how nature was so much more familiar and accessible than in Los Angeles, and how the streets and shops reminded them of home. There they could take long walks among trees and beside rivers. And what was even better was that they had chosen this city together. They sat down, talked it out, and found a place they could both call home. In the end, as their lives in Atlanta were just getting really started, they had time to reflect on the last year. Sometimes they didn't feel so affected by COVID-19, but then they'd remember that just wasn't true: of course, they were. They still would be in California, reaching for the impossible, unsure if they really wanted that. The pandemic was scary, and difficult, and harmed a lot of people. Matthew and Camilla learned how to take the sourest lemon the world had to offer and make it into lemonade.

Their passion to find a better life together showed them that they could do whatever they set their mind to. Some people are too scared to move. There is value in sticking around and sticking it out, and there is also a nobility in knowing when to move on, knowing what the relationship not only needs, but what the individuals need. Camilla was not afraid to move out to California and work in a job she never pictured herself doing, and Matthew was not afraid to go after her. But when all was said and done, they came back to the East Coast with more perspective and more conviction about who they were and what they wanted. They were changed, made whole, and uplifted. If you want to be happy, you may just have to risk unhappiness to get there. At the end of the day, if there is still a smile on your face and a hand clasped tightly in your own, maybe you did something right. Maybe, just maybe, everything would be okay. That is something everyone needed to know when the word "Corona" first entered the public consciousness in a very new way.

---

1. "Unique Facts about Old Faithful Geyser," Yellowstone Holiday, June 13, 2012, https://www.yellowstoneholiday.com/yellowstone-hiking/unique-facts-faithful-geyser/ (accessed June 27, 2020).
2. "Why Is It Called "Old Faitherful?," Wonderopolis, https://www.wonderopolis.org/wonder/why-is-it-called-old-faithful (accessed June 28, 2020).

11

MOVING ALONG OUT WEST

Voodoo Donuts is home to one of the weirdest and most bizarre bakery attractions in the country. It was conceived in 2000 by Kenneth "Cat Daddy" Pogson and Tres Shannon as a shared entrepreneurial idea. They were a wacky and fun duo living in Oregon, trying to make a name for themselves. They dug into the niche markets of Portland and discovered that downtown Portland did not house a single donut shop. In 2003, they changed all of that by opening their own small shop squished between two exotic night clubs. They began by offering the classic donuts, while balancing those offerings out with some of their own creations. They also began hosting various social gatherings, including weddings, concerts in the loft above the air duct, and weekly Swahili lessons. Within a month, the cultural hodgepodge was mentioned in the national press and began to grow from there. Years later, Voodoo donuts now has nine locations in five states with almost every location attracting a line of people that wraps around the block. So in the second week of June 2020, when we arrived in Portland, that was the first stop on our list.

On the way into downtown I had a sinking feeling that the shop would be closed due to COVID-19, but they kept up the CDC guidelines, and the doors were open when we walked up. The kids' eyes lit up at every odd, wacky, fun donut sitting in the window display. There was a donut of every design imaginable: Voodoo Bubble (a pink frosted donut with a piece of bubble gum on top), The Homer (an exact replica of the donut Homer Simpson eats in the TV show *The Simpsons*), Voodoo Doll (a doll-shaped donut made in the fashion of a real life voodoo doll), Oh Captain My Captain (a white iced donut with captain crunch breakfast cereal toppings), and of course, a Glazed Old Fashioned for the fans of the classic donut. As I gazed at all of these wonderful choices, my eyes and the eyes of the kids got the better of me. I walked out of the shop carrying three boxes with forty donuts in total. It was worth it.

We had been doing a lot of driving in heavy traffic at times and sleeping squished together in an RV. It was not lost on me or Michael that the kids missed their own home and their own beds. Nevertheless, they had great attitudes, and Michael and I were happy to reward them. So things like donuts and candy and campgrounds helped keep them interested and occupied. As they ate their second and third donut, skipping lunch that day, we headed over to the Portland Japanese Garden and drove through the open route to gaze at all the beautiful flowers, little waterfalls, tiny bridges, and the mountain view above it all. We then continued our drive out of Portland, taking in the highway view of the mountains that overlooks beautiful Oregon. On the last leg out of the area, I spotted Multnomah Falls coming off of a mountain, and I tried to get the kids to see it in time, but when I turned around, they were either asleep or staring at an iPad screen, almost asleep.

C'est la vie.

After a few more hours, we finally arrived at a campground

with an ocean view on the edge of Oregon. We unloaded the kids' bikes for the millionth time of the trip and they rode around while Michael and I cleaned up the RV a bit. I did some laundry in the nearby laundromat opened to campers for fifty-cents a load while enjoying an ocean view of the Oregon coast from our RV that sat on the side of a cliff.

The next day was spent at the beach and visiting some of the attractions nearby. I was able to finally get coffee from the infamous Dutch Bros. Coffee (I highly recommend this place), and we even got to try ice cream from Tillamook Creamery, which had just opened back up that day after being closed in March. Later that day, we visited Cannon Beach and Haystack Rock from the movie *The Goonies*.

As we crawled into the RV that night, I couldn't help but think about the state of the world. It felt like we had snuck away from the classroom while everyone else was forced to sit and take a test they had not studied for. I almost felt guilty for all the fun we had been having. My family was experiencing and seeing things we'd never seen before. We were together all the time, and despite a few small fights over blankets and iPads, the kids were in generally great spirits. I felt guilty, as though I had cheated my way out of the pandemic.

COVID-19 was wreaking havoc everywhere, and it was visible to the eye. As we drove through the country, we saw shutdown businesses, closed up motels, and vacant movie theaters all along the way. There were signs posted on doors and messages on gas pumps about keeping your distance and wearing masks. Just about every museum or indoor activity possibly was forbidden. But it somehow felt like we had found a loophole, an underground tunnel to crawl into while the rest of the world was forced to live through it. As Michael and the kids slept soundly across the RV beds, I picked up my phone and opened the WhatsApp messages. I had done my best during the long car rides to keep up with and respond to the messages coming through. I was surprised to find that people who did not know each other, from different parts of the world, were taking turns encouraging each other over a message board I had created. Strangers were offering words of wisdom and comfort to one another. The compassion people could feel for their fellow human was not lost due to any language barrier or cultural differences. But that does not mean people were having an easy time. People in places like the Philippines were being fined for not wearing a mask, and people on the American/Mexican border were being sheltered and almost illegally detained by border patrol just for seeking asylum in the U.S. Even in America people were losing jobs, going out of business, and living off of savings as they waited for their unemployment checks to be issued, which were backlogged due to the unprecedented influx of unemployment applications. As I stayed up until past midnight staring at my phone in the dark of the RV, I began to wonder what this all meant.

I had devised the idea for this trip as a way to give the kids a fun summer and distract our family from COVID-19. We still had plenty of work to do, phone calls to make when we stopped for gas or food. The ultimate plan of escape was working for the whole family. I still couldn't help but feel immense guilt about it. Was it the right thing to do when the rest of the world was suffering?

I woke the next day with only one answer: yes. This trip had begun as a pipe dream for me. But with Michael's help, my drive to do crazy things, and the kids' great attitudes, we had made it a reality. And I knew as we drove to our next location that we were making the right choice, for our kids and for ourselves. Yes, we were escaping, but during this time, we were doing whatever we could to help make a better life for our kids. Isn't that every parent's mission? The guilt I felt over the luxury we had of being on the open road was outweighed by the days of happiness it gave them, as opposed to the days of depression they may have felt stuck at home. I recently read that the rate of suicide in nine and ten-year-old children was increasing due to quarantine.[1] I didn't even know children that young commit suicide. I knew that I was doing the best thing for the girls and husband I loved so much.

And I looked forward to the days to come. And so did Cody Archer after his life got turned upside down.

Cody Archer:
A Story on Navigation

New Year's Eve 2020. Cody Archer and his boyfriend, Ryan, went to a party that night. They were having a good time, but something began to happen to Ryan that sent shockwaves into their lives. Around dinner time that night, Ryan started feeling "odd." He started sweating, and he could feel his pulse racing, something Cody had never seen in their three years together. "We thought it may be an allergic reaction to seafood, but it kept getting worse," said Cody.

It got so bad that they eventually went to Atlanta Medical Center. The doctors took Ryan straight back, and Cody had to wait outside because of COVID-19. It turns out that Ryan's blood pressure was in the 150s, which was not only high but also extremely abnormal for him. "He's a healthy guy that eats well, does CrossFit, and has no other history regarding heart issues," described Cody when asked about that time. The doctors got Ryan stabilized and observed him, ran a few tests, then eventually discharged him. Ryan did his best to take it easy, but three days later, it all started again. The symptoms were immediately bad enough that Ryan was scared and knew he needed medical help. Cody quickly left work, took him to Kennestone Hospital, and the doctors took Ryan back into the ER right away. Cody still couldn't go in, and the doctors there said it would be a while, so Cody went back to the office since it was close by.

Eleven hours later, he was discharged and told that he had hypertension. He arrived with a BP of around 157/100; it was higher than he ever had before. Ryan's resting heart rate was typically around 55, but now wasn't going below 85. It seemed to come from out of nowhere. After a follow up appointment, they related it to possibly being a "post-COVID-19 symptom." They said there wasn't much they could do since this illness was still so new, but they could treat symptoms as they arose. After a positive COVID-19 diagnosis in June and a full-recovery in August 2020, now Ryan was continuing to suffer from unexplained, frequent (weekly) flare ups of chest pain with drastically increasing heartbeat.

Backing up to March of 2020, Cody and Ryan were not surprised with the lockdown. It all happened at the same time they were in the market to buy a home. They had lived in the same apartment together for a number of years and they wanted a change, a place to truly call their own. In his own life, Cody was in the process of leaving the Georgia Bureau of Investigation (GBI), looking for something with a lot less blood and a little bit more windows. He was also taking care of his grandmother at the time, who was close to the end of her life and needed more of his time. But on March 13, 2020, a day the world would soon remember for years to come, things took a drastic turn for the already transitory nature of Cody's life.

The first major change was just two weeks into quarantine.

Cody's grandmother passed away. Her loss was not a shock to those who knew of her ailments; the shock came with how exactly they would handle the aftermath. She was quickly brought to a morgue where an autopsy was done, and her body was cremated. However, when most ashes are returned to the family within a twenty-four to forty-eight hour span, the remains of Cody's grandmother were not returned until almost a week later. This was due to the overwhelming death counts and brand-new precautions for all medical examiners due to COVID-19 restrictions.

The Archer family had been planning the funeral for a little bit of time before his grandmother had even passed, as she was thought to succumb rather soon. But now, because of the social distancing guidelines and "stay at home orders," it was nearly impossible for the family to carry out the funeral as planned. In the end, they held a private graveside visit with just Cody, his siblings, his parents, and Ryan. It was better to honor her with an intimate group than to expose everyone to this new virus spreading around.

The next phase of her passing's aftermath was the move-out process. When a single woman has died at an old age, her house is left completely as it was. The next of kin, Cody and his immediate family, were left with the task of cleaning the house out and putting it on the market. Typically the family would have held an estate sale for the community to come by and take items right out of the house for a price. But this was in full-blown quarantine, and no estate sales were allowed. The only other option Cody and his family had was to sell things online, left out on the porch for contactless pick up by anyone who paid over Apple Pay, PayPal, or Venmo. It was a tedious process, and the items moved slowly. Sometimes it was hard for one of the Archer family children or parents to find time in their day to drive over to their late grandmother's house to put a randomly purchased item on the front porch in time for the buyer to pick it up. After about a month of this, they rented a storage unit close by and moved everything into there for the time being. It wasn't perfect but it would have to do for now. Cody had much more pressing matters to get to.

As an employee in the GBI, Cody was considered an essential employee and kept his schedule for the time being. However, because of COVID-19, the death investigations always had a risk of COVID-19 being the cause of death. The spike in cases raised the risk of death, and the spike in deaths raised every death investigator's workload to another level. It was overwhelming for Cody, someone who had already been looking to leave the field behind. Now he was stuck investigating deaths where any one of them could be caused by a virus that the entire world did not quite know what to make heads or tails of. Luckily, he had an apartment to come home to, but that was soon to be gone too.

During their free time together at night, Cody and Ryan would plan out their dream house. They spent a lot of time on Pinterest, looking up model homes and deciding how best to decorate theirs. It was a fun outlet for both of the overworked, underpaid twentysomethings who needed solace in their life. But thanks to COVID-19, even the actual purchase of the house did not go over as well as they'd expected. When one typically enters the process of buying a home, they have several walk throughs and can find things to improve upon the house before they move in. These walkthroughs can also help bring down the price, like if you find issues with the home that aren't visible initially. But for Cody and Ryan, this did not happen. They were forced to close on the house without ever doing a final walk-through. They had put an offer on the house before quarantine, but they still wanted that final chance to take a look once the previous owner had moved out to make sure they moved in on the first day to a house that looked good. They didn't get that luxury and without it, they moved into a house with lots of little issues, otherwise fixable by the previous owners if not for the lack of a final walk through. It was a hassle, as both Cody and Ryan did their best to settle into their first home together against the backdrop of thirty gallons of paint leftover from the renovations. Instead of sitting down and breathing a sigh of relief, they first had to add up how much it would cost for a garbage company to take the paint away, at $5.00 a gallon. And then the hits just kept on coming.

In June of that year, less than a month after moving in and finally getting the house close to their liking, Cody was at work in the morgue, performing an autopsy, when he saw his phone light up on a table nearby. It was Ryan, describing a headache he was experiencing that was unlike any other. Cody knew it must be bad, as Ryan rarely got headaches. He immediately told his supervisor, who advised him to go home, to be on the safe side. Two days later, Ryan reported that he had lost his sense of taste and smell. It was not even twenty-four hours later when Cody began to experience a sore throat and headache. The day afterward, they both went to get tested. They expected results to come a few days after that, but they were wrong. It took eight days for Ryan's results to be returned, and twelve full days for Cody's. "You just feel really weird. You're sick with a possible virus and you sit around for two weeks waiting to know if you actually have it," Cody remembered.

When they did come back, both reports were positive.

According to a new mandate, all state employees must report two consecutive negative tests before returning to work. This took some time, since they first actually had to get over the virus. During that time, Cody was forced to work from home, which meant he was not surrounded by all the typical tools, monitors, phones, and other investigators to turn to. He was alone in a new house all day long, taking calls at random times of the day, and trying to perform toxicology reports and autopsy reports through telecommunication. It was eight long weeks of positive COVID-19 tests and many hours spent stressed out. During that time, Cody continued to feel sick. It was hard for him to focus, and oftentimes he just felt like sleeping and watching television. Plus, not being in his normal working environment made it difficult for him to focus on work at all. The one silver lining was for Ryan to be at their new house with him, also working from home. This time in their lives was hard for both of them. They had moved and were dealing with an intense sickness. It was still the early days of COVID-19, early enough that neither of them really knew what to expect. They did their best to push through it together. While at home, with time to sit back a bit more and ruminate, Cody decided emphatically at this point that he needed to make the plunge towards that different direction in life.

In August 2020, nearly six months into the quarantine, Cody quit his job at the GBI and started working in the real estate industry as a transaction coordinator, handling housing contracts and conferring with agents about money. It was a completely different pace from his previous job. He was in front of a computer all day in an office. It felt like being more a part of the real world. He was happy there, despite the different stressors that came with the job. As the months went by and he learned how to perform at the job, he found his life began to get better. He began to feel settled again. The house was starting to look the way he and Ryan had envisioned it. Ryan had a new job as well, and things were looking up on the outside.

On the inside, however, Ryan noticed symptoms of the virus that did not go away when the sickness itself did. He had trouble breathing months after he got a negative test back and he did not regain his sense of taste or smell for a good portion of the year. By now he was taking daily medications to regulate blood pressure and regulate vitamin levels in his body. He also had to routinely monitor his blood pressure and pulse. By this time, Ryan had already been in the ER twice in one week for sudden cardiac issues.

Despite all of these setbacks, Cody and Ryan began the new year with relief. They were both glad to be through the hurdle of transitions that had been thrown at them all throughout 2020. And then, in February of 2021, Cody received a call.

It was the office of Death Investigations from the GBI, asking if Cody would come back. He felt his stomach turn over at the thought of it. The things he had seen at that job were disturbing, often grotesque even in the typical cases of suicides and overdoses, not to mention murders. He did not relish heading back into that world, and he was finally comfortable. But he knew the opportunities they were offering were too good to pass up. So he reluctantly took the job but not before embarking on a company trip to Florida with all the other transaction coordinators with the real estate office. He bid them farewell and walked back into the crime lab, ready to resume his role as a death investigator.

Looking back on all of it, Cody says it was more overwhelming than he could have predicted had he known about what would be coming. Every time he turned around in 2020, something new was happening, and he had to work through it; he had to find his way to the light at the end of each and every tunnel placed in front of him. "It is all about navigation, finding your way around a lot of little things and even a few big things," he said. "There was never a time when I have been tested more than in the year 2020." But for Cody, he knows there is no choice but to keep fighting, keep pushing, and to keep your head up. "You have to navigate this life carefully," he says, "or else you will lose yourself in all of the wrong turns and pitfalls. We just have to keep looking forward with hard work and a good support system." And Cody hopes he can begin to find comfort again in the remainder of 2021, but he knows that no matter what happens, he will have Ryan, his family, and his courage to navigate whatever comes his way. Because with family comes helpfulness.

Judy Webb: A Story on Helpfulness

On March 28, 2020, *The New York Times* released an article describing just how much South Africa, and specifically the city of Johannesburg, was responsible for the Coronavirus on that continent.[2] At that time, Johannesburg alone had just locked down their five million-plus residents for three weeks. It was said, "Three weeks after the first infection was discovered in South Africa, the country is now the epicenter of the outbreak in the continent, with more than 1,000 confirmed cases, double the cases in Egypt," (Chutel, Dahir 2020).[3]

Judy Webb lives with her husband in Johannesburg. At the time of lockdown, they were both retired and spent their time working for various organizations around South Africa. Judy has two daughters, one son, and seven grandchildren. She was used to traveling often to the United States to visit with one of her daughters that lives there with her three daughters. Judy's other daughter had emigrated to New Zealand the year before COVID-19 hit with her twin girls, and Judy had started making visits there as well. Her life was running full steam ahead before the virus came and shut everything down. The lockdown order was issued by South African President Cyril Ramaphosa. When news of the virus came out, and the lockdown began, Judy was not worried. "I didn't overreact, thinking it would only be a few months and that was manageable," said Judy of that news.

At the beginning, Judy described what she observed in South Africa. There was the typical panic buying like everywhere else. The biggest shock was the banning of alcohol and cigarettes. This quickly led to contraband sales and lots of intense reactions from people in the area. The reason for the ban came from the government. It was strongly opposed by both alcohol and tobacco firms, but medical experts supported the ban right away. The reason for the support and idea behind the ban was that South African government officials believed people should be leading healthy lives during a health crisis, and things like cigarette smoking and alcohol poisoning put people at a higher risk for COVID-19 infections and would further the spread of the virus.

Judy recalls the first ban on these items came at the same exact time as the lockdown, and most residents were given twenty-four hours to buy what they wanted before it became temporarily banned. A few weeks later, the ban was eased, and alcohol and cigarettes were sold, but at restricted times only. A few months after that, the lockdown for these items was lifted completely. However, just before Christmas, the lockdown orders were issued again. This time the cigarettes were permitted but the alcohol was banned immediately, with no twenty-four hour window to buy beforehand. The second ban on alcohol was lifted again in late January. It was one of the most peculiar cases when it came to lockdowns, as no other country had a ban like this. However, Judy says it accomplished what it was supposed to because it freed up room in the local hospitals because there were less cases of alcohol poisoning and other trauma cases related to alcohol, like drunk driving.

Judy observed these government mandates with a keen eye but kept mostly to herself and the life she led with her husband. And for good reason as she was busy enough taking care of her husband who was already dealing with his own medical issues before the lockdown began. Not to mention, Judy had a plethora of house projects to work on from her large old home, to her vegetable garden, to her small cottages on her property that she rented out as long term rentals. She did not have much need for alcohol and tobacco. Instead, she had a need for the basics, like toilet paper, which was a universally difficult thing to come by during the first Coronavirus wave. Despite Judy's best efforts, life didn't go as smoothly throughout the pandemic as she had planned.

Halfway through the year, Judy's husband came down with a severe fever. When faced with this issue, Judy decided not to take him to the hospital because of the overcrowding from COVID-19 patients. Instead, she took care of her husband at home, thanks to significant help from their general practitioner and the fact that prior to retirement, Judy worked as an active nursing sister with ICU training, both for large hospitals as well as some family-owned businesses, so she was well equipped to help him. Her husband was ultimately cured through the use of intravenous antibiotics. It was hard on Judy to care for her husband as well as their property. She was used to running her home and land with domestic help. The lockdown left her to handle all the upkeep herself while the help stayed at home with four months of full pay. Judy paid this to her staff. There were government grants available, but they were small and very slow to receive. Judy didn't even spend the time applying for them. She knew she couldn't consciously leave her staff hungry and chose to pay them and focus her time managing her home rather than applying for grants. Being left to do all the extra work put so much of a strain that at one point during the lockdown, Judy damaged her back. It was a difficult time for her all around, but still she stayed strong. She knew she had it better than some other people around South Africa, where the rural areas were a hotbed for infections.

"Our people have lost jobs and have literally been struggling to survive, so the pandemic became secondary to survival," said Judy, describing life in lower-income areas of Africa. When it came to things such as schools shutting down, the people in the rural areas and parishes could not even attend virtual schooling because their area had no immediate access to the internet and a data plan was too expensive for them. They simply put school on hold. Eventually, many months into the pandemic, schools began to reopen with many restrictions.

Throughout COVID-19, Judy worked with organizations to keep projects going in spite of the restrictions. International Service Organization (Inner Wheel) was one group Judy supported with various projects around South Africa for the elderly and for children. Another group Judy supported was the "Book Project," which had been bringing in millions of educational and children's books from Houston, Texas, over many years. "Books are free, but we need to raise money for transport of containers to the Humanitarian Centre. It has been a great project and has supplied many books to underprivileged schools throughout Southern Africa," says Judy.

Aside from helping those in need that she does not personally know, Judy and her husband also just do their best to stay close with their children and grandchildren. "Thank goodness for technology," says Judy. "WhatsApp videos and instant messages were helpful. We are in contact daily, but I yearn to hug and hold them again." She has learned that there is nothing more important than family, a theme she sees in many people's lives since the virus came about. But for someone living in South Africa, where poverty is rampant, Judy feels truly blessed to have the kind of life she has and to support those who need more help. When asked about the future, Judy simply said, "We must keep our guard up and pray this doesn't happen again anytime soon." Because for Judy, all you can do is hope and work your hardest for your friends and loved ones. At the end of the day, that is what will help countries that are as in need as South Africa become whole again. The best way to see that through is to trust those in charge, and not everyone did.

Ling Wú: A Story on Trust

Ling Wú never wanted to be famous, recognized, or interviewed. She simply wanted to go to work and come home. She enjoyed a simple life. She worked as a real estate agent in between two major cities in China. One of those cities would become the most talked about cities on the planet: Wuhan. The other city was Hong Kong. When the global spread of Coronavirus turned everything on its head, what changed most for Ling Wú was her ability to trust those in charge.

At the time of the Wuhan outbreak in 2019, the world did not know yet what had happened. But as the reports came through, word spread quicker than the virus itself. Now, In order to understand how the virus spread, you must understand Wuhan itself. Wuhan is the capital of Hubei Province in the People's Republic of China. It is the largest city in Hubei and the most populated city in Central China. The estimated population is over eleven million people. It is home to big business, lots of real estate, and universities[4]. As the outbreak began, Ling did not know that an invisible virus was infecting many of those eleven million people. Once it was known, she did her best to stay safe. She watched from a safe space in her home. But as the months went on, the impact of the virus was unavoidable.

The government began releasing mandates for the People's Republic of China and the people were told to stay indoors. "It was boring," she said later. Anytime you wanted to go outside, you had to check your temperature and dare not exit your home unless absolutely necessary. This went on for several months, and she watched while the rest of the planet received similar mandates from their governments and everyone collectively entered a new phase of life. But she did what she was told, careful not to step outside the laws set forth by the Chinese government. Eventually, the government began relaxing the rules a bit, and the city of Wuhan attempted to move on and get back to normal as best they could. Around this time, a mutual colleague of Ling's reached out to her from the United States to ask her for an account of what life was like in Wuhan during the year of COVID-19. Ling was already in Hong Kong then, far enough away from Wuhan. Or so she assumed. Perhaps, she thought, I could say a few things to help her out. Little did she know how dangerous her brief, careful words would become. And how quickly that danger would come to her front door.

The first mention of the virus in Wuhan came in late December of 2019, the first mention of it in the United States was in January 2020.[5] It was nearly a year later when Ling decided to share her account of what life was like during the year of COVID-19. Ling figured that enough time had passed and she could speak openly about how she felt the Chinese government handled the virus, so she decided to share the good, bad, and the ugly. How could the government deny it now, it was all anybody could talk about, Ling thought. So, as the first few simple messages came over from WhatsApp in December 2020, she responded. She agreed to share information, and she answered a list of questions. She was careful, as always, but honest. She agreed that the first reported case, which was now common knowledge, began in Wuhan. She spoke openly about how little the higher ups in Wuhan actually did initially to stop the spread and how the Chinese government took little action to combat the disease. She was fair to both the citizens and the government. She did not mean for this to be a form of protest. If anything, Ling was just retelling what everyone already knew.

The one thing Ling explained that most people do not know, was how the virus spread throughout Wuhan in a surprising way. "There were still one million college students in Wuhan at that time [December of 2019]. Later, the college students returned to their hometowns in various parts of China during the holidays." She later spoke about how the Chinese government handled it better than, for instance, the American government did. But the Chinese government also did not tell the citizens what was going on. She thought that they should, as far as the public conscience was concerned. The conversation went on over messages for several days, and throughout that time Ling remained courteous, to the point, and honest.

A few days passed without a tip from anything on her social media platforms and messages. But then something strange happened. She attempted to log onto her Facebook and found something downright strange. Her profile was gone. Not logged out of, not blocked, not hacked, but simply gone. Up and vanished. But how? Even if she wanted to delete her Facebook, she never thought she'd be able to. Now she had no choice one way or the other. Any digital fingerprint she had left on the social media universe had been erased, right under her nose. How odd. She spent the next few hours thinking about it, wondering what it could mean. She was a bit worried because, as a real estate agent, she relied on the outreach the site provided between buyers and sellers. So why, of all things, was her Facebook deleted? A sinking feeling in her stomach brought her back to the conversation she had with the outside world. She had been willing to speak about her country's politics to someone outside the country. She did her best to ignore the aching worry in her stomach.

Still the feeling would not leave her. She went to open her WhatsApp page to reconnect with the lady from the United States that she had been in contact with and see what she might think about it. When she tried to put her information in, the same thing that had happened with Facebook was happening right before her eyes. She tried to put in her email and password but neither was recognized. She tried to use the "forgot password" button at the bottom. When asked to input her email for verification, an error message came up: "no contact listed under that email." Now she knew something was wrong, but she still did not know what. And that is when she logged into her email, the basic use for a computer ever. It was still logged on—luckily—but she noticed something strange as she read through a list of her new emails. At least four people were pulling out of their housing search with her. All of them were courteous but brief. "Decided to go with another agent for our future searches" was the general gist from them. Ling could feel her fingers trembling as she held the phone in her hands.

This was not a coincidence. She knew why this was happening. Ling knew that her disappearance on Facebook and WhatsApp, platforms she connected to most often with clients, made her seem suspicious. Perhaps some of the clients had seen other people's Facebook's deleted and knew she must be under heavy suspicion for one reason or another. Either way, she knew they did not trust her anymore. And if you can't trust your real estate agent, then you certainly don't want them to be your agent.

Still, the question of *how* the government did this remained at the forefront of her mind. She was not sure how to find out, but she so desperately wanted to. Who could she call, the customer support line for The People's Republic of China? Yeah, right. Good luck with that, she thought. The truth was that she had no help, no idea. She was not able to log in, and she knew this was the way it would go. She knew that she was being watched. She was not a government employee, she worked in real estate. She did not have any secrets to reveal, but that had been her whole point: the government told them nothing. She figured, in some ironic way, that the government wanted its citizens to follow suit. Don't talk to anyone, about anything, or else you're in trouble. Period.

Weeks went by and still no luck. Not everyone on her client list pulled out, but there was a decrease in her rising sales quota, eventually putting her into some trouble with her brokers. She knew they would not understand what was going on with her. Even if they had something similar done to them, she would have never found out about it. People in China keep their private lives private, end of story. Except of course, she had learned, the government was allowed to interfere whenever necessary. The more she ruminated on it, the more she knew that she had not been brought in for questioning because she had not technically done anything wrong or divulged any secrets. She realized, as the invisible dust of this electronic stampede began to settle, that they'd only silenced her platforms to speak out, because she had made it clear she was not against speaking out in the first place. If she had actually said something to put her in hot water, she had no idea where she would be now.

She sat down at her small, modest kitchen table one night a few weeks later and pondered how this would affect the rest of her life. Could she build a new Facebook profile, or a new WhatsApp contact? She was only able to get this story to us for the book by way of one email from a new account she set up to send from and never use again. Would this all blow over and be forgotten? Or would she be on a watchlist for the rest of her life? She thought about it for a moment and decided that it would probably be the latter. And that was okay. She knew she had pushed the very small limits she lived in. She had been warned. It scared her, that is for sure. If she had kept her mouth shut, maybe she would have been able to see baby pictures of her former buyers in their new homes; maybe she would have had more clients in general; maybe she would still trust her government. Who really does in the first place? Not me, she thought as she walked to bed and climbed under the covers that night. Not one bit. But nobody would hear a word from her about it again. No way. She would learn how to balance her life on her own terms. And she wouldn't be the only one.

Bjorn Westman:
A Story on Balance

Bjorn Westman was born in Sweden and lived there most of his life. At the time that COVID-19 became a worldwide pandemic, Bjorn was still living in Sweden but not for long. He lived there with a wife he loves. He has eight children altogether, one with his wife and seven from previous relationships. A good number of his family, including his wife, daughter, eldest and youngest sons, work in the medical community. Bjorn works as a truck driver for a living and is on the road for a large portion of the year. He averaged 340-360 clocked hours and drove upwards of 800 miles every trip before COVID-19. His highest hour count on record, for a single calendar year, was 3,885 hours. At the time COVID-19 hit, he was making short distance deliveries for construction materials around Sweden and Norway. It is his life's work, and he is proud to do it. But as time moves on and he is getting older, he is beginning to look forward to his retirement alongside his wife, who has worked as a nurse for almost the same amount of time he has been driving trucks. Bjorn is a simple man with a very complicated relationship to the opposing governments of Sweden and Norway. A relationship that was put to the test because of COVID-19.

The border between Sweden and Norway is razor thin, yet for the last several decades, their responses to just about everything is almost opposite. To talk to Bjorn about something as catastrophic as COVID-19, his opinions and statements can volley back and forth like a table tennis match. He was a Swedish-born farm boy who now lives and works out of Norway (since early into the pandemic), with a personal belief in science but a set-in-stone reliance on the men and women in actual power. There is nothing about Bjorn that is one-sided, so when it comes to a worldwide pandemic, he is one of the most interesting subjects to question about the matter at hand.

The Swedish people pride themselves on their humility and consider a mere job title announced in public a form of bragging. To hear it from Bjorn himself, if someone makes a lot of money in Sweden, most people will assume he must have cheated on his taxes. Norwegians are the complete opposite. If that same man makes the same amount of money in Norway, the people around him will be happy for him and move on. This example may make Swedes look resentful, but it is simply a matter of refinement for them to not talk about wealth or power. They want everything and everyone to lay low, and they rely on the politicians in high offices to take care of everything. That is why, when COVID-19 came to Sweden, the response of the people was like nothing had happened.

Bjorn however was bordering the two countries, and from the response he saw in Norway, he knew something must be actually going on. He would listen for signs or directions from the Swedish government, but they never said boo. They legitimately told the people of Sweden to not worry, that they didn't need to social distance or wear masks, that the deaths were not from COVID-19. In Norway, masks and social distancing were immediate and mandatory. Bjorn, the man of two worlds, was automatically torn. Lucky for him, however, because he was self-aware enough to know his place in all of this, he did what he learned to do long ago.

"I am always annoyingly factionally interested," Bjorn says describing himself. In other words, he doesn't rely on the people's opinions from either side of the fence. He looks at the data, the stats, the numbers. He wants answers in a logical, fact-based document, not from the lady in the supermarket talking to him to make small talk. He said he is old enough to know that not one side is 100% right at every turn. He disagreed with both the viewpoint of Norway, which, to Bjorn, acted like this virus was the end of the world, and Sweden, which acted like nothing was even happening. Bjorn's objective in early 2020 was to find a common ground between his two opposing countries.

The psychology of Sweden makes their response to a pandemic understandable. From the outside, Sweden is a very peaceful country, completely neutral on almost every front. When Norway was occupied by the Germans during WWII, Sweden stayed out of it. It is this function that has kept them from having a war in over 280 years. But Bjorn knows that this outside peace only creates internal turmoil for the Swedes themselves because they believe that past peace will continue into the future, and they leave no room for the idea of something going wrong. Bjorn describes the Swedish mindset as such, "Their past peace influenced Swedes in such a way that they can sit behind the kitchen curtain cursing at the world, but don't do much to change anything about the problem."

Bjorn knows he is not like that. Growing up on a farm led

him to constantly learning new things and to discovering new ways of how something worked. And that is how he continues to look at the world today. So when the two countries he calls home began to separate their objectives in response to COVID-19, Bjorn began taking it upon himself to learn what he could. And what he found was more in line with the Swedish mindset than he might have expected. While he didn't agree Norway was overreacting at the time, he continued to study the virus for himself. Bjorn saw some reasons why Swedish healthcare professionals may, in fact, be right about the virus not being as harmful as first expected by most people around the world.

Bjorn learned that the virus, much like the common flu, is treatable, and that most people who died from it did in fact have severe, underlying issues when they got the virus. Therefore, the virus may have pulled the trigger but there were plenty of bullets loaded in the gun beforehand. He began to read about the way pathogens take up room in a person's body and how important it is to allow ourselves exposure to these pathogens of COVID-19 in order for our body to build up the correct immune system to fight it. To Bjorn, if we hide in our homes all day and night, we will never get past Coronavirus and it will linger for much longer than it needs to. However, there are still precautions that Bjorn thinks Sweden should implement. For example, social distancing is important for people who do have those underlying issues in their bodies, and just because we should expose ourselves to the disease, does not also mean we should antagonize it and act as if it is not real. In other words, there should be a balance in dealing with such a complex virus.

That is how Bjorn views his life as a whole, even before this pandemic hit. For him and his family, it is all about balance. As previously mentioned, he is a working man, but most of his family are professional healthcare workers. He believes that this balances out the way the family is perceived socially. In other ways, Bjorn tries to balance his work-life spectrum, spending as much time with his wife as he can while home but also clocking in the right amount of hours on the road in order to carry his weight in the finances of their life. There is nothing in life more important than a healthy dose of balance for Bjorn.

But not everyone sees this virus as an extension of that. In Sweden, it took the citizens working independently of their government to begin social distancing. Norway, on the other hand, said almost immediately that it was unlawful for crowds over a certain number to gather together. In Sweden, the government did not release numbers of deaths due to COVID-19 partially as a way to keep things calm. In Norway, every death had a possibility of being linked to COVID-19. Bjorn knows that there is a happy middle, and he hopes that one day, the two polar opposite worlds he travels between will find it.

During the first lockdowns, Bjorn had a conversation with a Norwegian police officer who told Bjorn that most of the police force in Norway received COVID-19 and other health updates from the media before their own bosses told them. Bjorn could tell from this conversation, as well as others he has either had or overheard in Norway, that people got sick and tired of the way things were being run because they felt the virus was taken too seriously. Even the Norwegian "statsminister," aka the Prime Minister, was fined 20,000 Norwegian Kroner for breaking the COVID-19 rules during her birthday celebrations. It is a whirlwind of issues that go from top to bottom in Norway. For Bjorn, he just had to keep his head on straight and continue to do the best he could.

In other words, Bjorn continues to drive his truck, stay as close as he can to his wife, and he is simply counting down the days until retirement. He does not *disbelieve* that COVID-19 is a thing, but he is skeptical of its actual impact upon the world at large. He hopes that the people around him will take it more seriously where it is being ignored and that the ones guarding the country of Norway will relax a little and give its citizens some legitimate breathing room. There are two sides to every story, two ways of looking at a problem. Nothing can lean too much in one direction, otherwise things fall down. He knows this because he's lived it. And he will continue to live it as an example of someone who not only found balance for himself, but wants to share the importance of it with others. But to stay balanced, you must stay strong. You must be willing to fight those tough battles in life, just like a warrior.

---

1. Tyler Kingkade and Elizabeth Chuck, "Suicidal thoughts are increasing in young kids, experts say. It began before the pandemic," NBC News, April 8, 2021, https://www.nbcnews.com/news/us-news/suicidal-thoughts-are-increasing-young-kids-experts-say-it-began-n1263347 (accessed April 18, 2021).
2. Lynsey Chutel and Abdi Latif Dahir, "With Most Coronavirus Cases in Africa, South Africa Locks Down," The New York Times, March 27, 2020, https://www.nytimes.com/2020/03/27/world/africa/south-africa-coronavirus.html (accessed March 28, 2020).
3. Lynsey Chutel and Abdi Latif Dahir, "With Most Coronavirus Cases in Africa, South Africa Locks Down," The New York Times, March 27, 2020, https://www.nytimes.com/2020/03/27/world/africa/south-africa-coronavirus.html (accessed March 28, 2020).
4. Maggie Hiufu Wong, "Wuhan: Inside the Chinese city at the center of the coronavirus outbreak," CNN, January 23, 2020, https://www.cnn.com/travel/article/wuhan-china-virus/index.html (access March 22, 2020).
5. Cecelia Smith-Schoenwalder, "What to Know About the Wuhan Coronavirus," U.S. News, January 24, 2020, https://www.usnews.com/news/world-report/articles/2020-01-24/what-to-know-about-the-wuhan-coronavirus-from-china (accessed on March 25, 2020).

12

WARRIOR

On June 17, 2020, an article was published on politico.com titled, "'It's just way too much to take on': School systems struggle with the politics of reopening."[1] In the article, many people in the school systems across America commented about the impossible situation COVID-19 brought to the education system. From life and death arguments to bureaucratic money-talk, the principals of various schools in all different states had overlapping issues that contradicted each other. "'I mean, it's like it's a lose-lose situation,' said Dan Domenech, who runs AASA, The School Superintendents Association. 'You have parents that are demanding the schools to open. And then you have parents that are saying, we're not going to send our kids to school. You have teachers that are saying we're not going to go back to work. Districts that are saying, with these budget cuts, we're going to have to lay off teachers,'" (Gaudino, Goldberg). [2] The rest of the article goes back and forth like this, with little in the way of answers to the multitude of questions. The article ends with, "There's a lot of anxiety and fear."

I thought about that article as we wished our oldest daughter a happy tenth birthday from our hotel room in Seattle, Washington. We had been on the road for almost a month, and things were going well. As I watched my girls dig into another one of Michael's homemade cakes, I pondered the next year's uphill battles. Each one of these girls would eventually have to go back to school and learn to live amidst the pandemic. We were on the other side of the world as far as they were concerned. We had taken them away from the cooped up house, the onslaught of new updates, and the worries of virtual schooling (we left the second the virtual 'school year' ended) for as long as we could. We still had plenty more to see and do, but I couldn't help begin to plan for their future. It was silly, I knew, because if the last few months had taught me anything, it was that the future is unknown and planning is only for peace of mind.

Over the next few days we busied ourselves by traveling through Washington State. We enjoyed the sites of Mount Rainier and also visited the state waterfall of Washington-Palouse Falls. Our oldest daughter was turning double digits and she wanted to see a new city she had never seen before for her birthday. She picked Seattle. We saw all sorts of fun things in and near the downtown Seattle area, including the town of Concrete, a shut-down Macy's department store, the very first Starbucks (opened in 1971), and Pike Place Market. Our RV needed servicing for the first and only time on the trip and so we stayed one night at the Westin in downtown Seattle, birthday girl's pick. Only three percent of the hotel was occupied.

The adventures continued as we entered Olympic National Park in Washington State. Established in 1938, this National landmark has become a popular sight due to its inclusion of just about every ecosystem over almost a million acres. We spent nearly all day at the national park, climbing up trees, standing over Glacial Lake and Lake Crescent. We saw signs for bear warnings and saw some of the tallest trees we had ever seen in our lives. One of the tall trees was also so large that it took all the kids to spread their arms out, hold hands, and just barely connect around the circumference of the trunk. This park made #2 in our top three list of favorite national parks for the trip, and it was mostly due to the hot springs we dipped ourselves in while there. We visited Sol Duc Hot Springs and took a dip in the 105 degree Fahrenheit spring waters. We had not expected it to be so fun, but to our surprise, it was one of our favorite national parks so far.

We then worked our way south until we reached San Francisco, California. The kids enjoyed watching cars drive down the steep streets. We visited the SF Bay and got to shop around in Ghirardelli's.

As I watched the kids experience newness at every turn, I deeply pondered the reality the education this trip would have on their lives. When the entire world shut down, my girls got to finally see a piece of it for the first time, and we were able to do it in a way that was safe. I couldn't imagine us visiting so many national parks in any other situation other than this.

That night in the RV park in California, parked 3,000 miles away from home, I thought about that article from a few days before. I thought about my girls and the children around the world. I thought about Alessandro and Camila, I thought about Benjamin Elbracht and his family, and baby still yet to be born. I thought about the children who had no parents, and the parents who had no children. I wondered how the children from around the world would fare in this new world, post-COVID-19. I feared for my children, when this was all said and done, how they would cope in the new world. I turned over in bed, looked at Michael sound asleep, and wondered how he would deal with the new world waiting for us when we returned home to Georgia. And finally, just before sleep took me that night, I thought about myself. I hoped and prayed that I would have the strength to help the girls through the next year of their lives with this disease being a threat to the world they knew.

Three days later we found ourselves in Las Vegas, Nevada after a quick pass through of the fascinating Redwoods National Park, which surprisingly, was mostly shutdown from cars being able to drive through "due to COVID-19". Odd, I thought, since driving through just meant enjoying the sites, socially distanced. When we arrived in Vegas, we found that the famous Strip was almost vacant. There was nothing but a few stragglers and street performers. We enjoyed driving around and showing the kids the large hotels that make up this unique U.S. city and we watched the Bellagio Hotel Fountain during the daylight hours and at night. It was quite a different and unique way of enjoying Vegas; nevertheless, it was plenty of entertainment and a fruitful experience.

The day in Vegas was great but the night was tough. While my kids slept that night, I was woken up several times by our dog, Luna, who insisted on being taken outside. I found myself walking an unfamiliar campsite at two, three, and four in the morning with a very poopy puppy. And the heat didn't help. It was late June in the middle of a desert campsite, right outside Vegas. Despite the agony of being up and down all night with a sick dog, I was still glad we were there that day, letting the kids experience all that they could.

Next stop, my sister Stefanie, the mother of my nephew who was on the trip with us for over a month, rented an RV of her own and we met up at a campsite in Utah with her other kids and husband. She even brought her in-laws and their dog along. The family trip out West doubled in size, and it was great.

We parked our RVs next to each other and had a fantastic time camping out, grilling yummy food, and roasting marshmallows. It was great having Stefanie there, but as I watched my girls and their cousins play together, I still had the nagging feeling of fear for their children's future. At one point during that first night, I pulled Stefanie aside, sister to sister.

"Do you think the kids are going to be okay?" I asked.

"What do you mean?" asked Stefanie.

"Do you think my kids and your kids and all the other kids are going to be okay when school starts back up?"

"Where is this coming from?"

I told her about the article I'd read recently about the school system.

Stefanie thought about it for a while. Then nodded. "Yes, I think the kids will be just fine."

"How do you know that?" I asked.

"Because," she said, "The school system is out of our hands. It's up to them to figure out how to take care of our children. And they will find a way, whatever it may be. But us, the parents, are doing the best thing for them right now. We're giving them an outlet, an escape for the time being. Sure, they'll have to go back to school, and we'll have to go back to work. While we're way the hell out here in the middle of the desert, the world is currently changing. People are dying, people are frightened, but people have seen things like this before. And we as people will get through it. You know why?"

I shook my head, tears coming to my eyes with what she was telling me.

"Because of the same reason we always fight hard to get through tough times. For the children. That is the age old reason for fighting against all of this, so that our children may have a better life. I sure as crap didn't want to haul a large RV across the country, but I know it's what the kids needed."

I nodded my head and couldn't help but laugh. "You're right. Michael definitely wouldn't be driving that thing all around if it wasn't for the kids."

"You see?" she said. "That's why we're all out here. Sure it's fun for us sometimes, but we're paying for it, we're planning it, we're taking care of it. And it's so the kids can enjoy the time they have in the best way possible."

I gave my sister a hug and thanked her for what she'd told me. I walked back to my kids, now dressed up in glow-in-the-dark rubber jewelry and let them dress me up in some as well. We spent the night as one big happy family, and I felt almost euphoric that we could see the stars that night; the kids were pointing up at them and smiling. I reminded myself I will take anything the Universe offers and do everything I can to make my children happy as the world changes around us.

We spent the next several days with our families combined, loading up the two RVs and traveling to different national parks and canyons all throughout Utah and into Colorado. We saw Zion National Park with its long paved roads underneath the large rock formations on either side of the road. Then we headed up into Bryce Canyon National Park where we looked out over the large cliffs and down into the vast canyons that seemed to go on for miles. The numerous group photos captured with cousins became priceless. This is where we parted ways with my sister and her family, and she took her son back home to Atlanta, and the remainder of the trip was my family of six. We then visited another one of our collective favorites so far throughout the trip: Mesa Verde National Park.

This National Landmark is home to some very rich Native American history. It was founded by Theodore Roosevelt and is considered one of the largest archeological preserves in the United States, with over 500 distinct sites and 600 cliff dwellings. The original settlers lived on the cliff of a mountain and their actual houses they built are still intact in some places around the sites. We saw some ourselves and it was intoxicating to see the remains of real, Native American history standing strong after all this time. Some of the structures we saw were once stone masonry towers that were said to have served as defensive structures for the early Mesa Verde settlers.[3] Starting as early as the sixth century, the farmers living in central Mesa cultivated corn, beans, squash, and gourds, which provided them with the amino acids of a complete protein. For meat, the Mesa typically hunted local small game, such as mule deer and rabbits. The crop gardens were built by hand and foraged for and by the sons of daughters of those who first built the land.[4] We found this park to rank #3 in our top three list and I believe it was because Mesa Verde was a world so far beyond what we knew.

It was hard to fathom how much work had gone into building a community so long ago. As we gazed out into this open, deserted terrain, I thought about this community, long ago that sits inside the walls of what is now the United States, and I fathomed how different the United States is now and particularly to each individual person.

I had been reading up on the COVID-19 news throughout our trip, seeing pictures of hospitals overrun with patients, homeless shelters overcrowded with people who lost their jobs because of the failing economy, large university campuses that had become ghost towns, and lines of people waiting outside the unemployment offices of several different counties, hoping to get a dollar from the government in order to eat the available food on otherwise bare shelves that had not already been ransacked at supermarkets across the country. I wondered how that could all happen at the same time that my family could look out over a large historical site that is now vacant. How is it that some places can be overrun with people, overcrowded and in danger, and other places are completely abandoned just a couple hundred miles from a large city like Los Angeles or San Francisco?

To me it seemed impossible to think that COVID-19 could affect the entire country when I looked out over all this empty land. It was rich with history but barren of today's society. And yet here we were, together as a family in the middle of a pandemic, away from the madness. The seconds ticked by with the miles we trekked back closer to home. Despite the happiness I felt and what Stefanie had told me a couple nights before, I still hoped that the world could get back to the way things were. And as I watched the sky meet the horizon in the far-off distance, I wondered if any of the people who died here could hear us. I wondered if they had any idea what had happened to our country and to the world.

Would the warriors who died on the forgotten battlefields below our feet tell us to give up or would they tell us to keep fighting? Then I thought again of what Stefanie told me: It is for the children. And I knew then that maybe the men and women who died in these lands, now forgotten and abandoned, would tell me that their children are the reason they fought so hard to live and work as well. So maybe I have to be more than just a mother to my daughters, a wife to my husband, a boss to my employees, or a woman to myself. Maybe I have to be like those that lived and died before me. Maybe I have to be a warrior. Then, as we walked back to the RV, my youngest daughter's hand in mine, I had my final thought for that day: Maybe I already am a warrior. And in order to be a warrior, you must exemplify resilience.

Johanne Boudreault:
A Story on Resilience

Johanne Boudreault is from Quebec, a primarily French-speaking province in eastern Canada. She has been a high school science teacher for over thirty years, with a concentration in biology. In early March of 2020, she had saved up enough money to take a well-earned sabbatical and go on vacation. She went to France to ski. It was a trip she had been dreaming about for years. She was overjoyed to be in another part of the world, away from teaching classes, grading papers, and displacing rowdy teens. She had planned the entire trip out to a T. But there was one thing she had not included in her itinerary; one thing that no one could have seen coming. It was March 14th, just as she had settled down for her three-month trip in France, that she got the urgent call from friends and families. When she turned on the news in her rented bedroom, she saw what everyone was calling about. There was a nationwide lockdown being set in place because of a new virus. Thanks to COVID-19, Johanne was forced to find a plane home as soon as possible if she wanted to make it back to Quebec at all. She didn't have time to pause and think about possibly staying locked down in France. It didn't even feel like a possibility at the time.

There were immediate problems with her return trip, things she could not have predicted and certainly was not prepared for. The first major issue was her house. Because of her three month trip to France, Johanne had rented out her house to another couple as a long-term Airbnb and she could not force them to leave. Until the three month's stay was over, Johanne and her boyfriend, Alain, had to find an apartment to rent month-to-month. It took some time because, since there was a pandemic, the lockdown kept most people from wanting to let people sublease their apartments around Quebec. Finally they were able to find one. So, they flew home and stayed there for the time being. But now that she was back home, there were other issues to attend to. Some of them were not so bad though.

While most teachers from the schools around Quebec had to learn to teach virtually, Johanne was relieved of this duty given the sabbatical that was still active. However, she was facing three months in an unfamiliar apartment, with nowhere to go because of the "stay at home" orders issued by the Canadian government. She spent the first few weeks split between keeping her eyes on the news and doing many puzzles to keep her mind active. She worried about the children, all of whom had been ordered to go home and learn virtually. She heard through the teacher grapevine that high school students were not required initially to attend virtual classes, and while some did, most did not. She feared for the future of their education and how that choice to be absent would affect them in the long run. "I was just worried about a lot of things during that time. And I was pretty lonely."

Johanne describes herself as a sensitive person, and the beginning times of the virus were a scary time for her. Not to mention, she felt depressed often over the loss of her long-awaited trip to France. It had been her dream for years. She had saved up enough money to go there and thoroughly enjoy herself, and instead of three fun months, within three days it was all over. And for the next few months, she was stuck in limbo. It was, in a very unfortunate way, very anticlimactic. All she could do at that point was look forward to this lockdown ending and to step back into her classroom. Little did she know what was waiting in store for her when the time to go back to school finally came.

After several months indoors, in September, after a long and locked down summer, school began again in-person. It was finally time for Johanne to rejoin her colleagues and kids in the classrooms. She had been teaching at this point for twenty-nine years, and she thought she had seen just about everything a school teacher could witness. But what she saw the first day of school after the pandemic felt surreal, in a bad way, and brought tears to her eyes. "I could not believe the sight of all these young girls and boys in masks. It was heartbreaking." She was devastated by the enormity of the pandemic, of what it had done both globally and locally. It had infected the major organs of older people and the lives of younger people. She made sure not to cry that first morning as the masked children walked into her classroom. But she certainly had a hard time not doing so.

In the beginning, the kids had to wear the masks in the hallways and in bigger groups, but once at their desks they were allowed to remove them, as the desks were separated enough for safe social distancing. That changed quickly, as did a lot of other things in the coming months as 2020 came to an end. Just a few months after school began, in November, the school had a few too many reported cases and the school was put on a one-to-one schedule. This meant that the kids went to school once every other day, and the rest of the school days were spent at home, doing virtual school.

Johanne had a hard time with this new change because now she was behind. While all the other teachers had already taught themselves how to teach virtually, using the correct platforms and websites, Johanne had to learn it all very quickly. She received a little bit of help from her fellow colleagues and began teaching virtually sooner than she would have expected. Another major change to Johanne's way of teaching is that instead of having one class to herself and then having different kids each new class period, the school began exercising the reverse. Now the kids stayed in one classroom all day and the teachers were the ones who rotated. The logic by the school board was that when the kids were being taught in person, they should have the fewest number of people walking around in the halls as possible. Since the students outnumbered the teachers thirty to one, the teachers were the ones to rotate. It made sense, but the other challenge was how it changed class schedules so the kids who were previously in some advanced classes were no longer getting those. Now they were all just lumped into one group. Johanne was forced to teach in a new classroom each period, throwing off her concentration even more than it already was. And then on the virtual teaching days, although stationary, her concentration suffered from that dynamic.

Johanne was primarily a science teacher, and that meant that a good number of her lessons involved projects to demonstrate her education. For instance, one year she had the students conduct an assembly of PVC pipes together and push water through them to exemplify how the human heart pumps blood through the body. Because of these new restrictions, the kids were not allowed to share materials and certainly not allowed to use materials brought in from outside sources, in case of cross contamination. As a way to continue to teach the kids through her illustrations, Johanne took on the task of filming herself completing these experiments from home and uploading them for the kids to watch as part of the virtual lessons. It was awkward for her to film herself but she knew that so long as the kids got to learn something as important as biology, perhaps they may remember it better if they could have a good laugh at their teacher.

When asked about the children and their perspectives, Johanne became emotional. The truth is that the kids were not doing well during the school year of COVID-19. A majority of them were, as she says, "resilient," but many were not. For instance, the once outgoing children who played sports after school and went to after school clubs were experiencing severe distress and depression. It was hard for them to stay motivated throughout the school days. Some of them did not even come in on the in-person school days because it was too hard for them to learn in the heavily restricted ways that schools had been re-designed to be. Some of the kids who used to be very engaged had become so withdrawn and "out of it" that they face the real possibility of failing a few of their classes. And many of them did fail. It was hard for Johanne to witness. Many of the teachers took on a de facto guidance counselor role because of all the strain the children were being put through. One positive amongst all of these negatives is that in order to facilitate the virtual learning process, the government of Quebec handed out Google Chrome laptops to every household that had a child in school. While that was very helpful, Johanne knew that it was not enough.

For the upcoming school year, she made it her goal to stay in-touch with her students more and to learn as many ways as it would take to push them further towards a better adjustment in their educational careers. As a veteran teacher, she knows the saying, "There is nothing I would not do for my students." And while that phrase sounds nice, the COVID-19 pandemic really reframed that mindset entirely. Johanne lost out on a long-planned trip she had been looking forward to. And she is upset about that. But she is also old enough to know that the loss of her trip is in the past. What lies ahead in the future is the question of how to help her students and live by her veteran mantra.

Education is important, but how to best educate the kids when the world looks ready to fall apart, is more important. Johanne says that there is no bottom to the barrel when it comes to what distracts us nowadays, high school students included. Everything is a distraction. Especially if the students are at home, not in the proper school setting. For the first time in her teaching career, Johanne knows that it is her responsibility to educate beyond the classroom and to touch the lives of each and every one of her scared, depressed, anxious students as best she can. "I just want to be there for them in any way that I can." And that is what she plans to do. Because when all is said and done, they are the future, and they have to be taken care of because it certainly feels to those of us who currently inhabit the earth that the future is more unknown now than it ever has been. Johanne Boudreault teaches by example and must show her students what true resilience looks like, and as long as they stay strong and find their passion, resilience will always win out.

Leticia Ramierez:
A Story on Passion

Ever since Leticia Ramierez was a young child, she worked herself harder than anyone else around her. No matter the challenge, she had an internal drive to overcome any obstacles and succeed. With that pressure brought anxiety, almost all of it internally generated. She would stress over bad grades, even at the age of six. So at seven years old, when her mother noticed this behavior was giving her daughter a hard time, she encouraged her to learn to swim as a way to rechannel and relieve her anxiety. Leticia took up the sport tentatively at first but soon learned she was a natural. At nine she joined the local swim team in her hometown of Monterey, Mexico. She was very good and only got better. By the age of fourteen, Leticia went to the National Championship and placed fourth in backstroke. Every one of her peers and family members were proud of her, but all Leticia could see was that she did not make it to first place.

As the years went on, this competitive nature drove her to other interests, specifically in the world of science. She applied and was accepted to the local university where she began studying Bioprocessing. There, her passion turned from an interest in swimming to an interest in learning. During her third semester, she stopped swimming and put all of her attention into school. She left the university with a PhD in Bioprocessing and landed a great job as a chemical engineer. Over the next few years she got married, had two kids, and in 2016, opened one of the first escape room attractions in Mexico with her business partner, Ricardo. Around this time, in the middle of running her own business and raising two daughters, Leticia's husband mentioned that she was putting on a little bit of weight. She took a look at herself and decided that maybe he was right.

Over the next few weeks, Leticia began working out but could not find anything that made her happy. Eventually she tried swimming again for the first time in over ten years. It was incredible, exhilarating, and exactly what she needed. But she also realized what she did not need, and that was a husband who did not appreciate her for what she was before she began working out again. She divorced him soon after that.

By 2018, she was swimming three days a week and having one of her most profitable years from the escape room. But that was not enough. Leticia knew she wanted more. So she approached a friend of hers and asked him to coach her. She wanted to get better at swimming so she could move onto Nationals again in Mexico. He accepted, but with one condition: She had to start swimming every single day for three months leading up to the competition. No exceptions.

Leticia accepted the challenge and began swimming every day. She told herself that she would only do this for the three month commitment and then, after Nationals, she would go back to swimming three days a week instead of seven. In 2019, when she finally made it to Nationals, she placed fifth place in open water swimming at the World Championship. This time, unlike when she was fourteen, the fact that she had gotten even this far excited her. She continued swimming every day after that, knowing full well that the training was what made her happiest, not the trophy or glory, but also knowing that with the training she would continue to improve. She could feel her life was going in an amazing direction. And then one day in early March of 2020, she read a news article, and her whole world stopped.

COVID-19 was not as rampant in Monterey as other parts of the world, but suddenly Leticia's childhood anxiety began to overpower her again. Before she knew it, she had to close her business indefinitely, help her kids learn from home, and stop swimming altogether. It was a miserable time for her, and she could not help but watch the news updates incessantly from reports all over the world. She researched statistics, read early reports that even walking your dog could transmit the virus into your home and that food shortages might take the world out before the virus did. She was a wreck for the first three months of the worldwide pandemic. But there was irony in all of it when she finally had a chance to look back on that time.

While Leticia's reaction to the virus was so chaotic and full of fear for the first three months, at that same time, the place she grew up and still lived, Monterey, Mexico, was acting almost as if nothing had happened. She and her neighbors were wearing masks and social distancing but not because of any government order. For the first three months, life in Monterey seemed almost normal. It was almost as if Leticia was experiencing anxiety brought on by the rest of the world, while stuck in the safety of her own world. And then things began to change.

As case numbers rose in and around Mexico, Monterey began to take a new approach. But now that she was months into the pandemic, Leticia had found ways to cope and she was learning how to calm down. So by the time her surrounded area was actually locked down and the fear settled in the area outside her closed front door, inside her home, she was fine. Her daughters, ages seven and fourteen, were the ones who needed the hand-holding. But there was an issue with that. The seven-year-old just needed guidance and a watchful eye from her mother. The fourteen-year-old, however, did not want anything to do with her mother. It was a terrible case of bad timing, where the ugly teen years collided with the lockdown months, forcing her very confused and upset daughter to be stuck inside all day. "She would spend a lot of time in her room during the day," said Leticia of those early days. It was a very tense situation for the whole family. She was trying to do her best to support her kids with school, she had a business to try and figure out a way to save, and she was not about to chance going out and swimming. She knew she had to adjust her life, and quickly.

In April, she felt she needed to close the escape room doors and the business didn't make a dime, but luckily, the landlord only required her to pay half of the month's rent. This was a blessing in and of itself, but it still did not keep Leticia from losing money. Around May, when she and the rest of the world realized the virus wasn't going away anytime soon, Leticia got an idea. It took her a few months to do the research and plan it out, but she eventually opened up a virtual escape room.

The idea for an online escape room was even more new-age than escape rooms themselves, and she had found a loophole that allowed for businesses stuck on Zoom to participate in team building exercises through her platform. It worked for quite some time, but it still did not make the kind of money she had been making before March. Then, around September of

2020, she got another idea. She noticed that movie theaters around Monterey were slowly, carefully opening back up. Leticia took a page out of their playbooks and began monitoring when they opened back up, and for how long, and at what capacity. Then she did the obvious, she mirrored that for her own escape rooms. This plan slowly but surely began to work. She and Ricardo started to see their profits increase steadily again, split between the virtual rooms and the physical ones. It was not ideal, but there wasn't a better option at the time.

As Leticia worked hard to put her life back on track, something was holding her back. She was itching to get back into the water. It had been months since she had swum a single lap, and this was taking a toll on her. Luckily, the pool nearby eventually opened back. When she arrived for her first day back in the water, the pool was already crowded. While the rule was four people to a lane, this was too much for the health-conscious chemical engineer. She left that pool and researched some farther from her home. She found one days later that was half an hour away, and when she arrived, she was met with little in the way of people. She thanked her lucky stars and dove into her own, almost-private swimming lane. She began swimming again every day and has ever since.

From the fallout of COVID-19, Leticia learned a lot about herself. She always knew she was driven, she knew that she was a hard worker, but she never knew she was so innovative. At every dead-end turn in 2020, she managed to plow her way through the brick wall and pave a new path. She studied what the rest of the world was doing and mimicked what the successful ones did. At the end of it all, Leticia knew it began and ended with her internal drive to seek reassurance, just like when she was seven years old, stressed out over first grade homework assignment. It all went back to swimming.

Leticia never lost her passion for swimming, and from that

she gained new passions as well. She learned that when you take a chance, you can't just stop after the first step into the unknown. If you choose to do something new, you have to put your all into it. She knew that having kids would mean working as hard as she could to raise them the right way. She knew going to college meant pushing herself to earn the highest degree she could. She knew that opening an escape room in Mexico meant she had to be creative and driven with her business. And that all started when she first learned how much she loved swimming. It is not enough to simply love something you took a chance on; you have to take that love all the way. Now, as the world learns to adapt to a new normal, Leticia knows she must push herself even harder in everything she does. It is not always because she's anxious, worried, or scared, it is because she has fallen in love with certain things in her life, and she must work hard for that love, one stroke at a time. For herself, for her life, and for her family. Because nothing can break love or family.

---

1. Nicole Gaudiano and Dan Goldberg, "'It's just way too much to take on': School systems struggle with the politics of reopening," Politico, June 17, 2020, https://www.politico.com/news/2020/06/17/reopening-schools-coronavirus-327020 (accessed Jun 29, 2020).
2. Ibid.
3. James A Lancaster and Jean M. Pinkley, "Mesa Verde," NPS History, May 19, 2008, http://npshistory.com/series/archeology/2/sec2.htm (accessed August 2, 2020).
4. Linda Lange, "Traveling across Colorado is a nature lover's dream," Knox News, August 25, 2021, https://www.knoxnews.com/story/entertainment/2021/08/25/traveling-across-colorado-nature-lovers-dream/8248154002/ (accessed September 14, 2021).

13

NOTHING BREAKS FAMILY

The Great Sand Dunes National Park is located in southern Colorado. The massive sand dunes are yet another way to enjoy the outdoors in such a great state. They counterbalance the ski slopes of northern Colorado; you can slide down them on a board or sled, standing or sitting at high rates of speed. These unique natural wonders are often joked to be an alien landscape. So much so that NASA has actually tested rovers on the geological conditions. The two Viking spacecraft that first landed on Mars were tested in these dunes. In early July 2020, we spent an entire day there. And it was, without a doubt, a pure blast. I had so much fun watching the girls and their dad fly down the large dunes with their feet sticking out ahead of them and their bottoms planted on the boards that slide effortlessly forward. I even took a few turns gliding down the dunes, and I must admit, it was a bit unnerving. I admired the kids every time they ran back up to take the plunge again. Unfortunately, the sand dunes weren't a hit for everyone. Our poor dog, Luna, wasn't so happy as the sand was irritating her by getting in her eyes and nose with the wind.

On the flip side, I was able to award the girls their national park junior ranger badges myself. Because of this program being put on hold during quarantine, I was allowed to take the oath and swear that they would complete the checklist to earn their badge. We did this for each National Park we visited on the trip. We would go to the Welcome Center, I would be given the badges to hand out when it was time, and the girls would receive workbooks to complete for each park. At the end of each trip, when I pinned the badge on each one of their shirts, I was overjoyed and humbled. It felt absolutely right to award them for being so brave, not only to ride down the sand dunes so freely or to explore big tree forests, but more deeply, to go on this journey with their parents like this. I felt as if these badges represented how hard these girls were working to enjoy themselves, despite the heat and despite the restless, long drives. They were troopers and they had certainly earned a badge to show for it.

Later that night, at yet another campsite, we sat outside the RV and had a pizza making contest. Each girl was given enough dough, sauce, cheese, and toppings to design a personal pizza exactly to their liking. It was fun to watch them create such wonderfully childish pizza designs, with pepperonis in the shape of flowers and sausages in the shape of smiley faces. At the end, I rewarded each girl with a prize for their decorations. Luna was happy to lap up the remains of the food that fell in between the cracks of the picnic table. At the end of that night, with the sun setting low over the vast Colorado horizon, we bathed the girls and combed their hair into neat little braids before bed. We felt so at home in this RV that had just two months ago been a stranger to us. Like the settlers I imagined the other day, I had learned how easily you can make something foreign your home, as long as you have a family with you.

I got a taste of just how big those settlements are when I

looked out over the tip of Pikes Peak just a few days later. The winding dirt roads led us up to the top of the mountain ranges that spanned the horizon. We were dizzy from the drive but exhilarated from the tops of the mountains that crossed through the lands. Each mile marker we passed told us about a different kind of plant or animal we could potentially find on our journey along the trails, including coyotes, big-eared bats, elk, mountain lion, and a Golden Eagle. Each mile marker we drove past brought us closer to the top of the mountain range, providing us with an even better view of the terrain below. I was elated when we made it to the top. Not just because we were at the top of Pike's Peak but because we had officially made it to the highest and lowest points of the United States, which, if you remember back to the conversation between Michael and me prior to leaving, had been Michael's only request for the trip.

We had recently visited the lowest point below sea level right before Vegas, in Death Valley National Park. It was 122 degrees Fahrenheit and we could barely stand to be outside. Now, within an hour's time we had driven up Pike's Peak from a warm eighty degrees Fahrenheit below to a frigid thirty-five degrees Fahrenheit at the top. We had not been prepared for that change and we were cold, but we had done it. We accomplished this feat and could now say we had been to both the top peak and the lowest valley in the United States. Reaching that goal felt satisfying.

Another interesting note, albeit less interesting but still a bit fascinating to me about Pike's Peak, was that driving back down the mountain we had to stop for brake checks at pull offs along the way where a person would measure the heat on the brakes to determine if the brakes are too hot and we needed to pull over and let them cool down to avoid them giving out as we go further down the mountain. It was the first time in my life that I had ever had to stop and have my brakes checked when driving down a mountain. At one point, our brakes were too hot, and we were advised to be even more careful with how we were driving down the mountain or we would have to pull over and wait twenty minutes at the next stop.

After Pike's Peak, each day continued to bleed into another and we were beginning to near the end of our epic journey. We drove on the highways that ran through Nebraska because if we didn't make the effort to go out of our way to hit that state, it would have been the only state not visited as a family in the entire continental United States. Then we drove through Kansas and down into Texas.

We visited the panhandle of Texas and stayed the night in a city called Amarillo. We stopped at a nearby Walmart and picked up a few cans of spray paint, then headed out to Cadillac Ranch. The lot was created back in 1974 by Chip Lord, Hudson Marquez, and Doug Michels, who were a part of the art group, Ant Farm. The entire lot consists of ten Cadillac vehicles that are buried nose first into the hard, Texas ground. Over several decades, tourists have stopped by with cans of spray paint and gone hog wild, painting over the cars with whatever design or words they want. We all took turns that day leaving our marks on the cars. And the girls even left their marks on Michael's plain, white T-shirt, but it was all in good fun.

We spent the 4th of July at a campground near Tulsa, Oklahoma on our way back across the country. We enjoyed the day swimming, feeding chickens, cows, and goats that were at the campground and cooking out over an open flame. We made toasted s'mores, roasted hot dogs, and dressed up in our best red, white, and blue. It was the most relaxed way we had ever spent that holiday, and we quite enjoyed it. The girls enjoyed the freedom of the campground, including getting to ride their bikes with me along the trails surrounding the site. Overall it was a good day, full of patriotic camaraderie. The best part of all: it was simple, traditional, and familiar. There was something happening again inside my heart and mind that had never happened before. I was beginning to call everything home.

The saying that home is where the heart is seems trite after hearing it all your life. But when you begin to travel, especially with your family, you do understand it more and more. I have spoken with sons and daughters that come from military families, and they speak about how easy it is to make yourself at home wherever you are when you are constantly moving. And that's how I had begun to feel over this last month and a half. When I traveled to different countries on my own, or with my family, I had experienced an inkling of that sensation. But out here, in the campgrounds that squat between cities all throughout America, I could feel myself making a home out of the land itself. It was almost akin to how it felt to first become a mother. You begin your journey with the first child as a weary traveler, not sure what choices to make, with no instincts to guide you. With each passing year of the child's life, and the children you have after the first, you become seasoned and wise. All of us were growing used to the changing scenery, just as I had once grown steadily used to the changing landscape of raising the girls. This trip was showing me that home truly is where the heart is because my heart had been in the desert landscapes of the West Coast, the watery landscapes of the Mississippi River, and the tree-lined landscapes of the Southeast. But it was also inside the girls and my husband. My home lay where they lay, whatever RV, campsite, hotel, or home we found ourselves in. Together, we are a home, just like together these United States are my home.

I thought about the homes and lives of others as Michael drove us back East. The WhatsApp messages were still flooding in from all different people all over the world. Some people were having an easier time than others. While one family might be catching up on books and movies they had not had time for before, others were sitting in isolated waiting rooms as their wives or partners gave birth. As we passed through Louisiana and into Arkansas, I read up on everyone's updates. I was astounded even more than before at the support that the messages were providing for people, typically by total strangers.

On July 8, 2020, a dear friend of mine from Guatemala wrote about how badly the virus was affecting her and her family. She told the group that she was fifty years old, living in the United States, and was in fear for her life due to the lack of health concerns by most people living in the States. But even in her times of struggle and doubt, she told the group the positive things that had come out of this quarantine. She said that she and her friends had become more sensitive, more encouraging, and more giving. She had created a way for her and her close friends to send money to those in need. It was sobering to read her story and learn how hard she was fighting to be strong. Her message itself was greeted with even more kind words of prayer from people who had never met her but cared for her deeply.

As we were in the middle of the East Coast, getting closer to home, it spoke to me how much people care for one another. I had seen that myself with the way people in grocery stores had treated my children over the last several weeks. I had seen it in Michael with the way he put aside his worries over the unknowns in our businesses and focused on getting the girls to another incredible site, while also playing with them when they got there. And I had seen it in the girls when I was worried or stuck in my own head. Like a sixth sense, the girls could see my stress and pull me over to ask for help on their arts and crafts or to their bed for some cuddles. I was amazed at the power a person can have on another, and not even a pandemic can stop a person's kindness towards another. If anything, when pushed to the extremes like we all had been, people find it in themselves to push back even harder against the negative flow of energy and find the radiant spirit that lives inside. I was amazed at the power a person can have on another, and not even a pandemic could stop a person's kindness. I just hoped, as we came closer to the end of our trip, that I could carry that same spirit with me back into my old, normal life. Whatever normal would end up meaning.

July 10, 2020, concluded our fifty-five day trip across America. Our last night was spent at, you guessed it, another campground. This time at a beautiful spot on the Mississippi river near Memphis, Tennessee. We woke up, drove through Missouri in the morning, and capped off the trip by visiting Elvis Presley's home. And finally, after two months on the road, we made our way into Georgia. In all, we drove nearly twelve thousand miles (nineteen thousand kilometers) and visited thirty-eight states. That concluded visiting the forty-eight continental United States, or "the mainland" or "lower forty-eight" for our family. We had visited the other ten New England states the summer before. Now, we just had to find a way to visit Alaska and Hawaii one day.

Together, the six of us had gone on an epic voyage together. We had sailed the highway seas, flew high through the cityscapes that stuck out across the states, and roughed the terrains of the Old West. We had not just been tourists. We had been on this adventure as voyagers, pirates, and princesses. We had been foragers and roughriders, collecting our goods and escaping on foot. It had been an adventure that felt like an entire lifetime, every day another battle, every state a new journey. We had seen so much and left no man (or cute little girl) behind. It was not just a field trip with Mom and Dad, it was an Odyssey; a great tall tale with great tall buildings that rose from the streets and long bridges that rose from the sea. It was an experience I never thought in a million years that I would get to have with my kids; never did I imagine we could visit so many national parks together in one summer, and it all had been born and ultimately happened because of something terrible. And now, thanks to time's inescapable grasp, it was all over.

But I knew then what I still believe now. That in the minds of us all, as a family unit and as individuals, no matter the ages, we would never forget that trip. There are some journeys you go on that live inside your bones, that ache inside your heart to be revisited, experiences that yearn to be reborn. I knew I would always carry with me the realizations I came to accept and completely let go of the notions I learned to ignore. I did not believe in just one home anymore, nor did I believe in just one type of life. I had learned that I was a warrior, for my girls, for my husband, for my business, and for myself. I had forged paths with my children that had never once been touched, and ones that could never be paved over again. And I had fought the battle of the divide that had been driven into my marriage. This journey across our great, big home had drawn all of us closer.

As we settled into our own, more permanent home, one more intimate and full of older memories, I knew we had to learn to live now in the new normal we never imagined. But this trip had taught us to understand what home really is and how to trust each other in order to feel strong.

As we pulled our bags into the house and I went about putting the dirty clothes into our trusty washing machine, I knew that my life was about to get a lot more complicated than it had been on our trip. We were going to have to navigate the real world of the Coronavirus, which none of us was truly prepared for. The journey across those thirty-eight States had been an exciting challenge. The new challenges of being in the world during the pandemic was going to be difficult. But if we could stay happy together in the RV, so far from home, then I knew that all of us could stay together happily in the home we had built for one another. Because nothing breaks family, not time, not distance, and certainly not this virus. It is what I learned through the WhatsApp messages, and it's what I learned in all different walks of life we came across on our trip. Without family, there is no home. But here we were, the six of us still together, under the same roof of the home we knew would return home to.

Now came the hard part. I would be going out into the world without my family by my side, Michael would return to work, and the girls would be headed back to school. As I turned the knob and heard the water begin to rush over the clothes, washing away the dirt from the trip, I prayed quietly to myself that we could all be warriors without each other constantly by our side. We had felt safe together in the confines of the RV, socially distanced from the rest of the world. But that was over, and now life in the real world, a world still rapidly changing day-by-day, was going to begin at the end of summer.

I ultimately knew we were going to be okay. We made it home. I had learned on the road that home is truly where the heart is. Only family can truly make a house a real home, which leads me to the story of the Barrero sisters.

Cecilia and Natalia Barrero:

MEGAN BECK

A Story on Family

When sisters Cecilia And Natalia Barrero first heard the rumors of this new virus, they were not sure what to make of it. They wondered how one single virus from China could spread so quickly. It sounded to Cecilia like one of those over-the-top movies. Not real life—certainly not real life. To Natalia, it sounded like a bad cocktail for what she already saw as an increase in anxiety. But both of them had their perspectives when this thing began, and the perspectives quickly changed as the events of the next year unfolded before them. Despite being divided into two different geographic locations, the sisters experience life together as best as they could, caring for those close to them and those far away.

Cecilia's real life was simple, happy, and safe. Cecilia lives in Newton, Massachusetts, (just fifteen minutes outside of Boston) with her husband and two daughters. Her husband, Christian, works for a large Pharmaceutical company, and before the pandemic he was used to traveling a lot for his job. When COVID-19 hit, her oldest daughter, Camile, was about to graduate high school and her youngest, Annika, was about to move into the fourth grade. Cecilia herself is a lawyer and she does marketing for law firms.

Cecilia describes herself as reserved but confident. Before the lockdowns, she loved to play volleyball with people from her community and had traveled a lot in her life, living in five different countries before coming to America. Her sister lives in Atlanta, Georgia, and they connect as often as possible. Cecilia also enjoyed regularly visiting Buenos Aires, Argentina, to see her mother and father who have lived there since before she was born. She stayed busy and kept a tight circle of friends around her, many of whom she enjoyed visiting often all before the lockdowns. This was Cecilia Barrero's way of life before the word "COVID-19" became a household name.

But as the rumors of the virus turned to facts, she watched the world turn upside down. From her modest home in Newton, Cecilia watched the news religiously, fearing the worst every time she refreshed her news apps or changed the channel. She saw the images of supermarkets ransacked, the streets of New York City deserted, and the hospitals overrun. Suddenly, her and her family's life of traveling and visiting with friends was over. She could no longer play volleyball and took up walking instead. "By the time the year of Covid was over, I probably walked the distance from Boston to Atlanta and back again," she said of her walking routines during that time. And a year was a lot longer than she expected. When the President labeled it a national emergency, she expected a few months indoors. She had no idea what this would become, how it would change her life and the lives of those she loved.

Meanwhile, in Atlanta, Georgia, Natalia was finding this new pandemic just as difficult. She was just finishing up her Master's and working as a counselor for her internship. At the time, she had been married to her husband for twenty years and had two children, Lola, who was eighteen, and Andres who was fifteen. Before March, 2020 was a big year, expected to cap off with some pretty great endings, including Natalia's completion of her Master's, and Lola's graduation from high school. Needless to say, all of that changed.

"It was hard on everyone because suddenly we were all in one house," said Natalia, looking back. Her husband, who used to travel once a week to Puerto Rico, was restricted from flying, and had to work at home. He became cooped up very quickly. And Natalia had her own issue finding a private space inside her home. It took a little bit of time for them, but eventually the family found out how to live in their space. But just because they had good physical arrangements did not mean every problem was solved.

The person that Cecilia and Natalia worried about the most was in an entirely different part of the world. From across the globe, the sisters feared for the health and safety of the woman that brought them into this earth.

Cecilia has lived her last twenty-four years as an expatriate, but she made sure to keep in touch with her mother and father. She would often visit them in person, flying to Argentina every year. But when international travel was banned due to COVID-19, it was difficult living with the unknown of when she could go back. Instead of calling her family there once a week, she began calling every single day. She had in-depth knowledge about how intense the virus was there from her family members experiencing and seeing it firsthand.

Argentina was more strict than the United States, at least at first. There was a curfew inflicted upon citizens from 1:00 a.m. to 6:00 a.m. It was specifically difficult in Buenos Aires as it is a major city in Argentina and most of the families live in apartments. So when the schools were shut down and all the kids had no choice but to learn from home, it was difficult for the parents to keep their children in a small apartment. As the virus raged on, many of those families moved into the more rural areas and began living in houses. Not only were the children affected but many people lost their jobs. There were some government assistance programs for people and small businesses, but Cecilia was informed by her mother and father that the government assistance was not consistent, and not all businesses or people who needed the assistance received it. Crime also began to spike to higher levels than ever due to job loss and increased poverty. What was once a peaceful place to live with low crime rates became a more dangerous environment with a government making bad choices. The sudden change in her home country affected her family members in a much more personal way as well.

Cecilia and Natalia had to watch from afar as their seventy-nine-year-old mother was diagnosed with depression for the first time in her life. Someone who was an outgoing, strong woman became cut down emotionally by the multiple negative impacts from a fatal virus running rampant through the country that she loved.

As Cecilia learned this through many phone calls over long, isolated months, a fear began to set in. In more ways than one, she felt she was watching her life quickly become unreal. She felt saddened that this virus could affect her mother so deeply in an emotional way. She also felt horrified that the place she called home was being hit this hard by the virus. She feared it was only the beginning.

As the months grew longer, Cecilia and Natalia, though separated by thousands of miles, did their best to grow accustomed to this new way of life. During the first summer of COVID-19, neither of their husbands traveled at all, and their children stayed home. This made for interesting living. With both parents working from home, both sisters individually devised a living room/office set up. It was hard for both of them at first, mostly because if there was ever a time that Cecilia needed her own space, ironically, it was during the lockdown. Her law firm became busier than ever, and Cecilia had loads of work to do each day. Natalia, on the other hand, being that she is a counselor, all of her clients and conversations had to be in private, by law. But with their husbands stuck at home, and working in the same space, being in a much-needed private space was almost impossible. Just like everything else, they learned to work with it.

When fall came, Cecilia's daughter Camile chose to go to a local university in-person, as opposed to doing virtual classes.

As for Natalia, her daughter, Lola, also chose to move to campus in search of a normal college experience. Cecilia's youngest daughter, Annika, was a harder decision.

All summer long, Cecilia kept her eye on the public school her daughter had been attending before the lockdown. She decided to give the school time to adjust to the sudden protocols and health concerns, but by August 12th, she knew the school would not be safe enough and decided to try another way to provide education for Annika. She knew neither she nor Christian had the time at home to homeschool her. So in late August, Cecilia turned to her husband and said, "I am sending her to private school." And so the search began.

She started with a list of eighteen schools but soon found that there was only possibly room in two of them. She was able to get onto the waiting list for those two, but it was not promising enough as the start date was fast approaching. She decided to go back to square one and search again. She came across a British private school that she had ignored at first, because of the expense. Since the other schools offered her little choice, she began to consider this more expensive school. She waited a week before calling the two other schools to ask if any room had opened up. When both schools said "no," she called the more expensive private school and was relieved to learn that they did in fact have room for a fourth grader.

Things then began to happen very quickly. Within two days, the school conducted two separate interviews, one with the parents and one with Annika. By the end of the second day, Cecilia was able to officially enroll her daughter. Annika began classes two weeks later on September 8th. Despite not having a chance to look more into the school, Cecilia says, "It was the best decision I ever made." Annika is very happy at her new school, making new friends and learning the right way. The only thing she doesn't like is having to be tested for COVID-19 once a week.

During this time, Natalia was having an even more difficult time staying positive in regards to her career. She was diagnosing more and more people with anxiety. Some who had never experienced it before were reporting the same symptoms that people with Generalized Anxiety Disorder report. Natalia diagnosed those who had never experienced it until COVID-19 as "seasonal" — meaning it was happening for a reason, for a period of time in one's life. But whether it was new or heightened, the anxiety her clients began to experience only brought with it some depressive moods for Natalia. It took a lot of patience and courage for her to stay a helpful mother and wife while also coaching her patients through one of the hardest parts of their lives every day, in a quiet part of her overcrowded home. And her clients were not the only people to experience anxiety either. Her mother was beginning to experience anxiety along with her depression, and so was Cecilia.

Cecilia described how much it helped her to stay focused on keeping those around her safe. It was not time to throw in the towel but time to roll up sleeves and get to work in every way possible. The long walks she took were not alone but with her neighbor whom she made sure to check in on as they were able to support each other equally during walks around their neighborhood. The phone calls to Argentina always were about the health and safety of her parents. For her mother, the depression was harsh. Luckily, Natalia, being a counselor, was there to help their mother deal with the depression better than Cecilia, taking that burden off of her.

After many months in lockdown, with friends and family abroad on different lockdown timelines, things did seem to get better. Camile enjoyed a year away at school, and Annika adapted well to the new private school. While Christian continued to have trouble dealing with the new home-base work system and loss of travel, he was able to find balance where at first he had none. Even Cecilia's job got a little less insanely busy. As the vaccine news began to crop up, Cecilia kept up with the news every day still. "I think that the US Federal Government did little to avoid COVID-19 spread. I was lucky to live in a state that handled the virus a little bit better than others," she said of her perspective on what she saw during the quarantine time.

Towards the end of December 2020, for the first time in over a year, Cecilia was able to travel back to Buenos Aires and finally embrace her mother and father. Just nine months earlier, the curfews had been in place, and now everything almost looked back to normal. That was due to the rumors of the virus dying down in the summer (which, for Argentina, begins in December and ends in March), people had begun to relax about masks and social distancing. She was shocked at how all the strict protocols her family had told her about were already being ignored. Cecilia felt that the government should have continued to enforce mask wearing and stricter social distancing protocols.

Another poor choice she saw from afar, many months later from the Argentinian government, was that they released a vaccine from the Russians that had not been put through Phase 3. Argentina then had an extremely difficult time vaccinating its citizens in a timely manner. In March of 2021, less than two percent of the entire country had been vaccinated whereas more than fifteen percent of the total U.S. population had been fully vaccinated. Her father, being eighty years old, was in an age group that received his first Russian dose on March 1, 2021, and he was so elated about it. But her mother, a seventy-nine-year-old lady, being in a different age group, had to wait her turn. Eventually, a few weeks later, she received her dose. Then, they were both waiting for their second dose. After three months, they were still waiting, and with the rumors that the Russian vaccine wouldn't be accepted for travel to western Europe (which their parents had been planning to visit), Cecilia and Natalia flew their parents into the United States the summer of 2021 where they each received two doses of the Pfizer vaccine.

For Natalia, because of her practice, she could not get out of work to go visit her parents with her sister when she went in December 2020. It was hard on her, but she was proud to stick around and still be there for her immediate family. Luckily, she got to see them when they came to the United States for their vaccine.

As 2020 transitioned into 2021, Cecilia could finally reflect back on the year that changed everyone's life. When asked about how her perspective shifted over the year of COVID-19, Cecilia had this to say: "The year taught me to be patient, resilient, and I also learned not to plan, and to live one minute at a time. During Covid, rules changed so easily that it was impossible to know what was going to happen tomorrow."

And the same goes for Natalia, whose outlook and perspective on the worsening anxiety in her patients taught her that we, as people are not alone, and we are also not that much different. What matters is that we are there for our neighbors the best we can be and that we are always there for our friends and family no matter what.

14

THE DAYS OF SUMMER

The arrival back to Georgia was met with almost utter exhaustion from every one of us. We were reluctant to get back to our normal lives and could not fathom the idea of school and work that loomed over us as we settled back into our old rhythms. Naturally, we started small. The night of our return, Aunt Judi came over, and we made fried green tomatoes with peppers and eggs—all fresh from our garden and farm. We spent that night eating healthy food and relaxing at home. Aunt Judi got the low-down on the trip from all the girls, while Michael and I just sat back in silence. It was nice to be home, but my mind was beginning to pile on its internal to-do list.

We began our remaining summer days at home slowly, getting back into the swing of things. The girls enjoyed time with their pets, and Michael and I enjoyed working on home projects. On July 13th, a few days after our return home, one of the girls (I'm still not sure who the culprit is) left the hamster cage door open and one of them escaped. He was able to climb into part of the ceiling and get stuck inside our walls. We could hear him scurrying around and crying through the walls in our living room. It would have been funny in a movie, and it is in retrospect, but it was disturbing at the time. When I asked Michael to free the poor hamster by cutting a hole in the wall, his first reaction was "absolutely not." But one look at his daughters' pleading faces and he caved. We were able to get the hamster out with some small drywall removal, and just a few weeks later, the exact same thing happened again, with the same hamster! Soon after a second rescue, the hamster died. We held a funeral for him in the backyard where we buried him.

The day after the hamster first escaped and was retrieved from the drywall, another animal escaped, but this time we were not as lucky. As I'm sure you remember, early on in the start of quarantine, my vacant offices were infested with mice and rats and to solve the problem, we adopted two cats and let them live in our space while no one was using it. But now, as we were set to open back up for in-person business, the cats had to go. I decided to bring them home. I had someone I know go fetch the cats and bring them to my house, but as she was leaving the office, the door to the cage was not fastened enough, and one of the cats jumped out and ran off. The search began that day for the poor little feline, but we never could find him. We brought his sister home, and the girls were happy to have another pet in the house. They officially named her Autumn, but to this day she is simply called, "Kitty."

The rest of the summer was filled with as much fun as we could have, both in business and in our family. On July 18th, Michael brought home the biggest slip-n-slide I had ever seen. No, seriously. Bigger than anything I have ever seen on any YouTube video search, too. It was 20' x 100', and we unrolled it down the slope in front of our house. The kids spent all day on it and couldn't get enough. The day after that, we took our boat to the lake and the kids went tubing while Michael and I enjoyed a few beers under the warm sun.

My business consumed my focus just a few days after that. On July 21st, Stefanie (she is a real estate agent for our company) and I hosted a socially distanced broker open house for a listing we had. It was a very good turn out, and as a sign of our gratitude, we handed out free wine bottles to all the guests that day. It would be another two months before the house was eventually sold, but it was only the very next day that something equally as wonderful happened.

On July 22, 2020, my business was named the 2020 Stewardship Partner of the Year with Cobb County. We had set up goals to be a more sustainable company (for instance, using reusable plates and cutlery for all of our meetings and events, committing as a business to use reusable water bottles, recycling everything possible, and committing to lower water usage indoors and on the landscaping of our property). We were very pleased to be the first recipient of this award in over a decade. The last time the award had been given out was in 2008.

As the start date for school mounted, I could feel the nervous energy radiating from all of us. I knew the girls were as anxious to return as Michael and I were to see them off. It had been six months of having them home every day, and it was time for the fun to end. On July 30th, Michael and I went to the kindergarten parents and teachers meet-and-greet. The other grades in the school typically had a meet-and-greet day as well, but they were canceled this year. It worried us to be around so many people, but we put on a happy face for the kindergarten event and did our best to stay positive, despite news reports and people's assumptions that in person school would end up being canceled again.

The anxiety levels in the house permeated throughout every room and out into the yard and pool. While Michael had plenty of work to keep him busy, I split my time between the girls, the pets, the office, and my own sanity. The girls did their part to keep busy as well. A couple of days before school started, I walked into the bonus room to find that Jane and Maddie had used all the extra toilet paper I had ordered months earlier from whogivesacrap.com to build a castle for their barbie dolls. I was elated to see them hard at work despite the pressure we all felt. It reminded me to stay calm. No matter what happened, I had kids who would not let a little pandemic craziness affect their lives too much. Even if all they had was lots of toilet paper, they would work with what they had and make something beautiful.

On August 10th, the day before school was set to start, we took the kids to a friend's local hibachi restaurant to celebrate and get out of the house. I can still remember the feeling I had on that drive to the restaurant. For the last month, I had wanted nothing more than for life to get back to some sort of normal. But suddenly, I was overcome with a sense of panic. I could feel the regret and longing mounting in my chest and stomach. I was worried that six months of having the kids all to ourselves had gone by so fast, too fast for my own sake. I needed more time, I needed more togetherness, I needed more memories. It was like the fifty-five day trip in that cramped, crowded RV had not been enough. The endless days of summer since then had been too short. I wanted them back home, on the slip-n-slide or covered in face paint and making silly faces. I wanted, needed, ached for just one more summer-filled quarantine day with them.

I felt this way all through dinner. I watched the girls eat and thought about how this would all change soon. Before I knew it, Michael and I would be picking them up and dropping them off, signing permission slips, and checking math homework all over again. And the house and my life would go back to an old-fashioned kind of noise that I had not heard in a long time. It was that dull roar of work that penetrated my brain all evening long. It was that roar of emails and texts and calls and meetings and calendars. I could hear the click clack of my shoes on the floors of our offices. I could hear the click clack of the keys as I typed up new contracts and spreadsheets. It was this incessant dull roar that had been so much a part of my last ten years, but in just six months had been wiped clean because of COVID-19. A new noise had taken over my brain. It was the noise of my children laughing and arguing and cheering and snoring. It was the miles and miles of tires on an open road for nearly two straight months as we crossed the country together. All of this new noise was what might go away the next day. And I wanted it to stay, to set up shop in my ears and never leave.

In the final moments as I walked out of the restaurant, a place we had come for dinner for years, I happened to spot a framed piece of paper on the wall. It was something our second oldest daughter had written about how much she loved eating there two years ago. I had completely forgotten about that little note. I had smiled as it was written by her, I had congratulated her as it was put on the wall, and then I had moved on with my life. And then two years had gone by before I ever noticed it again. And here she was, along with her sisters and Michael, 700+ days later. And we had all moved on. And I knew then that that was what was expected.

In this world of COVID-19 and news and rumors and fear and hope, we had to move on. Tomorrow we would all wake up in a different world, a different time than any of us had ever known. As I left the restaurant that night, I decided against the loss of what once was. I would welcome the future with open arms just the way I had learned to do over these first six months. Otherwise, I would not be able to look back on the past and smile just as hard as I do now, and that takes commitment.

And the person I learned the importance of commitment from best is none other than a dear friend of mine, Dr. Michael Good.

Dr. Michael Good:
A Story on Commitment

Dr. Michael Good was raised unlike many others. He was born in Indiana to a single mother who was a devout Jehovah Witness. As part of their faith, a Witness does not celebrate any of the major holidays, including Christmas, Easter, Halloween, etc. They don't even throw birthday parties. As these are typically communal experiences, besides their church, Michael was not exposed to many group settings, making his search for fellowship and friendship unusual. As a way to cope with feeling lonely, Michael sought out and cared for animals. What began as a search for connection quickly became a passionate obsession. His love for his mother and devotion to taking care of animals gave him a comfort that the outside world could not offer him. It was not until he was much older that he learned the truth: Some experts have estimated the rate of suicides associated with the Jehovah Witness society to be five to ten times the rate of the general population, especially in children.

At a much younger age than most, he learned how to care for all different types of animals and raise them according to what each one needed. At nine years old, Michael saved up all his money from his paper route and purchased a pony for $25.00. To some it may have seemed odd, but nobody in his small world seemed to mind. And this new pet meant so much more to him than it might have for some other little boy or girl. It gave him not only a type of friend but also a responsibility. He could learn to take care of something besides himself, a skill that would stay with him for all his life. Michael has always had a natural instinct in taking care of the animals, and those instincts only deepened and matured into pure skill the older he got. This outlet kept him happy when his surroundings and upbringing did not offer what he needed mentally and emotionally.

Against all odds, Michael was the first person from both his mother and father's side to go to college. The challenge to simply be accepted into Veterinary School was harder than one might expect. "At the time, it was easier to get into Harvard Medical School than a vet school," says Michael. But he paved the way not only for himself, but for his son, Phil, who also became a veterinarian when he came of age. Michael was always working against expectations and assumptions about what he could achieve in life. People around him saw him as someone who came from nothing, but that did not limit his social skills. From early on, Michael was always personable and charismatic, and that helped him through school. It also later helped him open his own veterinary clinic, where he quickly built a loyal client base that became a large practice. In the forty-plus years, Michael has established six other veterinary practices, and on top of that, he runs his own animal rescue program. He has treated patients all over Georgia, saving pets lives when he can and taking good care of the pets who cannot live past their ailments. Everything was running smoothly until March 2020. At that point, Michael had been expecting the worst, but he was not sure he could handle just how much of a loss he would initially take when COVID-19 became a pandemic.

He and his staff were very quickly considered essential employees by the United States government and the state of Georgia. Therefore he did not have to close his doors for business. However, three of his vets were Hispanic women who had children. They were deemed at a higher risk of complications and did not want to endanger their kids. So when the virus hit, it did not matter that they were able to keep their job as essential employees, the three of them left to stay safe at home and take care of their children who no longer could be looked after by the school. Many of the administrative staff left too. To Michael, a man who had taken the reins and run the show since he was a kid, he knew this was not about just saving his business, it was about helping those in need who could not help themselves. That meant the animals and the veterinarians who worked for him. However, very quickly the business was in jeopardy. Michael ran one of the largest veterinary practices in the southeast. Michael and Phil were well trained veterinarians, but that did not mean they knew how to juggle schedules and make follow-up appointments as well as their previous employees did. Phil was the first one to suggest that they close up shop for a little while and wait for this virus to blow over.

"No, Son," said Michael. "We're not doing that. We can't do that. We have to stick around and work through this."

It became a very difficult decision for the both of them. Michael knew it would be hard to stay open, and Phil knew that too. But Michael no longer had young kids, and Phil had just begun that phase. They knew that they could not let Phil expose his kids, Michael's grandkids, to COVID-19. So they came up with a solution. Phil proposed that he would come in at about noon every work day and only handle the animal patients but not interact with their human owners. With this in mind, Michael devised a new set of rules for the new way their world would work.

The first thing he did was shut down his waiting room. Before COVID-19, the waiting room was full of people and their pets waiting to be called back to the exam room. With the room taken away, people were told to wait in their cars with their pets and were called directly into the exam room that had been disinfected, passing quickly through the disinfected lobby. He also told clients that if they wished to be in the room with their pet, they must make an appointment with him only. The pets could come with no more than two people, and the owners must wear masks. This was the only vet clinic in the area that was open for the public, every other one at the time was a drive-through type. Michael would arrive early in the morning to set up and would stay all day until the last client scheduled had been seen. "I was pretty much running what was typically a five-man veterinarian practice with just my son here part-time and me here full-time," said Michael of those COVID-19 months. He later went on to speak to how crazy people must have thought he was. But he wasn't crazy; he was just devoted.

As the months marched on and the world learned how to work around the virus, Michael was able to get a few of his staff back but only about half. What was once a staff of forty-five became a staff of twenty-two. But Michael pulled himself up once again. And he did it all "without a sniffle." Michael attributes his very good health to his childhood dog affiliation. When he was growing up, he was always around one breed of dog or another. He later read a study that was done to prove that dogs can actually help enhance your immune system the more you're around them because of the nature a dog can provide. They go out and play in the dirt and come back to their humans, and that may actually be improving humans' immune systems. This helped Michael all his life stay safe and healthy when others did not feel so good. There was only one medical issue that flared up for him throughout the entire quarantine experience, and it had nothing to do with COVID-19.

In the middle of working nearly fourteen hour days, Michael began to feel pain in his hip. It started mildly but quickly got much worse. At the age of sixty-seven, Michael was not surprised. He had been working on his feet for over forty years and played all kinds of sports. This wear and tear possibly put him at a disadvantage compared to other men his age who perhaps hadn't put so much wear on their bodies. Yet, he was still on his feet all day working the job of four other people. So while the rest of the world was laid back watching Netflix, Michael was gritting his teeth and working hard through the pain. When he finally did go for a diagnosis, the news was even worse than he was expecting.

A doctor informed Michael that what he thought was a pulled groin from his years of playing sports was actually a degenerated hip and he would need a total hip replacement. This news came in mid-November of 2020, still well into the lockdown phase for most people. He could not stop to have the surgery despite the pain. He made another decision on behalf of the clinic. He informed his doctor that he would wait until after the holidays to have the surgery done. This would allow him time to help the clinic with the pet boarding, which increases heavily over the Christmas season. It is very typical, and many people do this with a vet they know. And since most vet places had been closed up, Michael's was one of the few clinics people trusted to bring their pets to, making him and his small staff very busy. It was not time to throw in the towel and get a surgery.

Of course, when late January came and went and the surgery was completed, the first words from Phil to his father were, "Take it easy, relax, I'll handle everything." Eight days into a planned, one month rehab, Michael got a call from his son, "Dad, please come back, this is out of control. How did you do this?" And since that time, Dr. Good has been working at the office every day. He takes off the time that he can, and he does not stay on his feet as much as he used to. But for Dr. Good, it is his mission in life to bring health and wellness to animals and families as much as he can.

. . .

Speaking about the year of COVID-19, Michael says, "It was a moral victory for me." But even though it was for him, he knows that the reason he worked so hard, through scary times and painful feelings, was due in large part to his passion for the animals themselves. His love for them won out over everything else, even if it meant taking a risk. There were even a few times where Michael did something no clinic owner had the courage to do.

Whenever a family pet had to be put down, new protocols put in place during the pandemic said that this had to be done without the pet's owners present. Michael's love for animals and compassion for animal lovers, encouraged him to make a dangerous choice with Michael taking care to stay as safe as possible. Despite the COVID-19 rules, his age bracket, and the urging from others that it was not worth it, Michael allowed all the family members into the room to say goodbye to their pet. Of course, he had them sanitize their hands and wear masks, as did he. Michael would do what needed to be done and would then exit the room for the family to say their goodbyes, and he would shut the door behind him. He would allow the family a few moments of peace as they wished their little friend goodbye because Michael knows how important pets are to humans.

Dr. Michael Good's entire life has been about animals. He has opened pet rescue centers, he has nursed sick pets back to health, and trained healthy pets to be man or woman's best friend. He does all of these things because no matter how old he gets, or how much the world can change, Michael is still that little kid from Indiana, trying to make the world a better place than he found it. All he wants is to share his passion about the wonders of pets and the greatness of the human spirit. "The COVID-19 pandemic has been a scary time for all," Michael says. Moral victory, to Michael, is only skimming the surface to describe just how proud he is of what he did to save those pets, from the day he was born to today. Because it was not the end of the world then, and it isn't today. It's just another day full of priorities.

Yasunori Hirabayashi: A Story on Priorities

Yasunori has always been an old-fashioned type of guy. He likes shaking hands in business meetings and hugging his mother when he comes to family gatherings. He likes going out to baseball games and watching them in the big stadiums just outside Tokyo. He and his family live in Yokohama, the second largest city in Japan. It lies on the Tokyo Bay, east of the island of Honshu. At the time the virus hit, he was one of the directors for his company. He was living with his wife and son, age thirteen. He liked his life and would not have changed a thing about it.

Some might call him a people person; he just says it is because of his age, being in his mid-forties, but he likes the person-to-person contact that this virus was said to be taking away. For him, in early March, as news of the virus began to spread, Yasunori's biggest concern was being unable to do all of the things he enjoys doing.

Before mid-March, life did not change as drastically as he expected it to. He continued to go to work, but he did actually have to self-restrict himself and his family from going out to eat and visiting with friends. It was hard for him, because he saw others going out. He knew that something serious was happening, and he had heard word from the government that changes were coming fast. In order to stay on the safe side, Yasunori started reading up on everything he could about the virus. As he read, the world around him did change, but by then he was ready.

Yasunori learned that the first reported case of COVID-19 in Japan was on January 16, 2020 from a resident in Kanagawa Prefecture who had just returned from Wuhan, China, weeks earlier. The threat of the virus was immediately recognized by the Japanese government, which Yasunori reflects, took severe preventive measures in extinguishing the spread as quickly as they could. On January 30, 2020, then-Prime Minister, Shinzo Abe, established the Japan Anti-Coronavirus National Task Force. Life went on normally, if a resident was not paying much attention. But on April 7, 2020, the Prime Minister instituted a strict, one-month State of Emergency for Tokyo, Kanagawa, Saitama, Chiba, Osaka, Hyogo, and Fukuoka. This was not surprising for Yasunori; he could have easily guessed that this was coming, and he kept himself as calm as he could.

Eleven days later, the State of Emergency was declared indefinite and ordered to oversee all of Japan. As every country took severe measures in stopping the virus, Yasunori was glad to see that Japan was strict enough to have one of the lowest death rates around the world, despite the higher age population per capita. Yasunori trusted his government and kept his own employees positive by staying positive himself. By May, everybody worked from home unless you were essential to life and death careers. Yasunori's son also attended school virtually. Things changed fast. Yasunori was glad that he had been keeping up with the news and had felt certain the inevitable was coming down the pike, otherwise it would have been more of a shock to him.

His personal life was still affected heavily. As his sister and mother lived in other parts of Japan, the lockdown kept him from seeing them in person. This made the relationship harder to keep up with, but it made it that much more important to work for. His own hobbies were also affected, like going to baseball games and playing sports at the local parks with his son. These things just forced him to focus on what he could control. Yasunori did not become a leader at his company without a hard work ethic and a positive mindset. And he knew that a positive mind was the only way to make it through this pandemic and still remain right side up.

"It is all about priorities," said Yasunori, when asked about that time. He was stuck at home with a wife and son who looked to him for guidance. He also had employees over Zoom and on emails who were asking him about the future of the company. He could not let them down. It was almost a form of self-care, he said, because he knew that if he kept those happy around him who look up to him, he could feel better as well.

The rest of Japan was not as lucky. As the country went into lockdown, the economy plummeted into a very difficult recession. Tourism, one of the biggest industries to the country as a whole, was eliminated. The 2020 Tokyo Olympics, which were expected to be a huge tourist boom, were postponed until summer 2021. The stock exchange around the world also took a large blow to every country's economy, making the recession in Japan even worse. According to *S&P Global*, an American corporation located in Manhattan, New York, responsible for financial information and analytics, the worst hit stocks were for travel, cosmetics, and retail companies. [1] Nippon Professional Baseball (NPB) also hit its lowest economic year, as one of the major tournaments, typically held in Osaka, was switched to an indoor field with no visitors allowed. [2] It was a devastation to a lot of fans, but most importantly it pushed the economy even farther into a dark hole. And as Yasunori watched this all happen over the year 2020, he knew he had no other choice but to stay positive and keep his priorities straight.

One of the hardest outcomes of the Coronavirus in Japan

was the rise in suicide rates.[3] For many years, it had been known that Japan had one of the highest rates of suicides than anywhere else in the world. In the past, it was attributed to people being overworked by many companies. The awareness of this in recent years has brought the companies to finally appreciate their employees better, thus lowering the rate of suicides significantly. But then, as Coronavirus swept through every major part of life for Japan, the suicide rate rapidly increased again for the first time in many years. This time, it was women who were responsible for the rising rates, as opposed to the overworked men who had been known to be the reason before.

Yasunori knew that eventually the world would rise out of the ashes from COVID-19 and carry itself back to better days. He knew this. His peace of mind came from a hard fought war against priorities. He could sit and worry all day long about the bad news or he could use it as a way to encourage himself and those around him to stay strong despite what the news said. He remained a good leader for his company, a loving husband for his wife, and a father for his son. And in order to do that, he had to make sure his priorities were in the right order. If not, then the virus would win, and Yasunori was never going to let that happen.

And I knew that feeling very well, because there were things in my life that I would not let happen either.

---

1. Soon Chen Kang, "Chinese coronavirus fear spreads over luxury, retail sectors," S&P Global, March 2, 2020, https://www.spglobal.com/en/research-insights/articles/chinese-coronavirus-fear-spreads-over-luxury-retail-sectors (accessed April 8, 2020).
2. Kaz Nagatsukam, "Coronavirus blow to Japanese sports industry may hit ¥274.7 billion," Japan Times, May 15, 2020, https://www.japantimes.-co.jp/sports/2020/05/15/more-sports/coronavirus-blow-japanese-sports-industry-may-hit-%C2%A5274-7-billion/ (accessed October 18, 2020).

3. Selina Wang, Rebecca Wright and Yoko Wakatsuki, "In Japan, more people died from suicide last month than from Covid in all of 2020. And women have been impacted most," CNN, November 29, 2020, https://www.cnn.-com/2020/11/28/asia/japan-suicide-women-covid-dst-intl-hnk/index.html (accessed January 11, 2021).

15

"I DON'T KNOW"

The start of school was scary for everyone. The day finally arrived and my children's school did indeed open its doors to all enrolled students on August 11th. There were many guidelines for the kids to follow; it did not feel like the first day of school, it felt more like the first day of boot camp. Every child was required to wear a mask any time they were moving around, either between classes in the halls, to use the restroom, or to go outside to get in the car after school. I was worried my kids would hate it, but I also knew that kids are quite adaptable, and they ended up dealing with it just fine. They were ecstatic to be back at school. As for my part in all of it, I was the health coordinator as soon as the kids got home. I had each child stand in the mud room, strip off their clothes and take off their mask for that day, and then I immediately put them in the wash and had the kids wear fresh new clothes for the remainder of the day. Like I said, it was a bootcamp.

There were highlights, though, to these crazy new times we found ourselves in. Just a few days after school started, Maddie started ballet and tap classes for the first time and very quickly fell in love with it. That, plus the other kids' activities they were still allowed to do, made life feel a little like old times again, even though we all knew it wasn't. The girls school did an excellent job at maintaining the health and safety of each student, by doing their part at home alongside their parents. But it was impossible to do enough. Despite the first quarter being COVID-19-free, by the time the first break from school began, on September 24th, the principal sent out an email to all parents saying that he had contracted the virus. He had fallen very ill, and he had not been able to return to the school for seventeen days. After that, the virus felt even closer to home. If the man who ran the school could get it, maybe my innocent girls and their equally innocent little friends could pick it up. Despite a lot of false reassurance, nobody could really tell what was going to happen next.

Most weekends were spent at home where the kids could go mask free around the house and dress up in their fairy princess costumes and have a ball. By September and October of 2020, people we observed were as strict as ever, and the idea of canceling their holidays was not off the table for most of the people we know. We continued to mostly stay home and still have fun. That is when the chickens and guinea pigs came in handy. They were a way for the girls to interact with something outside of school, be outside, and still stay safe. But it wasn't always easy. Things like birthday parties and trips to the mall were off-limits at that time. In other words, the kids had plenty to do around the house outside of school, they just didn't have a lot to look forward to—maybe not even their usual holidays.

Before I knew it, the end of October arrived. By then the girls were wiped out from the new school routine and the constant health concerns that floated around them like buzzing flies whenever they left the house. I could tell they were bummed and very tired of this new way of life. I also could tell how much pressure there was from the outside world to not let their kids go trick-or-treating on the 31st. But seeing the longing in the girls' eyes for something normal, anything that reminded them of life before COVID-19, I could not say no. We got costumes and masks and went out that night. The streets were not completely deserted, although many of the houses that were typically decked out didn't have any decorations out nor did they even have their lights on.

The girls still had plenty of homes to visit and many of the homes opted to put a table at the end of the driveway with candy already laid out (versus the communal bucket). It felt a little wrong to be out and about like we were, but the joy of my children enjoying Halloween overshadowed my concern there, and it was nice to enjoy some part of life that wasn't so heavily mandated. From the limited crowd I saw on that Halloween night, I knew the holidays were not anywhere close to going back to normal.

Close to the end of November, I began to get a bit anxious. Besides Halloween night, life during the week seemed to feel as normal as it was bound to get. The girls were in school, and Michael and I went to work. Real estate sales had picked up like crazy. COVID-19 caused people to make moves all over the place. When stuck at home working, people realized features they wanted in a new home, and they started packing up, selling, and moving. People also got permission to work at home indefinitely, allowing them to live wherever they wanted to in the country. I have said many times that COVID-19 was like a big shoe stepping on an ant hill. We were the ants, and we came out running to a new location. Most of the money and clients that my mentors said we would lose we did not, and business was actually busier than ever. We hired a handful of new employees to help lighten the load. Everything felt like we were finding a new rhythm, a new pattern to this masked-up rat race we were living in. Settled in our routine, my anxiety was not about the life we had now, it was about the holidays to come.

I had been keeping a close watch on the news for word of what the experts like Dr. Anthony Fauci would tell us about spending Thanksgiving and Christmas with family and about traveling. I was not surprised when Fauci advised the nation not to travel, along with the CDC that claimed how dangerous traveling was, especially with months of winter ahead where the typical flu usually ticks up higher than any other time in the year.[1] [2] But this was America, and the mentality here, especially in the blessed South, was that no one could tell someone where to go and where to stay. America was the land of the free, and certain people felt it was their God-given right to travel wherever they pleased within the boundaries of this sacred Nation. This worried me more than I could have expected, sky-rocketing my anxiety levels for the health and safety concerns of family, friends, and employees. Even if none of them moved an inch during the holiday season, when it was all said and done, and everyone who *had* traveled returned, they were bound to come into contact with someone that had traveled and picked up the deadly virus along the way.

For Thanksgiving, we decided to go stay at our Florida home. The only risk we took was inviting a few family friends to stay with us. We all stayed in the house, fished, and swam in the private pool while we were there. On Thanksgiving Day, we had dinner at the house, with family and friends. The day went well and spirits were high. It was peaceful that in spite of all of our messed up plans this past year and the scary way things looked from the outside; we had the fortune of fellowship.

By December, everywhere I turned, it seemed the entire world was fighting over whether to have Christmas and New

Year's or not. Inside the home, things were only becoming more tense. Work was stressful, the girls were always in fear of going back to school virtually, and the holidays only meant more threats of infection. We had one enjoyable night that I can distinctly recall, a night that let our family and some friends let their hair down. It happened on December 11, 2020.

We went to a dinner at a friend's house with five couples from our group of friends for a five-course dinner party. There were no masks and no COVID-19 to worry about. Everyone had assured us ahead of time that they were clean. It was exactly the kind of night of fun that I needed, especially with what was to come next. But on the way there, I received an email. It read:

"Given the news about Jane and next week, I wanted to touch base with you. We will miss her SO much. In order to keep her engaged and learning, the school has offered to let her join the virtual Kindergarten class next week. She will send you an email with a schedule tomorrow and specific details Luna. We put a bag with materials in Jane's backpack today. You will use those materials for class next week. Please let me know if there is ANYTHING you need. I can always drop things by your house or send it home with one of your other girls. I will be praying for health and for your family. We will miss Jane! I will make sure to send home Christmas things next week."

I was confused. What did they mean about Jane? After some digging of my own, I learned that Jane had been accidentally looked over on a list of kids who had come in contact with COVID-19 at the school. As a precautionary safety measure, she was forced to return home for two weeks to quarantine. That would mean a month out of school, as the quarantine would back right up to the school's Christmas break. Then the second shoe dropped.

The next day, December 12th, I received a text from my

oldest daughter that said, "Mark just threw up." Our two oldest daughters had spent the night before at their cousin's house and now he was throwing up, which meant that those girls had also been exposed to COVID-19. Now two more of our daughters would have to quarantine with the other. The only daughter left unexposed was the youngest, Maddie. But seeing as how the rest of us would be stuck inside, we didn't see a point in sending the three year old to school. So she stayed home as well for the next month. It became a month of quarantining that led right into Christmas break. By the time the actual holiday came right up in our faces, I was exhausted but blessed that none of us actually got sick.

It felt like by the time I looked up from my computer again it was December 23rd, two days until Christmas. And we still had plenty to worry about. The first issue on the agenda was our church's annual Christmas Eve service. I was split down the middle on whether I wanted the family to attend. On the one hand, it could potentially be a large virus mosh-pit, on the other hand I wanted to do the best I could to give the kids a normal Christmas. I debated back and forth with Michael. Finally, after enough talking, the family dressed up, masked up, and went to the first service on Christmas Eve. I would live to almost regret this decision entirely.

As we neared the church, we could tell the weather was not looking so good. Cracks of thunder and flashes of lightning soared over the top of our car all the way to the church. As soon as we arrived, it began to snow, which it rarely does in Georgia. The church had devised two ways in which to lessen the flow of people. One was to post the service live via webcam for free to any families that wanted to watch from home. The second was to split the Christmas Eve service into three separate events (it was usually just one large service). This was at least the plan, and to avoid the crowd and to be amongst the first people in the sanctuary, we decided to take the girls to the first one. However, the church's second attempt became a moot point when, just five minutes before the first service was even set to begin, it began sleeting. The church quickly canceled the second two services, hoping to save the lives of its flock. Nonetheless, the sheep didn't listen and came in herds to the first service. So, what began as a simple way to lessen the crowd and stop the spread of COVID-19, ended with a packed church full of rain-soaked, sniffling churchgoers, crammed together seeing God's plan for our final days. Or should I say, *day*, since based on the amount of people in that service who could have spread the virus, we'd all be dead by tomorrow.

Luckily, the next day went much smoother. On Christmas morning, the girls awoke to presents that Santa Claus had delivered. Aunt Judi came by to visit with us, and we enjoyed watching movies most of the day. So, despite all of my trepidation leading up to Christmas, and the fallout thereafter, I was able to put it on hold and enjoy the day with family.

After Christmas Day the world continued to be in limbo. I watched the news, monitored the expert's opinions, and tried my best to figure out what would happen in the next few months, or even the next few days. The CDC was trying to halt everyone from having a New Year's Eve celebration, Facebook users were spouting freedom of America, and my kids were asking me if we were going to stay up and watch the ball drop with friends like the last few years. As it had become so common in the last few months, I looked at each of the girls and simply told them a new phrase I had learned: "I don't know."

It was true, I didn't know what would happen for New Year's Eve, I didn't know what would happen in 2021, and I didn't know when this virus was going to go away. I looked to my friends on WhatsApp. Some were saying they celebrated Christmas but wouldn't be celebrating New Year's, others were saying the opposite, and still some were saying they didn't care and would celebrate all the holidays they wanted to. When I was asked what I would do, I tried to give my take on the topics, tried to sound as if I had a plan. But I didn't have a single one. All I had was a good dose of hope and a moderate ration of fear. I did my best in the final days of 2020 to lean towards hope.

Hope is sometimes all we can rely on when we have no real answers. I believed it was more noble to tell my children that I didn't know, than to lie and tell them I did. I did not want them thinking I had all the answers, because sometimes mommies and daddies just do not have any. It's not the parent's fault, it's not the children's fault, it's just a time of not knowing. And in the not knowing, I learned how to teach myself and my girls to simply just hope for the very best. Little did I know that the very best was yet to come. But I was happy right then, just like a friend of mine by the name of Romola Jain.

Romola Jain:
A Story on Happiness

Before March 2020, Romola Jain lived an ordinary life raising her remaining two school-aged children and helping her husband, Neera, run their two-person garment business. In her day-to-day life she would daydream of her first loves: art, cooking, and teaching. Although she believed one day she could combine her love of teaching and cooking and art by starting workshops to share her passions with others, she had no idea when she would ever have the time. Little did she know her world and everybody else's would change on March 13, 2020.

Originally from India, Romola moved to France twenty-seven years ago with Neeraj to start a family. Together they have always lived in the North of France near the Belgian border in a little-known town called Lille. When the pandemic hit in 2020, and her town was shut down along with the rest of France, things seemed dire. The two-person run business could no longer afford to keep up with the restrictions and health risks and was forced to shut down temporarily. In the beginning of the pandemic, French schools had not quite mastered the art of virtual learning, so her two young boys like the rest of French children were stuck at home left to their own devices along with baffled parents like herself and her husband.

As the world saw gloom and uncertainty, Romola saw a silver-lining. With her kids around all the time and her business temporarily shut, she finally had the time to pursue her original passions for cooking and art along with two eager students of her own. She remembered how her parents always instilled in her a sense of curiosity for learning and excellent work ethic, and she wanted to impart the same to her young and newly bored boys.

She began her pursuit with drawing, teaching them patience and peace through making their own mandalas.

In the ancient Sanskrit language of Hinduism and Buddhism, mandala means "circle." Traditionally, a mandala is a geometric design or pattern that represents the cosmos or deities in various heavenly worlds. "Every person is their own universe. The essence of mandalas is the ability to find peace within yourself by exploring symmetry and patience."

Seeing the effect that her home workshops had on her boys with the passing months, she yearned to reach others. She decided to turn those once closely-held daydreams into reality. She started to create books and she self-published them on Amazon. Her life was beginning to come full *circle* like her mandalas. She went from the young girl who loved arts and crafts, to a mother given the time to teach her own children this same passion, to teaching others by selling books.

Today, her book, *Atelier Mandala for Everyone* teaches just what it claims: the process to grow patience and discipline through a creative self-care routine for everyone of all ages. She thanks art for being her mental and emotional support while her world was changing. Art allowed her to not only adapt but to evolve in frightening times. She went ahead and added her passion for cooking in her entrepreneurial endeavor and began to have very small classes to teach art and Indian cuisine to her peers around her area. It was not long until word of her wonderful workshops and beautiful drawings quickly spread.

As the months of quarantine drew on and on, Romola began to feel better and better about the new life she had been afforded by this otherwise disastrous virus. Thankfully, her children as the tech-savvy youth of today, picked up virtual learning relatively easy, so she suddenly had all the time in the world to design mandalas and teach cooking.

By November 7, 2020, there were over 86,000 reported cases of COVID-19 in France alone [3] and Romola felt the same pain that everyone else was feeling at a global level—pandemic fatigue. She felt that she could help others through her art and cooking as ways to relinquish some of that hurt that most were feeling. People around the world began finding Romola on Amazon and beginning their creative self-care journeys at their own pace through her book.

By the time that it was safe enough for her and her husband's business to open back up, she no longer had time for it. Her supportive spouse took it over entirely so that she could continue to pursue her dreams of educating people through art and food. She began workshops of Indian cooking classes that involved no more than five people per week. Word had been spreading quickly around her little corner of the world, and requests to attend her classes skyrocketed. She was astounded that something as simple as cooking lessons by someone as unknown as she was could be in such high demand.

When she thinks of the why behind her dreams, Romola could only come up with one reason. "I just really like making people happy," she says. "The mandala art pieces I design are supposed to calm one's soul, and food is very similar." She knows that people are in need of community, and 2020 was ironically the best time to take a chance on one's own unexplored passion that would fit into this mold. For Romola, to be able to create art, make food, and share all of that with friends and family, she feels overwhelmingly humbled.

Romola's passions have become such a hot topic around the north of France that people are asking for her in all different mediums. She was able to help edit an adult art book aimed at helping people combat anxiety through coloring the mandalas she designs. She also has been asked by several schools to come once a week and teach cooking classes for students of all ages. What began as a daydream to pass the time has become a reality. She could have only ever dreamed that she could use her passion to inspire others and make people happy, and happiness to Romola is the most important way to overcome the struggles we all face. And to make others around her happy makes Romola the happiest person she knows.

---

1. Libby Cathey and Anne Flaherty, "Government response to coronavirus: Fauci backs Trump travel ban, says testing system 'a failing,'" ABC News, March 12, 2020, https://abcnews.go.com/Politics/government-response-coronavirus-fauci-backs-trump-travel-ban/story?id=69557417 (accessed April 30, 2020).
2. Savannah Behrmann, "'Convinced': Fauci says there will be coronavirus in the fall after Trump says 'it may not come back,'" USA Today, April 22,2020, https://www.usatoday.com/story/news/politics/2020/04/22/coronavirus-

dr-anthony-fauci-says-i-am-convinced-second-wave/3009131001/ (accessed April 30, 2020).

3. Vishal Tiwari, "France Relaxes COVID-19 Restrictions, Begins First Phase Of Easing Lockdown Measures," RepublicWorld.Com, November 29, 2020, https://www.republicworld.com/world-news/europe/france-relaxes-covid-19-restrictions-begins-first-phase-of-easing-lockdown-measures.html (accessed January 4, 2021).

16

PEOPLE

As the New Year came into our life, our family looked ahead into the future. Into the unknown. I was very much stuck in the present, of course, but there was a collective, universal sigh of relief that I could feel that was sweeping through America, and the rest of the world, as 2020 turned into 2021 and the clock started over. The year had been arduous for some, decent for others, and quite eye-opening for me. And everyone had been through *something*. My question now was what to do next. I knew externally that I would run my business—we would sell the houses, sign the contracts—and that I would get the kids to school, make dinners, go to bed, and then do it all over again. But something had to be done, something had to be said about this irregular, unrecognizable, unbelievable year. But *what to do* bugged me. This ultimate question continued to nag at me as the first days of January greeted us with a chill breezing its way through the city of trees.

Throughout the days leading up to school starting back, we did what we could to stay busy. Maddie enjoyed painting my nails, all the girls helped me tend to the chickens and guinea pigs outside, and we baked all kinds of new desserts and breads together. It was fulfilling and exhausting to be around them again for long periods of time— it had already felt like years since the RV trip. And yet I knew it was not the same. The sheltering wasn't as typical as it had been over the last year. Stores and restaurants were getting busier, people were buying more homes, and the vaccine was on its way.

As January turned into February, the world held its breath for the virus to die out. But that is when the virus decided to spread on its third wave. Up until this point, at our real estate office, we had been allowing everyone to remove their masks when working at their desks, but by mid-February, we required masks to be worn at all times. Everyone was happy to comply and many were relieved with the extra precautions being put in place.

Back at home, I watched my girls begin to learn their way around this new world. On February 4th, our third oldest daughter started her first practice for her new softball team. The next day was the Annual Father-Daughter Dance at school, a reimagined experience with three different drive-throughs picking up a box of goodies, a photo booth station, and finally a gift certificate pick-up for one of the nearby restaurants of the father and daughter's choice. Michael took the three older girls, and Maddie and I stayed behind to watch a movie and have some quality time together. Then, on February 11th, all four girls got to stay home over the weekend and build a very special Valentine's Day box for their classrooms, where they stored the treats for each classmate. Throughout that month, my initial, beginning-of-the-year fears began to subside as I watched our family continue to overcome the challenges that COVID-19 brought.

Time started to fly by. I started having way less time to worry about the news and stopped spending as much time checking up on my WhatsApp messages. I didn't mean to; it was just the way everything seemed to shake out. The girls were so busy with their school, homework, and extracurricular activities; Michael and I were entering into our busy season, taking on new agents and listing lots of houses. In other words, life had begun to go back to some sort of normal for my family.

As far as I could tell, despite the new normal we were in, technology had found a way to adapt for the people. When our two middle daughters had their first musical performance, the school taped the entire thing and streamed it for parents to watch later at home. When new buyers wanted to see a home but didn't want to go out into the world, we used a tool called Matterport to give a 360 degree view of the entire house from the outside-in. Solutions really could be found when facing a brick wall. If you can't go through it, you look up, you look down, or you look left to right, but you never look behind. Looking back meant repeating the past, making old mistakes, trying old ways that had failed or were outdated. It was true that this virus had ushered in a new era. I was seeing it firsthand everywhere I went, and I was not surprised at the rumors that some of these new "Covid-friendly" means of daily life were not ever going away.

I read once that survivors of traumatic events will mark the date of the event very efficiently for a while and then eventually stop. I have heard stories that for people involved in traumatic events such as 9/11 or a school shooting, on the anniversary of that day they wake up and mark the day in their minds, like clockwork. Sometimes they feel their years begin and end with that date. And then one day, ten, twenty, fifty or so years later, they stop. They look at the date on the calendar, perhaps having forgotten it was that day to begin with, and merely shrug their shoulders. I had never fully understood that idea until I saw the calendar read: March 12th. I almost lost my breath at the sight of it. How could it be that tomorrow it had been a year since this all began? It was the first time I learned the true lesson of how much time really does heal all wounds, both inside and out. And somehow, in some miraculous and ordinary way, people are able to simply move on.

And that is exactly what my family and I had done by the time we woke up on March 13, 2021. My brother's forty-first birthday. It was like any other day, with a partly cloudy sky, and a high of sixty-seven degrees Fahrenheit. As I drove the kids to the bus that morning and then drove to work, I thought strongly about that. I had a laundry list and a half of things to do that day, and not one of them had to do with COVID-19. Not anymore. Because, while it was still not gone from our lives, COVID-19 had simply become a part of our lives. Not like a sheep in wolf's clothing either, not something that snuck in and ruined everything for us. Instead it was something we had learned to build our lives around, the only way humans know how: one brick at a time.

So after the clocks continued past the COVID-19 year date, and life continued on, I was not surprised when my birthday was just a day away, March 18th. I was surprised however at the sense of humor God has for us sometimes. I had been marooned at home together with Michael for the past five days because of a possible COVID-19 exposure and that day, my birthday, was the day I would be scheduled for my COVID-19 test.

The test was held at a drive-through spot in Kennesaw, Georgia, in a shopping mall parking lot. The line was long, and the cars moved slowly. I felt fine, and I was pretty sure Michael felt fine, but we both had a little trouble believing everything was going to be okay. I mean, in some ways I thought maybe now was my time. Stefanie had just tested positive, and she had done her best to stay safe. What was in store for me? Maybe it was just karma. Maybe it was just life saying, "You had a good year?

Great, now that you're settled again, here's that virus you spent all that time worrying about."

My official paperwork let the nurse who performed my test see that it was, in fact, my birthday, and while the little test tube was stuck way up my nostrils, she sweetly sang a cute rendition of "happy birthday" to me until the time for the test was over. It felt more like a good omen than just a nice stranger making an awkward moment better. Both of our tests were negative and we drove away.

In the middle of the drive home, something struck me, and it all came back to that ultimate question nagging at me back in January. It was like being hit with a million water balloons, and I was soaked in this realization. People were how I survived the year of COVID-19 so well. *People* were the answer to the question of *what to do next*.

This entire year, from the people in my company, to my neighbors, to my family, to the nice grocery store employee in Florida who held my groceries, to all the people on WhatsApp who told me their stories, and to the million others caught in inspiring videos and on uplifting images. People were the entire reason that this world was still moving much like after the events of Columbine or 9/11. It was the connection, person to person, that made all of this worth it. This was the first major incident worldwide in over a hundred years that people had been physically cut off from one another when they needed each other the most. But that had not stopped me or anyone else. We had used technology and other inventive ways to reach our loved ones and were there when they needed or wanted to reach out to us.

This was a time of war, a time of combat against a virus, but this war was not just fought by the weapons in the medical field, like masks and ventilators and rubber gloves, it was fought by people. We had become so distracted, so utterly careless in *how* we communicated, just as long as we did *eventually* communicate, and it was only with people we *thought* were more important. The year taught us what was most important: the people around us, the people who loved us back — neighbors, friends, and family.

In reflection, despite all of the hardships and sadness that came with it, I was grateful for what this year had given me. I was grateful for the friends and family I grew closer to because of the hard times we were facing together. I was grateful for the new friends I made from around the world just from the ease of my phone. And I was grateful for the cherished time I got to spend with my children that we would have never spent had it not been for the virus. Those little girls would grow and never forget the year that the earth powered down just slow enough for their eyes to catch a glimpse of it in real time. I thought I was strong before, but this year empowered me beyond all expectations, and it was in large part because of other people.

I began and ended the year of Covid with a birthday to mark my passage of time through this life of mine. It was bookended with a deadly virus that is still spreading its way through our country. And as I watch it silently spread, unaware of where it is and where it will go next, I am able to stay strong through the company I keep and the people I love. Nothing is more powerful than human connection. And when a war in our life tries to take us down, be it a war for our heart, our mind, our soul, or our body, we have our fellow men and women to lean on. This virus tried to take that away. But this year taught me that it will never be taken away.

Nobody will forget what happened in the year 2020. The year the war began. The people who lived through it fought back like true warriors. I am glad I am one of those warriors. Glad I get to see how I inspired my young girls to be little warriors too.

Soon, they will have their own battles to fight, maybe

another war one day. And perhaps one day I will not be there for them. But for now, in the time I had this year and for the rest of the birthdays I have left, I want to continue training my girls to be warriors. To learn to laugh, learn to cry, learn to speak up, and learn to listen. I, alongside my fearless and wonderful husband, fought and continue to fight The People's War for ourselves and for our children. And one day, when they have children of their own, I hope they continue to teach the most important lesson they learned from us: You cannot do it alone. You always need people that you love to stand with you by your side. And that will never end, no matter what the future may hold.

EPILOGUE

A STORY ON THE FUTURE

On March 13, 2021, exactly a year after the day the world changed, Eliott C. McLaughlin wrote an article on *CNN* entitled, "10 Lessons Learned in a Year of Covid-19 Lockdown."[1] In this article, McLaughlin lays out all of the good and the bad that came from a year no one could have predicted to the full extent to which it actually occurred. McLaughlin explains how we came together as a world and worked towards helping others but also how this year exposed our "swagger" when it came to thinking we knew more than the experts. It was a year of racial tension, economic collapse, and worldwide panic. And yet, through all of that, little miracles happened every day. People invented new ways to say "I love you" and designed new ways to help make the world a safer place. It was in this year, with the people featured in this book, and the events that happened in my life, that I experienced a profound new outlook on our life on this planet and went through a paradigm shift of my own. So what happens next?

Where do we go from here?

I am in the present, my work completely laid out in front of me, too much to do with not enough time. However, I cannot help looking towards a future shrouded in complete and utter uncertainty. It's raining outside as I write these words. The window pane soaked as water drops from the sky and melts the leaves in the forest to my right. Only through the perspectives I have gathered in this past year can I fathom an inkling of what the future might bring. But as we have all learned, even one's greatest expectations can change on a dime.

In the *CNN* article, McLaughlin writes about the sacrifices made in all different areas of our lives. "...[w]e would be remiss to ignore the accompanying sacrifices that amounted to tiny acts of heroism and doubtless saved myriad lives." I am blessed to have been a witness to some of these acts of not only kindness but bravery and wisdom. Everyone I spoke to had insight that provided a fuller perspective on the overall pandemic, and everyone had a story to tell. Each time I got to speak to a person on the list who was bold and willing to speak about their lives, I was honored and humbled all at once. Some of these stories moved me beyond words, and yet, the words they spoke told stories full of meaning. I could not have done it without their compassion and their composure during a time when the world was unfair and each person's life was unbalanced. But again, it was not enough to look back into the recent past and reflect; I was amazed to witness the powerful visions each of these people around the world had about the future.

Mike Stiles, who came face-to-face with death in an unexpected COVID-19 attack in early 2020, spoke about the future: "Doctors fight every day to save lives, but the Coronavirus taught me that everyone should first fight for themselves. Because in the end, we are the General and the Private in this battle for our lives. We don't always know when the battle will begin, and we certainly do not know when the battle will end. But if we fight, we have a chance."

Marian Balthazar, who works nights on the other side of the world in the Philippines, witnessed some of the toughest times during quarantine, but yet she stays positive to this day and still looks forward to the future.

Bruce Marden, the self-proclaimed "simple man," who at eighty-five received both vaccines, is still doing well and keeping his spirits up by spending time with his granddaughters, sticking by his son's side no matter what, and enjoying his loving wife more every day.

Anne Cardell, the doctor from New York who gave birth during peak COVID-19 times, knows that her little girl, Magnolia won't have any recollection of that first year of her life, but it would be wrong to say she won't know anything about COVID-19, and she will most likely experience life differently than any of us who grew up prior to it. Anne knows that children as well as adults have an internal need to be together, and as a nation and a world, we will always find ways to fellowship.

Those are just a few of the many people I had the honor to speak with over this past year who were optimistic about the future, who believe in a time when things like COVID-19 will no longer hinder our way of life.

But the future may not be positive if we are not careful. At the end of his article, McLaughlin wrote: "There's an old saying about history repeating itself, and there's no reason to believe it won't apply in post-pandemic life. If we engage in denial or fail to heed the lessons handed to us, we could do this all over again —and maybe sooner than we'd like."

I do worry about this. We can come out of a tough experience with our heads held high, but that does not mean we should forget what led us to the experience in the first place. We have to keep our eyes open and be vigilant for the next pandemic that may be on the rise. We cannot lose sight of what kept this virus from getting worse, and we have to learn to take care of things when they are good, not wait to fix them after they have broken because we have stopped looking.

There are questions that I ask myself often: have we learned, will we do better, and will this just be the first of many pandemics in our lifetime? Over time, I have come up with my own ways of sticking to best practices, and Michael and I do our best to keep instilling those best practices into our daughters. But sometimes, I need to look outside of myself for inspiration. And there is one person who always inspires me to believe in a better future. And I met him in a little shelter just inside Mexico on the Mexican-American border.

Alessandro Cavedoni is one of the first few people I spoke with about the pandemic. Today, he is gearing up to study Political Science at Texas A&M and working towards becoming a major influence in the political spectrum of Venezuela and American relations. I know that Alessandro has a bright future ahead of him and also has one of the most resilient and impassioned spirits I have ever met. If anyone can speak towards a bright future, it is this young man.

I reached out to Alessandro in late July of 2021, just a year and four months after the COVID-19 outbreak. After all that has happened in his life, all that he has been through, he has never lost a strong belief in himself nor the power of his voice. This is what he had to say: "The truth is that, to me, the future looks brighter. I can say from my experience that hardship is always needed to trace the route from where we are to where we want to be. We are all human beings, equal to one another. And as humans, we'll improve, and it shall be a transcendental change for humanity that will mark the division between 'before' and 'now.'"

1. Eliott C. McLaughlin, "10 lessons learned in a year of Covid-19 lockdown," CNN, March 13, 2021, https://www.cnn.com/2021/03/13/us/lockdown-lessons-learned-covid-19/index.html (accessed March 15, 2021).

POSTSCRIPT

With a heavy heart, I am sad to announce that my dear friend, Dr. Good, the vignette of the veterinarian in *The People's War,* passed away before the publishing of this book due a sudden heart attack. He is greatly missed by all who knew him.

PLEASE LEAVE A REVIEW

Thank you for taking the time to read about the many experiences that were had by myself and others around the world during this trying time. If you enjoyed "The People's War", please leave a review.

ACKNOWLEDGMENTS

I want to express my gratitude to all of those who opened up and shared their stories with me during this period. Your camaraderie has played a significant role in allowing me to reflect on these years with genuine fondness.

To my family, thank you for always being ready for new adventures, whether that be a cross-country trip or hundreds of baby mice.

ABOUT THE AUTHOR

When **Megan Beck** is not writing, she can be found traveling, spending time with her family, gardening, or spending time with her many beloved pets. She looks forward to releasing more books in the near future.

@authormeganbeck

www.ingramcontent.com/pod-product-compliance
Lightning Source LLC
Chambersburg PA
CBHW051722040426
42447CB00008B/937
* 9 7 8 1 9 5 6 9 5 2 0 3 2 *